THE THEOLOGY OF THE BOOK OF GENESIS

The book of Genesis contains foundational material for Jewish and Christian theology, both historic and contemporary, and is almost certainly the most consulted book in the Old Testament in contemporary culture. R. W. L. Moberly's *The Theology of the Book of Genesis* examines the actual use made of Genesis in current debates, not only in academic but also in popular contexts. Traditional issues such as creation and Fall stand alongside more recent issues such as religious violence and Christian Zionism. Moberly's concern – elucidated through a combination of close readings and discussions of hermeneutical principles – is to uncover what constitutes intelligent understanding and use of Genesis, through a consideration of its intrinsic meaning as an ancient text (in both Hebrew and Greek versions) in dialogue with its reception and appropriation both past and present. Moberly seeks to enable responsible theological awareness and use of the ancient text today, highlighting Genesis's enduring significance.

R. W. L. Moberly is Professor of Theology and Biblical Interpretation at Durham University. He is also the author of *Prophecy and Discernment* and *The Bible, Theology, and Faith*. His writings have appeared in scholarly journals such as *Vetus Testamentum*, *Journal of Theological Studies*, *Harvard Theological Review*, and *Journal of Theological Interpretation*.

University of Hertfordshire

College Lane, Hatfield, Herts. AL10 9AB
Information Hertfordshire
Services and Solutions for the University

For renewal of Standard and One Week Loans,
please visit the web site http://www.voyager.herts.ac.uk

This item must be returned or the loan renewed by the due date.
A fine will be charged for the late return of items.

OLD TESTAMENT THEOLOGY

GENERAL EDITORS
Brent A. Strawn,
Associate Professor of Old Testament,
Candler School of Theology, Emory University
Patrick D. Miller,
Charles T. Haley Professor of Old Testament Theology, Emeritus,
Princeton Theological Seminary

This series aims to remedy the deficiency of available published material on the theological concerns of the Old Testament books. Here, specialists explore the theological richness of a given book at greater length than is usually possible in the introductions to commentaries or as part of other Old Testament theologies. They are also able to investigate the theological themes and issues of their chosen books without being tied to a commentary format or to a thematic structure provided from elsewhere. When complete, the series will cover all the Old Testament writings and will thus provide an attractive, and timely, range of short texts around which courses can be developed.

PUBLISHED VOLUMES
The Theology of the Book of Jeremiah, Walter Brueggemann

FORTHCOMING VOLUMES
The Theology of the Book of Exodus, Dennis T. Olson
The Theology of the Book of Leviticus, Brent A. Strawn
The Theology of the Book of Judges, Joel S. Kaminsky
The Theology of the Book of Psalms, Patrick D. Miller
The Theology of the Book of Ecclesiastes, J. Gerald Janzen
The Theology of the Book of Daniel, Anathea Portier-Young
The Theology of the Book of Hosea, Christine Roy Yoder
The Theology of the Book of Amos, John Barton

THE THEOLOGY OF THE
BOOK OF GENESIS

R. W. L. MOBERLY

University of Durham

CAMBRIDGE
UNIVERSITY PRESS

CAMBRIDGE UNIVERSITY PRESS
Cambridge, New York, Melbourne, Madrid, Cape Town, Singapore, São Paulo, Delhi

Cambridge University Press
32 Avenue of the Americas, New York, NY 10013-2473, USA

www.cambridge.org
Information on this title: www.cambridge.org/9780521685382

First published 2009

Printed in the United States of America

A catalog record for this publication is available from the British Library.

Library of Congress Cataloging in Publication data
Moberly, R. W. L.
The theology of the book of Genesis / R. W. L. Moberly.
p. cm. – (Old Testament theology)
Includes bibliographical references and index.
ISBN 978-0-521-86631-6 (hardback) – ISBN 978-0-521-68538-2 (pbk.)
1. Bible. O. T. Genesis – Theology. 2. Bible. O. T. Genesis – Criticism, interpretation, etc.
I. Title.
BS1235.52.M63   2009
222′.1106–dc22   2008041848

ISBN   978-0-521-86631-6 hardback
ISBN   978-0-521-68538-2 paperback

For Jenny,
celebrating ten years

Contents

General Editors' Preface

Some years ago, Cambridge University Press, under the editorship of James D. G. Dunn, initiated a series entitled *New Testament Theology*. The first volumes appeared in 1991 and the series was brought to completion in 2003. For whatever reason, a companion series that would focus on the Old Testament/Hebrew Bible was never planned or executed. The present series, *Old Testament Theology*, is intended to rectify this need.

The reasons for publishing *Old Testament Theology* are not, however, confined solely to a desire to match *New Testament Theology*. Instead, the reasons delineated by Dunn that justified the publication of *New Testament Theology* continue to hold true for *Old Testament Theology*. These include, among other things, the facts that, (1) given faculty and curricular structures in many schools, the theological study of individual Old Testament writings is often spotty at best; (2) most exegetical approaches (and commentaries) proceed verse by verse such that theological interests are in competition with, if not completely eclipsed by, other important issues, whether historical, grammatical, or literary; and (3) commentaries often confine their discussion of a book's theology to just a few pages in the introduction. The dearth of materials focused exclusively on a particular book's theology may be seen as a result of factors like these; or, perhaps, it is the cause of such factors. Regardless, as Dunn concluded, without adequate theological resources, there is little incentive for teachers or students to engage the theology of specific books; they must be content with what are mostly general overviews. Perhaps the most serious problem resulting from all this is that students are at a disadvantage, even incapacitated, when it comes to the matter of integrating their study of the Bible with other courses in religion and theology. There is, therefore, an urgent need for a series to bridge the gap between the too-slim theological précis and the too-full commentary where theological concerns are lost among many others.

All of these factors commend the publication of *Old Testament Theology* now, just as they did for *New Testament Theology* more than a decade ago. Like its sister series, *Old Testament Theology* is a place where Old Testament scholars can write at greater length on the theology of individual biblical books and may do so without being tied to the linear, verse-by-verse format of the commentary genre or a thematic structure of some sort imposed on the text from outside. Each volume in the series seeks to describe the biblical book's theology as well as to engage the book theologically – that is, each volume intends to *do* theology through and with the biblical book under discussion, as well as delineate the theology contained within it. Among other things, theological engagement with the composition includes paying attention to its contribution to the canon and appraising its influence on and reception by later communities of faith. In these ways, *Old Testament Theology* seeks to emulate its New Testament counterpart.

In the intervening years since *New Testament Theology* was first conceived, however, developments have taken place in the field that provide still further reasons for the existence of *Old Testament Theology*; these have impact on how the series is envisioned and implemented and also serve to distinguish it, however slightly, from its companion series. Three developments in particular are noteworthy:

1. *The present hermeneutical climate*, often identified (rightly or wrongly) as "postmodern," is rife with possibility and potential for new ways of theologizing about scripture and its constituent parts. Theologizing in this new climate will of necessity look (and be) different from how it has ever looked (or been) before.

2. *The ethos change in the study of religion, broadly, and in biblical studies in particular.* No longer are the leading scholars in the field only Christian clergy, whether Catholic priests or mainline Protestant ministers. Jewish scholars and scholars of other Christian traditions are every bit as prominent, as are scholars of non- or even anti-confessional stripe. In short, now is a time when "Old Testament Theology" must be conducted without the benefits of many of the old consensuses and certainties, even the most basic ones relating to epistemological framework and agreed-upon interpretative communities along with their respective traditions.

3. Finally, recent years have witnessed *a long-overdue rapprochement among biblical scholars, ethicists, and systematic theologians.* Interdisciplinary studies between these groups are now regularly published, thus furthering and facilitating the need for books that make the theology of scripture widely available for diverse publics.

In brief, the time is ripe for a series of books that will engage the theology of specific books of the Old Testament in a new climate for a new day. The result will not be programmatic, settled, or altogether certain. Despite that – or, in some ways, *because* of that – it is hoped that *Old Testament Theology* will contain highly useful volumes that are ideally poised to make significant contributions on a number of fronts including (a) the ongoing discussion of biblical theology in confessional and nonconfessional mode as well as in postmodern and canonical contexts, (b) the theological exchange between Old Testament scholars and those working in cognate and disparate disciplines, and (c) the always-pressing task of introducing students to the theology of the discrete canonical unit: the biblical books themselves.

Brent A. Strawn
Candler School of Theology, Emory University

Patrick D. Miller
Princeton Theological Seminary, Emeritus

Preface

When I began seriously to think about the writing of this book, two things struck me. Neither was new, but each struck me with fresh force, in the kind of way that changed my thinking and so also my writing.

First, of all the books in the Old Testament, Genesis is probably the most appealed-to and most used in contemporary discussion. To cite a few examples, the biblical portrayal of creation, and the contemporary phenomenon of creationism, feature regularly in "science and religion" debates, such that the question of what to make of the first few chapters of Genesis remains a live issue. Global warming is directing enormous attention to our understanding of, and appropriate interaction with, the environment; in such a context, the implications of the divine mandate to humanity to "have dominion" over the earth, and what kind of stewardship is envisioned, becomes important in a way that it was not a hundred years ago. Greater population mobility raises issues about the interrelationship of different religious traditions, such that interfaith dialogue is increasingly on the agenda of those to whom faith is important; and dialogue among Jews, Christians, and Muslims regularly appeals to Abraham as some kind of "ecumenical" figure, who may represent common ground among the dialogue partners. Millions of Americans believe that the United States of America should support the state of Israel because of God's promise in Genesis to bless those who bless Abraham and his descendants.

Second, a strongly negative stance toward the Old Testament tends to be an integral element within the currently fashionable atheist critique of religious faith in general and Christianity in particular. To be sure, not all express themselves quite as eloquently and forcefully as Richard Dawkins: "The God of the Old Testament is arguably the most unpleasant character in all fiction: jealous and proud of it; a petty, unjust, unforgiving control-freak; a vindictive, bloodthirsty ethnic cleanser; a misogynistic, homophobic, racist, infanticidal, genocidal, filicidal, pestilential, megalomaniacal, sadomasochistic, capriciously malevolent bully."[1] Nonetheless, anxiety, suspicion, and hostility, not least toward famous stories within Genesis, are on the increase. Is not the story of Cain and Abel an archetypal example of the murderous violence that the biblical conception of God can generate?[2] If one can but stand back from familiar interpretations, should one not see that the God of the story of Adam and Eve, or the Abraham who is willing to reduce his son to smoke and ashes, is each alike a "monster"?[3] If these stories were merely museum pieces, their doubtful values perhaps would not matter so much. But it is because these are part of the sacred scripture of more than a billion people today that what these stories say, envisage, and possibly mandate *matters*.

---

[1] Richard Dawkins, *The God Delusion* (London: Bantam, 2006), 31. See further the discussion in Chapter 3.

[2] See Regina M. Schwartz, *The Curse of Cain: The Violent Legacy of Monotheism* (Chicago: University of Chicago Press, 1997) and the discussion in Chapter 5.

[3] So, respectively, David Penchansky, *What Rough Beast? Images of God in the Hebrew Bible* (Louisville, KY: Westminster John Knox, 1999), 5–20; and Richard Holloway's review of *After These Things*, by Jenny Diski, *The Guardian*, April 24, 2004, 26.

I have therefore decided against one time-honored scholarly way of writing on the theology of Genesis – namely, to focus primarily on a depiction of the religious thought and practice within Genesis as a constituent element within the wider history of the religion of ancient Israel. At the present time, this would mean distinguishing between Priestly and non-Priestly strands within the text; focusing on the nature of the Priestly perspective; discussing whether it is appropriate still to think in terms of a Yahwist and, if so, what particular emphases characterize the Yahwist; examining how the various Genesis traditions may reflect and relate to various contexts within ancient Israel and Judah; and so on. These are all valid issues. The difficulty is that they are increasingly issues of interest only to professional biblical scholars. The wider public interest that attended pentateuchal criticism in the nineteenth century has long since ceased. Even among scholars, interest in the wider issues about the nature and development of Israel's religion and its possible enduring significance, an interest that clearly motivated the nineteenth-century debate that climaxed with Wellhausen's famous synthesis,[4] is hardly to the fore of the many technical debates that continue. Yet it is not just the nonscholarly public that tends to put different questions to the biblical text, for scholars themselves are recognizing that many different questions may validly be put to the biblical text, depending on the purposes that motivate one's inquiry. And so, we are back at the first point.

Thus my approach to the theology of Genesis is via various contemporary debates about, and appeals to, the biblical text. My concern is still to discover and engage with the intrinsic theological

---

[4] Julius Wellhausen, *Prolegomena to the History of Israel*, trans. J. Sutherland Black and Allan Menzies, repr. ed. (Atlanta: Scholars Press, 1994 [German orig., 1878]).

meaning of the Book of Genesis, only to do so in the context of its reception and use. The debates I interact with are mostly scholarly debates, but scholarly debates that are more obviously engaging with the questions that many readers of Genesis are actually asking; even so, there is space for only some of those questions. I am also painfully aware that much of Genesis and its theological meaning remains undiscussed in the pages that follow, but I hope that the studies that follow are at least representative of Genesis and its theology as a whole.

I am grateful to my wife, Jenny, and my colleague Richard Briggs, for their reading and commenting on draft chapters and suggesting helpful changes, which I have generally (but not always) followed. I am also grateful to Brent A. Strawn and Patrick D. Miller, the series editors, for the honor of being invited to contribute this volume, for their putting up with my delays and idiosyncrasies, and for their constructive editorial improvement of my text. As a result of all this wise and friendly help, my text, whatever its continuing deficiencies, is much better than it would have been otherwise. My thanks also to Douglas Earl for compiling the indexes, which we hope will be user-friendly.

Biblical citations are taken from the NRSV.

Abbreviations

ACCS:OT	Ancient Christian Commentary on Scripture: Old Testament
ANET	James B. Pritchard, ed., *Ancient Near Eastern Texts Relating to the Old Testament*, 3rd ed. (Princeton, NJ: Princeton University Press, 1969)
ASTI	*Annual of the Swedish Theological Institute*
ATM	Altes Testament und Moderne
BibInt	*Biblical Interpretation*
BZAW	Beihefte zur Zeitschrift für die alttestamentliche Wissenchaft
BZHT	Beiträge zur historischen Theologie
BZRT	Beiträge zur Religionstheologie
CC	Continental Commentaries
CD	Karl Barth, *Church Dogmatics*, ed. G. W. Bromiley and T. F. Torrance, trans. G. T. Thomson et al., 5 vols. in 14. (Edinburgh, UK: T. & T. Clark, 1936–1977)
CSCD	Cambridge Studies in Christian Doctrine
ESV	English Standard Version
ExpT	*Expository Times*
HBT	*Horizons in Biblical Theology*
HTR	*Harvard Theological Review*
Interp	Interpretation: A Bible Commentary for Teaching and Preaching

Int	*Interpretation*
JB	Jerusalem Bible
JSJSup	Supplements to the Journal for the Study of Judaism
JSNTSup	Journal for the Study of the New Testament Supplement Series
JSOT	*Journal for the Study of the Old Testament*
JSOTSup	Journal for the Study of the Old Testament Supplement Series
JTS	*Journal of Theological Studies*
LHBOTS	Library of Hebrew Bible/Old Testament Studies
LXX	Septuagint
MT	Masoretic Text
NEB	New English Bible
NIV	New International Version
NJPSV	New Jewish Publication Society Version
NRSV	New Revised Standard Version
OBT	Overtures to Biblical Theology
OTL	Old Testament Library
OTM	Oxford Theological Monographs
REB	Revised English Bible
SABH	Studies in American Biblical Hermeneutics
SBLSCS	Society of Biblical Literature Septuagint and Cognate Studies
TOTC	Tyndale Old Testament Commentaries
VT	*Vetus Testamentum*
WBC	Word Biblical Commentary

CHAPTER 1

What Is a "Theology of Genesis"?

The book of Genesis contains some of the most memorable and moving narratives within the Old Testament, which have engaged the hearts and minds of (quite literally) millions of people down the ages. Neither Jewish nor Christian faiths – nor, more distantly, Islam – can be understood without some appreciation of the enduring impact of the Book of Genesis. Likewise, much of the literature and art of Western civilization, at least until recent times, is deeply imbued with motifs and images from Genesis.

In Genesis, God creates a world, which is the object of his approval, indeed delight ("very good"). Yet Eve and Adam listen to the serpent in Eden and eat the forbidden fruit, hide from God, and are expelled from Eden. Cain resents God's preferential acceptance of Abel's sacrifice, ignores God's warning, murders Abel, and is condemned by God to be a marked and restless wanderer on the earth. Noah builds an ark in wordless obedience to God and enables a faithful remnant to live through the unmaking and remaking of the known world. The great building project at Babel – Babylon, an early center of human enterprise – is overturned by God so as to scatter people and make human language and culture complex.

Against this backdrop Abraham is called by God to leave his Mesopotamian home on the basis of God's promise to make him the ancestor of a great people, in a land of their own, blessed by

God, and esteemed by other peoples. Abraham does many things, yet his life fundamentally involves waiting for a son by Sarah to begin to fulfil the promise; his son Ishmael by his servant-girl Hagar also gives rise to a people, but is nonetheless a false start. When finally the long-awaited son Isaac, the symbol of Abraham's future, is born and begins to grow, Abraham is told by God to reduce him to ashes and smoke in a sacrifice; Isaac's knife-edge survival anticipates that of his descendants.

Isaac himself does relatively little. The longest narrative in which he appears focuses on how his wife, Rebekah, conspires with his younger twin son, Jacob, to deceive him, so that he pronounces his blessing on Jacob rather than on his older, preferred, and intended twin son, Esau.

Jacob does not walk before God in the mode of Abraham. Rather, he appears to be relentlessly, and more often than not successfully, self-seeking, whether in deceiving his father Isaac or in trying to outsmart his uncle Laban to whom he flees to escape Esau's murderous anger. When God appears to fleeing Jacob at Bethel, Jacob thinks in terms of making a deal with God. Only years later, when Jacob, returning home, fears for his life and wrestles through the night with a mysterious figure does he appear genuinely to encounter God and thereafter builds an altar to God. However, Jacob remains a poor and querulous father of his twelve sons, the ancestors of the twelve tribes. Yet remarkably, he, and not Abraham, is the eponymous ancestor of the whole people of Israel.

Joseph, Jacob's favored son, pays for his youthful arrogance toward his brothers by being sold by them into slavery in Egypt, where he faces prolonged darkness, is traduced by Potiphar's wife, and is abandoned in prison. Yet eventually his interpreting of the Pharaoh's dreams gives him a meteoric rise to power. His brothers, seeking food in Egypt in time of famine, do not recognize Joseph, and Joseph appears to toy with them. Yet eventually Joseph's brothers and father are brought to food and safety in Egypt, and there is a family reconciliation (of sorts). When Joseph dies, the Genesis narrative comes to an end with Israel's ancestors established in Egypt, with the promise of settlement in Canaan left open for the future.

It is a rich and frequently surprising narrative. Though there are some comings and goings from and to the two great centers of early civilization, Mesopotamia and Egypt, the main action is in the seemingly insignificant land of Canaan. God makes promises and guides, and his blessing overarches the whole; yet for long stretches, God appears absent and inactive. Sinners at Sodom and Gomorrah perish; yet deceitful Jacob prospers and lives long. Younger sons are consistently favored over their older siblings, so that the "proper" order of things is regularly subverted. Significant space is given to Abraham's untypical military campaign, Jacob's breeding of sheep and goats, Joseph's management of the Egyptian economy. The more one looks at the material, the less it fits typical notions of what "God" and "religion" are all about.

TOWARD A "THEOLOGY OF GENESIS"

The Contested Nature of "Theology"

How then might one approach the task of articulating a "theology of Genesis"? This is tricky and controverted, for a variety of reasons. For example, people often point out that Genesis is not a work of theology in the sense that people usually understand that term – in the kind of way that, say, Origen's *On First Principles*, or Aquinas' *Summa Theologiae*, or Barth's *Church Dogmatics*, or even von Rad's *Old Testament Theology* are recognized as works of theology. But this means that it is vital at the outset to define what is, and is not, meant by "theology."

"Theology," like "history" and many of the other major categories that scholars use to interpret the biblical text, is not itself a biblical term; it originated in classical Greek and rose to prominence in the works of the church fathers. Of course, it need not be a problem to use postbiblical terms to designate and interpret the content of the Bible,[1] as long as the terms are used with appropriate nuance and sensitivity. But this already reminds us that biblical interpretation generally involves a dialectic between the content of the text itself and the categories and frame of reference within which one seeks to understand and perhaps also appropriate it. Notions such as the plain sense of the text have their place, but they can easily obscure the subtlety and complexity of what in fact goes on when people read any text from the past, never mind one that is held by Jews and Christians to be enduringly authoritative.

The term "theology" has a long and complex history from the Fathers to the present day, which makes it far from straightforward to use. Not least there has been a tendency from the early Enlightenment in the seventeenth century onward to use theology as a counterpart of religion, both of which are used in distinctively modern and contracted senses. "Religion" in the modern West is often used to denote a generic kind of thought, piety, and practices, quite distinct from those of politics, economics, and the natural sciences; it designates what happens primarily in an inward, subjective, and largely private realm, distinct from what happens in public – so that religious people who transgress these distinctions tend to encounter strong opposition. Theology is then sometimes conceived as an attempt to talk about religious experiences, which risks being a kind of psychobabble with religious jargon;

---

[1] Such terms even include the basic structuring categories Old Testament, Hebrew Bible, and New Testament.

alternatively, theology may be a kind of metaphysical speculation about invisible and intangible entities – an activity that bears no relation to, and certainly makes no difference to, the realities of everyday life. One reason, therefore, why it can be difficult to articulate a theology of Genesis is that so much of the content of Genesis does not conform to modern theological preconceptions of what one should find there. Only if one can recover a more classic sense of theology, as an attempt to understand everything in the world in relation to God, will one be better placed to start to make sense of the theology of Genesis.

Historical Criticism and Socially Valued Knowledge

One common scholarly approach, which tries to deal with the problem of possibly distorting preconceptions, is to understand theology in relation to the Bible as a primarily philological and historical discipline, a descriptive and analytic account of religious thought and practice. In this sense, to give an account of the theology of Genesis is to characterize its content in the categories of religious history: to show what certain terms and ideas and practices mean in their originating context, in the tenth or sixth century BCE (or whenever), and to map them in relation to each other and to other aspects of ancient Israel's developing religious thought and practice, and possibly those of Israel's neighbors also. Such a theology of Genesis is not in principle different from giving an intelligent account of the content of any religious text, biblical or otherwise – one would not in principle handle Augustine's *Confessions*, the Qur'an, or the Bhagavad-Gita differently. The task requires good philological and historical understanding, so that one can appreciate the content of the text for what it is, without prematurely assimilating it to the perspectives of other texts, ideas, and practices from other periods of history and different cultural contexts. Theology thus becomes, in essence, a history of Israelite religion in some form or other.[2]

There is obvious value in such an enterprise. Not least, those who hold the Bible to be God's self-revelation, a gift and a truth that is given to Israel and the church for the benefit of the world, have an interest in wanting to discern as accurately as possible what the text really says, lest God's word be misunderstood, or lest it be confused with their own preferences and predilections. On any reckoning, the insights of good philology and history will only be downplayed or despised by those who have never come to appreciate what those insights are or who have failed to master the disciplines necessary to acquire them.

Nonetheless, it is the thesis of this book that a theology of Genesis needs to be more than, and somewhat different from, this, primarily because Genesis is not a freestanding ancient text, like the Epic of Gilgamesh, but is part of the authoritative scriptures of synagogue and church, wherein there has been an unbroken history through the centuries of living with the text in a variety of ways, not least its incorporation into regular worship, both through reading aloud and in liturgical texts. Among other things, this means that one does not, indeed almost cannot, come to the text "cold," but only in the context of an enduring Jewish and Christian, and consequent wider, cultural reception. This reception forms a kind of

---

[2] There have been many twentieth-century debates as to how, if at all, to distinguish between theology and the history of Israelite religion. Usually those advocating the distinction have presented their theology in thematic/systematic categories, more recently also in synchronic form, as distinct from providing diachronic, comparative, and developmental accounts (history of religion). Yet it is doubtful whether any of these, even Gerhard von Rad's influential concept of retelling (*Nacherzählung*), succeeds in doing more than, as it were, reshuffling the pack so as to provide a fresh hand to set on the table of accurate historical understanding of ancient religious data.

plausibility structure, a context for bothering with the text and for taking it seriously, in a way that would not be the case otherwise. It means, among other things, that Genesis (or any other biblical book) is approached with expectations, or at least arguments, about its enduring significance and possible truth that are not the case when one approaches most other religious texts of antiquity.

Biblical scholars often take this plausibility structure for granted. Sometimes, however, they reflect on it, and one striking example is this excerpt from Brevard Childs:

> I do not come to the Old Testament to learn about someone else's God, but about the God we confess, who has made himself known to Israel, to Abraham, Isaac and to Jacob. I do not approach some ancient concept, some mythological construct akin to Zeus or Moloch, but our God, our Father. The Old Testament bears witness that God revealed himself to Abraham, and we confess that he has broken into our lives. I do not come to the Old Testament to be informed about some strange religious phenomenon, but in faith I strive for knowledge as I seek to understand ourselves in the light of God's self-disclosure. In the context of the church's scripture I seek to be pointed to our God who has made himself known, is making himself known, and will make himself known. . . . Thus, I cannot act as if I were living at the beginning of Israel's history, but as one who already knows the story, and who has entered into the middle of an activity of faith long in progress.[3]

Childs's formulation is rather distinctively Christian; Jews often express their own self-understanding in relation to the Bible quite differently. Yet for Christian and Jew alike, there is a common preconception. It is one thing to come to the biblical text without allowing church and synagogue to prejudge the outcome of one's

---

[3] Brevard S. Childs, *Old Testament Theology in a Canonical Context* (London: SCM, 1985), 28–29. Although the thought is basic to Childs's work, its expression is untypical, as Childs generally eschews such first-person "confessional" terminology.

philological, historical, and other inquiries. It is quite another to recognize that one might well not bother with studying this text in the first place were it not for the general assumptions and expectations with regard to its enduring significance and truth – assumptions that depend on the continuing health of synagogue and church, and their wider cultural recognition. As Jon D. Levenson crisply puts it, in the context of discussing the role of historical criticism in biblical study,

> [t]he very value-neutrality of this [that is, historical-critical] method of study puts its practitioners at a loss to defend the *value* of the enterprise itself. In a culture saturated with religious belief involving the Bible, this weakness was less apparent, for the defense was less called for. Now, however, after secularism has impugned the worth of the Bible, and multiculturalism has begun to critique the cultural traditions at the base of which it stands, biblical scholars, including, I must stress, even the most antireligious among them, must face this paradoxical reality: the vitality of their rather untraditional discipline has historically depended upon the vitality of traditional religious communities, Jewish and Christian.... Indeed, in the humanities today, every "canon," cultural as well as scriptural, is under intense suspicion, and every selection of subject matter is increasingly and correctly understood to involve a normative claim and not merely a description of value-neutral fact. In all cases, what scholars study and teach is partly a function of which practices and beliefs they wish to perpetuate.[4]

Ideological Criticism of the Biblical Text

What, then, of one of the fashionable trends in contemporary biblical scholarship, ideological criticism of various kinds? Ideological

---

[4] Jon D. Levenson, "Historical Criticism and the Fate of the Enlightenment Project," in Levenson, *The Hebrew Bible, the Old Testament, and Historical Criticism: Jews and Christians in Biblical Studies* (Louisville, KY: Westminster/John Knox, 1993), 106–26 (109–10).

criticism generally encourages readers to read "against the grain" of the biblical text, critique it in the light of the best cultural values of the present time, and bring to critical consciousness, with a view to repudiation, issues of, say, gender or power that are simply taken for granted within the biblical text.

Interestingly, proposals to read against the biblical grain tend to get their critical and rhetorical purchase from an apparent unwillingness on the part of mainstream scholarship to put hard questions to the biblical text or to take sufficiently seriously what the text might "do to you" – thereby apparently encouraging rather unthinking biblicism. So, for example, David Clines criticizes typical historical approaches to the Bible and insists that a reader can only maintain ethical integrity by reading the Bible against the grain:

> The practitioners of the historical-critical method, like the inventors of the atomic bomb, were ethically irresponsible. Their commitment was to the "truth," whatever that might be and wherever it might lead. And that is unquestionably a whole sight better than a commitment to falsity. But it systematically ignored the question of effects on readers, and it is about time we regarded such study as part of our scholarly discipline and task. . . .
>
> I am rather insistent on a programme of judging interpretations by standards other than their own; for if we do not judge them by our own standards of reference, we cannot be ethical. If we judge the references in our texts to slavery or to the oppression of women by the standards that operated in the ancient world, we might well find ourselves approving those practices, or at least being less antithetical to them. We do not owe any such debt to the past, however, and it is a more truly human activity to make serious and well-informed judgments than merely to acquire knowledge or "understanding. . . . "
>
> What it boils down to is this: To be truly academic, and worthy of its place in the academy, biblical studies has to be truly critical, critical not just about lower-order questions like the authorship of

the biblical books or the historicity of the biblical narratives, but critical about the Bible's contents, its theology, its ideology. And that is what biblical studies has notoriously not been critical about at all. To be critical, you have to take up a standard of reference outside the material you are critiquing; but, traditionally, biblical scholars have been believers, ecclesiastics or, at the least, fellow-travellers and sympathizers with the ideology of the Bible. When the academy begins to view the Bible as a cultural artifact, and is not seduced or pressured by religious commitments, the hallmark of criticism will be that it steps outside the ideology of the text.[5]

The issues at stake here are complex, and part of the force of Clines's rhetoric depends on some oversimplifications. For example, it is hardly the case that mainstream biblical scholarship has eschewed critiquing the biblical text in all sorts of ways. Clines's stance is reminiscent of the kind of critique offered by deists in the eighteenth century, which was the period in which historical-critical approaches started to dominate the field. Strong ethical critiques characterized this scholarship, and there are still historical-critical scholars today who see themselves as continuing within such a mold.[6] Moreover, one response to the pronouncement of the Bible's inadequacies from a modern (and often irreligious) European perspective has been precisely to promote a more rigorous and thoroughgoing historical awareness.[7] In other words,

---

[5] David J. A. Clines, "Why Is There a Song of Songs and What Does It Do to You If You Read It?" in Clines, *Interested Parties: The Ideology of Writers and Readers of the Hebrew Bible*, JSOTSup 205 (Sheffield, UK: Sheffield Academic Press, 1995), 94–121 (107–10).

[6] See, e.g., Heikki Räisänen, "Biblical Critics in the Global Village," in *Reading the Bible in the Global Village: Helsinki*, ed. Heikki Räisänen et al. (Atlanta: Society of Biblical Literature, 2000), 9–28; and John J. Collins, *The Bible after Babel: Historical Criticism in a Postmodern Age* (Grand Rapids, MI: Eerdmans, 2005).

[7] It is notable that the German Enlightenment, which quickly came to lead the field in the study of ancient history and the Bible, remained more religiously

there is a dialectical relationship between historical understanding, critical appraisal, and possible contemporary response to the biblical text.

In certain ways, ideological criticism often represents a secularized version of a religious rule of faith, an issue to which we will return. Moreover, in its own way, ideological criticism does not deny the force of Levenson's sociological observation cited at the end of the previous section. For, if one takes time minimizing the enduring significance and impact of the Bible, or denying that its deity is the one true deity, or at least querying some of its cultural (e.g., "patriarchal") presuppositions, then this is essentially a reactive exercise premised on Jewish and Christian affirmations and their historic and enduring cultural impact – and so, is unnecessary if writing about Zeus or Marduk and the religious ideas and practices respectively associated with them. Some indeed appear to study the Bible primarily so as to oppose the perpetuation of its beliefs and practices, whether in overtly religious or in secularized forms;[8] but the presupposition of the exercise is that there is something there that needs opposing. Of course, if such ideological scholars become a predominant voice, they could in the long term diminish the interest of universities, publishing houses, and inquisitive students in the Bible, and resources will be redirected to where they are considered more worthwhile.[9]

---

engaged certainly than its French counterpart and generally than its English counterpart. Thus German historical work on the Bible characteristically was articulated with an eye to the enduring significance, in one form or other, of the material.

[8] See the discussion of Regina M. Schwartz's work in Chapter 5.

[9] One might compare the recent book by Hector Avalos, *The End of Biblical Studies* (Amherst, NY: Prometheus, 2007).

A PROPOSAL FOR A "THEOLOGY OF GENESIS"

Biblical Text and Canonical Contexts

For present purposes, the significant factor in an ideological program such as that of Clines is that it brings us back to the point that the Book of Genesis comes to us, not as an interesting papyrological or epigraphic discovery from exploration of the Middle East that can enlarge our knowledge of ancient religion, but in the context of the canonical scriptures of Judaism and Christianity. In this context, Genesis has a seemingly inexhaustible history of interpretation and appropriation, which gives rise to continuing expectations and assumptions as one comes to the text. Whatever the complexities and ramifications of the debates about the relationship between scripture and tradition that have characterized both Jews and Christians down the ages, and however much it may become necessary periodically to reassert a certain kind of scriptural primacy over the formulations of continuing traditions of interpretation,[10] the fact remains that Genesis is received within the context of continuing traditions of faith, life, and thought, however variously these may be conceived.

Although there can be an undoubted heuristic value in imaginatively bracketing these contexts of reception, so that the meaning of the Genesis text as an ancient text can better be appreciated, the appropriate stance for a theology of Genesis is not only to bracket but also to incorporate. The task will certainly have dimensions of what might be included in a history of Israelite thought and

---

[10] This can take many forms. In Jewish contexts, the Karaites and modern Reform Jews have in differing ways appealed to scripture to relativize rabbinic traditions of interpretation. And apart from Protestantism's classic appeal to scriptural primacy, there are movements within contemporary Roman Catholicism to renew the foundational role of scripture.

practice, but it will also engage with the reception of the text as a resource for probing its significance and exploring its possible appropriation.

To be sure, a proposal such as this makes some scholars nervous. They may complain that this prematurely fuses what should at least provisionally be separated. One of the best-known twentieth-century expressions of such anxiety was Krister Stendahl's 1962 essay on "Contemporary Biblical Theology," which argued for the importance of separating what the text "meant" (the descriptive task) from what it "means" (the hermeneutic question).[11] The serious deficiencies in such a program have not infrequently been spelled out.[12] Nonetheless Stendahl has recently clarified his concern in writing the essay, which was to "dethron[e] the theological imperialism that biblical scholars often enjoyed, or presumed, in the heyday of Biblical Theology," with a specific view to preventing a particular (mis)appropriation of the Bible:

> The issue was the ordination of women in the Church of Sweden. And the triggering factor was the signing of a public statement to be signed by the New Testament teachers in Uppsala and Lund Universities. They declared ordination of women to the priesthood to be contrary to the Bible – with no if, and, or but! It was the early 1950s. I was a doctoral student at the time, also a part of the teaching staff. When asked to sign, I found myself in a strange position. I was quite convinced that the ordination of women was the right thing,

[11] Krister Stendahl, "Biblical Theology, Contemporary," in *The Interpreter's Dictionary of the Bible*, ed. G. A. Buttrick et al., 5 vols. (Nashville, TN: Abingdon, 1962), 1:418–32; reprinted in Heikki Räisänen et al., eds., *Reading the Bible in the Global Village: Helsinki*, 67–106.

[12] The most telling critique of which I am aware is Nicholas Lash, "What Might Martyrdom Mean?" in *Suffering and Martyrdom in the New Testament*, ed. W. Horbury and B. McNeill (Cambridge: Cambridge University Press, 1981), 183–98; reprinted in *Ex Auditu* 1 (1985): 14–24, and in Nicholas Lash, *Theology on the Way to Emmaus* (London: SCM, 1986), 75–92.

and that for many reasons. At the same time I found the arguments of teachers and colleagues exegetically sound. I did not want to make Paul and/or Jesus into proto-feminists. Certainly the overwhelming biblical perception of the role of women could not easily be brushed aside, for example by reference to those docile women in Luke's gospel. I had to give reasons for not signing on, and when you are in a minority of one, you have to think harder. Hence the urgent need to take the hermeneutical gap seriously.[13]

Whatever one feels about the ordination of women, one can concede Stendahl's point that there are problems in trying to resolve a significant issue in contemporary life solely on the basis of biblical exegesis – as though one could, as it were, take the biblical text and just lay it down on the table as the ace of trumps. Neither Jews nor Christians typically operate thus. The sacred and authoritative text must indeed be considered and appropriated, but *other considerations must also come in* – the problem is to articulate precisely what these are and how they might function. Stendahl argued for a certain kind of gap between biblical past and ecclesial present, whereas Clines (one imagines) would simply wield his ethical knife. But neither shows much appreciation of the difference that may be made by long-term living with the biblical text, its ever-renewed reception and appropriation in worship and study – at least the difference that can be made in principle and on a good day, for in none of this do I wish to deny that Christian interpretation and appropriation of the Bible has often been deeply problematic.

One key aspect of the canonical preservation and reception of a book such as Genesis is *recontextualization*. As part of a canonical collection, Genesis is read alongside other texts, with other

[13] Krister Stendahl, "Dethroning Biblical Imperialism in Theology," in *Reading the Bible in the Global Village: Helsinki*, ed. Heikki Räisänen et al., 61–66 (62–63).

perspectives and practices, many of which may not have been envisaged by those writers and editors responsible for Genesis (though on numerous points of detail, one can of course argue the issue either way, at least within the Old Testament canon) – but which now form part of the frame of reference within which Genesis is received. For Christians, this canon includes the New Testament, in which God becomes definitively understood in the light of the incarnation – the life, death, and resurrection of Jesus.

One of the features that characterizes the phenomenon of the canon and its appropriation by the church is the very thing that Clines insists on – perspectives beyond that of the specific text being commented on. To be sure, the perspectives tend not to be quite those that Clines seems to prefer, though both Deuteronomy and Qoheleth, never mind the Gospel of John or the Letter to the Ephesians, are all interestingly distinct from Genesis. Ecclesial reflection on Genesis, and mutatis mutandis that of the synagogue, is generally characterized neither by harmonizing nor by distancing but by a range of highly complex synthetic moves, many of which are fluid and open to varying kinds of reformulation; and questions of practical appropriation are always mediated by questions of the wider life of the community in relation to scripture as a whole.[14]

Among other things, this means that characteristic Christian and Jewish reading of scripture tends to be a complex matter that is always indebted to some kind of rule of faith, which provides a way

[14] A fundamental weakness of the biblical theology movement, to which Stendahl refers, was its tendency to separate "pure" biblical thought (of a Hebrew nature) from the distorting influences especially of patristic interpretation (of an unduly abstract Greek nature), without realizing that to separate the biblical text from the continuing tradition of Christian thought and practice is to deprive oneself of the necessary resources for responsible weighing and appropriating of the text – however difficult the exercise may sometimes be.

of relating the parts to the tenor of the whole.[15] Rules of faith can vary markedly in their application and are not separable from wider contexts of faith and practice. So, for example, Calvin's Reformed identity and resistance to the Roman Catholic Church and von Rad's Lutheran affiliation, membership in the Confessing Church, and resistance to Nazism influenced the ways they articulate their readings of scripture. But the basic point is that what is recognized to count as good theology in relation to the Bible is far more subtle and differentiated than is often recognized and draws, consciously and unconsciously, on numerous resources in the literature and life of the last two thousand years.

How this all may work is unpredictable. The fact that Genesis countenances, for example, polygamy, sharp practice in sheep breeding, or scattered construction of altars has not generally moved interpreters to suppose that they should adopt such practices. However, Noah's curse of Ham/Canaan did lead some Christians, most notoriously in North America and South Africa, to suppose that those who could be identified as Ham's descendants should be induced to serve those who identified themselves as descendants of Shem – though this has been abandoned not just

---

[15] There has been a resurgence of Christian interest in this issue in recent years. As introductions, see K. Greene-McCreight, "Rule of Faith," in *Dictionary for Theological Interpretation of the Bible*, ed. Kevin Vanhoozer et al. (Grand Rapids, MI: Baker Academic, 2005), 703–4; and Ephraim Radner and George Sumner, eds., *The Rule of Faith: Scripture, Canon, and Creed in a Critical Age* (Harrisburg, PA: Morehouse, 1998). There is, I think, less work from Jewish perspectives, and in any case the language and frame of reference of rule of faith is Christian rather than Jewish; nevertheless, a good example of an articulation of a Jewish rule of faith is Moshe Greenberg, "On the Political Use of the Bible in Modern Israel: An Engaged Critique," in *Pomegranates and Golden Bells: Studies in Biblical, Jewish, and Near Eastern Ritual, Law, and Literature in Honor of Jacob Milgrom*, ed. David P. Wright, David Noel Freedman, and Avi Hurvitz (Winona Lake, IN: Eisenbrauns, 1995), 461–71.

because of secular pressures (though they helped) but because it has also been seen to compromise the fundamental Christian understanding of God and humanity.

The theological interpretation of scripture – its reading with a view to articulating and practicing its enduring significance for human life under God – involves a constant holding together of parts and a whole which is regularly reconfigured. It is in the meeting of biblical text with canonical context and the ongoing life of communities of faith that theology is done – and where one may hope to try to articulate a theology of Genesis.

Text and Contexts: An Example

One consequence of the understanding of theology just outlined is that the context of the interpreter becomes significant in a variety of possible ways. The entrance point into working theologically with Genesis need not arise from systematic reading of the biblical text itself, but rather from some issue or challenge within continuing Christian life.

One example, typical of countless others, can be seen in the following recent remarks by Stanley Hauerwas, in the context of a discussion of the difference that Christian faith should make to education, with special reference to the work of Luigi Giussani:

> Consider the implications of Giussani's almost throwaway observation – "Luckily, time makes us grow old" (p. 72) – for how medicine, and the sciences that serve medicine, should be understood. I think there is no denying that the current enthusiasm for "genomics" (that allegedly will make it possible to "treat" us before we become sick) draws on an extraordinary fear of suffering and death incompatible with Giussani's observation that *luckily* time makes us grow old. Our culture seems increasingly moving to the view that aging itself is an illness, and if it is possible, we ought to create and fund research that promises us that we may be able to get out of life alive. I find it

hard to believe that such a science could be supported by a people
who begin Lent by being told that we are dust and it is to dust we
will return.

For Christians to create an alternative culture and alternative
structures to the knowledges produced and taught in universities
that are shaped by the fear of death, I think, is a challenge we cannot
avoid.[16]

My interest here lies in Hauerwas's appeal to the words of God
spoken to the first humans in Genesis 3:19b: "You are dust, and to
dust you shall return." This verse, probably known best from its
use in funeral services, may or may not feature in a conventional
theology of Genesis, although there can be little doubt that the
nature of human life as mortal under God is an important concern
within Genesis: It is central to the story of the Garden of Eden;
the repeated "and he died" has a key role within the list of long-
lived antediluvians in Genesis 5; the dying words and actions of
Abraham, Isaac, Jacob, and Joseph play a crucial role within the
overall narrative sequence.[17] Yet although this issue offers a real
entrée to the theological concerns of Genesis, it is the twenty-first
century context, with a Western culture increasingly influenced by
the fear of dying, that gives Genesis 3:19 the possibility of making
some real difference to how people today think and act.

[16] Stanley Hauerwas, "How Risky Is *The Risk of Education*? Random Reflections
   from the American Context," in Hauerwas, *The State of the University: Academic Knowledges and the Knowledge of God* (Oxford, UK: Blackwell, 2007),
   45–57 (53). His constructive engagement is with Luigi Giussani, *The Risk of
   Education: Discovering Our Ultimate Destiny*, trans. Rosanna Frongia (New
   York: Crossroad, 2001).
[17] I take the liberty of including Abraham's commissioning of his servant to find a
   wife for Isaac in Genesis 24 under this heading, as it is premised on Abraham's
   old age and incapacity to fulfil the task himself, even though it is not the kind
   of impending death scenario that we encounter in Genesis 27, 48–49, 50:24–26.

Moreover, Hauerwas is not appealing to the theology of Genesis as such, but rather to a particular Christian liturgical use of the Genesis text: It is the Genesis text as recontextualized within a frame of reference other than its own literary context that is significant, indeed authoritative. This other context indeed takes seriously the plain sense of the Genesis words in their own right, as a pronouncement of human mortality and a reminder of human continuity with the wider material environment. Yet as part of a Lenten liturgy, it does this within a frame of reference that looks to Good Friday and Easter where God's own entering into, and overcoming of, death is portrayed – a frame of reference beyond the ken of the Genesis writers.

So, if Genesis 3:19 is to have some contemporary cutting edge and allow some of the theology of Genesis to bear on a culture fearful of death, it will do so not by appeal to Genesis in its own right but by virtue of continuing Christian faith and worship providing a context within which an important concern of the Genesis text can still be meaningfully articulated and heard, in a way that may be timely.[18]

It follows from this that there is something intrinsically contextual and provisional about theological use of the biblical text. Theology is not a once-for-all exercise in finding the right words and/or deeds, but rather a continuing and ever-repeated attempt to articulate what a faithful understanding and use of the biblical text might look like in the changing circumstances of life. To be sure,

---

[18] Much of what I say here and elsewhere applies also, mutatis mutandis, to Jewish contexts for hearing and appropriating Tanak. My predominant emphasis on Christian understanding and use is primarily a reflection of my limited expertise and the constraints of a word count and is not intended to downplay the significance of Jewish contexts. My Christian reading of Genesis may, I hope, be heuristically useful for Jewish readers, who can then themselves articulate what a Jewish understanding and appropriating might entail.

philological and historical insights into the nature and meaning of the text should enter into these ever-renewed attempts, so that one does not say silly things willy-nilly; and one can always learn from the giants among earlier generations of biblical commentators. So, one does not start afresh each time, but in principle one has an accumulated wisdom to draw on. However, this is easier said in theory than realized in practice.

CONCLUSION

In the light of what has been said, I offer two final observations about the nature and scope of this study. First, the approach to the text of Genesis taken here will typically be via particular arguments about it and particular uses of it. In the dialectic between ancient text, reception, and contemporary context, reception and/or contemporary context will usually be the starting point. I hope that this will shed illumination on the theological significance of the biblical text in ways that would not be possible if a different approach were adopted.

Second, the discussion of the biblical text will necessarily be selective. Otherwise this book would simply need to be much, much longer. Although I have tried to include most of the famous passages whose discussion one might reasonably expect to find in a work such as this, I am painfully aware of what is not included; for this I ask the reader's indulgence (and forgiveness). What follows is a guide to, rather than a comprehensive coverage of, what theological understanding and appropriation of Genesis today may involve.

CHAPTER 2

On Reading Genesis 1–11

Before we consider the theological meaning and significance of the early chapters of Genesis, whose use within Christian faith has been enormous, it will be appropriate to say something about the genre of the material. For one cannot put good questions to and expect fruitful answers from a text without a grasp of the kind of material that it is. If one misjudges the genre, then one may produce poor and misguided interpretations.[1]

One initial difficulty, however, concerns the problem of finding a good classificatory term. All the common terms – myth, folktale, legend, saga – tend to be used in a wide variety of ways. Especially with usage of "myth," there is something of a chasm between scholarly understandings and popular pejorative uses. Thus, unless any term is carefully defined, it is unlikely to be helpful. Moreover, argument about the appropriateness of particular terms can easily displace attention to those features of the text that give rise to the use of the term in the first place. I propose, therefore, to eschew the use of any particular classificatory label and to focus

---

[1] See, e.g., John Barton, *Reading the Old Testament: Method in Biblical Study*, rev. ed. (Louisville, KY: Westminster John Knox, 1996).

rather on an inductive study of indicative features within selected texts.[2]

BUILDING ON THE HISTORY OF INTERPRETATION

At the outset it is worth noting something of the history of interpretation of the early chapters of Genesis. Among other things, this history can dispel facile assumptions, especially the assumption that difficulties with the genre of the text are solely the result of the development of modern historical and scientific awareness.

The first giant in the history of Christian biblical interpretation – Origen, in the third century – already addressed this issue. In the course of a general discussion of biblical interpretation, and in support of his thesis that "spiritual" interpretation could be hidden in the text and might be indicated by a narrative of events that could not have happened, Origen cites, among other texts, the early chapters of Genesis:

> For who that has understanding will suppose that the first, and second, and third day, and the evening and the morning, existed without a sun, and moon, and stars? and that the first day was, as it were, also without a sky? And who is so foolish as to suppose that God, after the manner of a husbandman, planted a paradise in Eden, towards the east, and placed in it a tree of life, visible and palpable, so that one tasting of the fruit by the bodily teeth obtained life? and again, that one was a partaker of good and evil by masticating what was taken from the tree? And if God is said to walk in the paradise in the evening, and Adam to hide himself under a tree, I do not suppose that any one doubts that these things figuratively indicate certain mysteries, the history having taken place in appearance, and

[2] I draw on my "How Should One Read the Early Chapters of Genesis?" in *Reading Genesis after Darwin*, ed. Stephen Barton and David Wilkinson (New York: Oxford University Press, 2009).

not "literally."[3] Cain also, when going forth from the presence of God, certainly appears to thoughtful men as likely to lead the reader to inquire what is the presence of God, and what is the meaning of going out from Him. And what need is there to say more, since those who are not altogether blind can collect countless instances of a similar kind recorded as having occurred, but which did not "literally"[4] take place?[5]

One does not need to follow Origen's distinctive construal of the way in which surface difficulties in the biblical text give rise to a deeper spiritual reading to appreciate the basic force of his observations as to the difficulties in a certain kind of face-value reading of the text.

More specifically, the value of reception history can be seen in the story of Cain and Abel in Genesis 4. The problem posed by this narrative is simple. Its internal details are in significant ways at odds with its present context at the outset of human life on earth. The problem has tended to be expressed popularly as the question, "Whence Cain's wife?" St. Augustine, for example, famously discussed this question, and his approach provided a conceptuality that was long influential; in essence, he argued that the problems of the text are to be explained in terms of omission because of selection and compression. Adam and Eve had many

---

[3] The Greek at this point (*ou sōmatikōs*) needs careful rendering so as not to skew it through categories that are eloquent of subsequent debates but not of Origen's frame of reference. I think "not 'literally'" is infelicitous in this regard, for Origen is indeed attentive to the letter of the text. It is the fact that the meaning of what the words say resists comprehension in terms of the familiar categories of action in space and time that moves him to read on a spiritual level.

[4] The Greek here (*kata tēn lexin*) seems to signify "in the terms of the wording of the text."

[5] *De Principiis* 4.1.16. The translation is Frederick Crombie's in *The Writings of Origen*, vol. 1, Ante-Nicene Christian Library 10 (Edinburgh, UK: T. & T. Clark, 1869), 315–17.

other children, details about whom are omitted in the biblical text, in its selectivity, even while it recognizes their existence (Gen 5:4b).[6] So, Cain and Abel married their sisters, and the world's early population expanded rapidly even though few details are given in the biblical text.

One major drawback with focusing on Cain's wife is that it can give the impression that the wife is the only detail of the narrative that is problematic within the wider context; this is clearly not the case.[7] For although the story does not mention any specific human characters other than Cain and Abel, it nonetheless presupposes throughout that the earth is populated. First, at the outset (4:2), Abel is said to be "a keeper of sheep" while Cain is "a tiller of the ground." Such divisions of labor with their particular categorizations would not be meaningful if there were only a handful of people on the earth; rather, they presuppose a regular population with its familiar tasks. Second, it is when Cain and Abel are in the open countryside that Cain kills Abel (4:8). The point of being in the open countryside is that one is away from other people in their settlements[8] – which is why most, though not all, manuscript traditions have Cain make a specific proposal for going out to the countryside; murder is best committed without an audience (cf. Deut 21:1–9), though Cain discovers that one cannot so easily escape YHWH as audience. Third, Cain complains to YHWH that if he has to become a "restless wanderer," then anyone who

---

[6] See *Questions on the Heptateuch* 1.1. The more general issue of the necessary marriage of brothers and sisters in early times is discussed in *City of God* 15.16.

[7] As Augustine himself recognized. He clearly saw that the reference to a "city" was the substantive problem needing discussion (*Questions on the Heptateuch* 1.1; *City of God* 15.8).

[8] The Hebrew term for open territory, *śādeh*, can be a kind of opposite to *ʿîr*, settled space (see, e.g., Lev 14:53).

finds him may kill him (4:14). Why? If the world were populated only by a few offspring of Adam and Eve, then they would naturally occupy a limited space, and so the more Cain wandered, the farther away he would be from these other people.[9] Rather, the implicit logic appears to be that someone constantly on the move, in the familiar populated world, lacks the protective support systems that go with one's belonging to a regular community; such an unprotected person is easily "picked off" by anyone in a merciless frame of mind.[10] Fourth, in the immediate aftermath of the main story, in the same context as the mention of Cain's wife, there is reference to the building of a "city" (*'îr*; 4:17). This familiar translation of the most common Hebrew word for a human settlement is potentially misleading because it can encourage the contemporary reader to imagine far larger populations and settlements than were in fact characteristic of the ancient world; with a few exceptions, most cities within the Old Testament would be comparable in population size to villages in the medieval and modern world. Nevertheless, this still presupposes the kind of population density and organization that is also presupposed at the outset by the roles of shepherd and farmer (4:2) and is at odds with the story's own location at the very beginnings of human life on earth.

How is this mismatch between the story's own assumptions and its present context best explained? The points I have raised, and

---

[9] Peoples are scattered far and wide only after Babel (Gen 11:9).

[10] One may compare the regular legal injunctions to care for the *gēr*, the "resident alien," that is, someone on foreign territory away from his or her own clan or tribe, who, like the orphan and widow, was a particularly vulnerable person because he or she lacked regular support and protection (e.g., Lev 19:33; Deut 10:17–19).

many others also, were fascinatingly discussed by a now-forgotten writer of the seventeenth century, who in his time had great influence, Isaac La Peyrère.[11] La Peyrère saw the consistent intrinsic problems of the text much more clearly than did his predecessors (such as St. Augustine, who only discussed Cain's city and Cain's wife). However, the conceptuality of La Peyrère's resolution remained in principle within Augustine's frame of reference – namely, that the difficulties within the text are the result of selective omission. Nonetheless, although in principle La Peyrère differed from St. Augustine in degree rather than in kind, he in fact stretched the conceptuality of selective omission to the breaking point. His key move was to argue that the Genesis text, in its selectivity, tells only the history of the Jews and not of humanity as a whole – and thus there were humans before Adam, "pre-Adamites" (a proposal that generated a huge debate for the best part of two centuries until a Darwinian frame of reference changed the shape of the debate); the details of the Cain and Abel story show that the Bible is aware of a larger human history that it chooses not to tell. Thereby La Peyrère was able to accommodate the recent European discoveries of a geography (especially the Americas) and a history (from the texts of the Chaldeans and Egyptians) that apparently did not fit within a biblical view of the world. According to La Peyrère's thesis, the apparent conflict between Genesis and new knowledge was thereby reconciled – a motivation that did not prevent his book being burnt in public and subjected to numerous rebuttals on the

---

[11] A convenient introduction to La Peyrère is Heikki Räisänen, "The Bible and the Traditions of the Nations: Isaac La Peyrère as a Precursor of Biblical Criticism," in Räisänen, *Marcion, Muhammad and the Mahatma* (London: SCM, 1997), 137–52.

part of the affronted faithful, both in his own day and for many years subsequently.[12]

On its own terms, the approach of St. Augustine or La Peyrère makes some sense and may still commend itself in one form or other to those for whom it still appeals to engage in a certain kind of reconciling of conflicts between the Bible and other forms of knowledge; the phenomenon of creationism attests, among other things, the enduring attraction of such an approach (however much creationists might – and no doubt do – dislike La Peyrère's particular proposals). However, the approach has been generally abandoned for the reason that its narrowly conceived view of how to handle problems does justice neither to the Bible nor to other forms of knowledge. For the present I would simply note that, if the story in itself presupposes a regularly populated earth, while its present context requires an almost entirely unpopulated earth, then there is a hypothesis that readily commends itself. This hypothesis is that the story itself has a history, and in the course of that history, it has changed location, moving from an original context within the regular parameters of human history – presumably the world of ancient Israel, familiar to the narrator[13] – to its present context at the very outset of human history. Such movement of stories is in fact a common phenomenon within the history of literature.

The basic point is simple: A story whose narrative assumptions apparently originate from the world familiar to the time of the biblical narrator has been set in a context long antecedent to that

---

[12] There was, of course, much else in La Peyrère's work that was provocative.

[13] For the purposes of the argument here, it makes no difference whether the story is ascribed to Moses in the fifteenth or thirteenth century BCE, the Yahwist in the tenth or sixth century BCE, or anyone else within the general historical context of ancient Israel.

world – the very beginnings of life on earth. From this it follows, *not* that one should not take the narrative sequence from Adam and Eve to Cain and Abel with imaginative seriousness as part of the developing storyline, but that in analytical terms one should recognize that the narrative is, in a very real and important sense, artificial and constructed out of originally diverse material.[14] The purpose of the literary construction would appear to be to juxtapose certain archetypal portrayals of life under God so that an interpretative lens is provided for reading God's call of Abraham and Israel that follows.

NOAH AND THE FLOOD

The story of Noah and the Flood also has numerous indicators as to its genre. On internal grounds, the story is clearly uninterested in those issues that have fascinated many interpreters who have sought to construe it as realistic or historical. To be sure, one or two of its details may appear to be so. If, for example, one takes the all-too-brief instructions in Genesis 6:14–16 to indicate that a transverse section of the ark would be virtually triangular – so that the ark should be envisaged "like a giant Toblerone bar," as one of my students nicely put it – then such a vessel would apparently be stable in floating, which is all that it would be required to do.[15] However, the instructions in 6:14–16 are open to widely differing construals

---

[14] Comparable is the way in which, when watching a movie, one can both imaginatively follow the storyline on its own terms and also reflect analytically, should one wish, on how the special effects are likely to have been produced.

[15] The contention that the design of the ark would give it stability is an ancient one. Cf. Meir Zlotowitz and Nosson Scherman, *Bereishis/Genesis: A New Translation with a Commentary Anthologized from Talmudic, Midrashic and Rabbinic Sources*, 2nd ed., 2 vols., ArtScroll Tanach (Brooklyn, NY: Mesorah, 1986), 1:231.

of the shape and seaworthiness of the vessel; the numerous picture-book depictions of the ark as some kind of houseboat derive entirely from modern artists' imaginative sense of what looks appropriate.

In any case, it is the consistent perspective of the story through-out that is most revealing of its genre. The omniscient narra-tor reports even the inner thoughts and words of YHWH (6:5–8, 8:20–21). But he says nothing whatever about Noah's thoughts or words – Noah says precisely nothing throughout. Further, the narrator shows no interest in practicalities such as the following: Which animals? What living conditions? or What sort of food, how much, and how to preserve it as edible? Admittedly, the narrator's disinterest in such details has not deterred countless interpreters across the centuries; and these questions are still amenable to inge-nious resolution today, as in the work of the American Institute for Creation Research.[16]

As for the nature of the ark itself, humans and animals within it appear to live in darkness. For, as far as we are told, the ark has only one openable hatch in addition to the door. The so-called window (ḥallôn) out of which Noah sends the birds (8:6) is probably not a window in the sense that one might readily imagine because it does not allow Noah to see out. If he could see out, then it is not obvious why he would need to dispatch the dove "to see whether the waters had receded from the earth"; and the text implies that Noah does not see what is going on outside the ark until he removes the covering of the grounded ark in 8:13.[17] Most likely, the text in 8:6

---

[16] See, for example, John Woodmorappe, *Noah's Ark: A Feasibility Study* (San Diego, CA: Institute for Creation Research, 1996).

[17] The use of *wĕhinnēh* (behold; NRSV: and saw) after *wayyar'* (he looked) is a common Hebrew idiom for shifting the perspective from the narrator to the character within the text. It is analogous to differing camera perspectives, specifically a shift from a general onlooker perspective to seeing with the eyes of one of the characters.

envisages an openable hatch in the roof, made of wood to keep the rain out. Noah reaches up his hand through this hatch to dispatch and receive the birds.

There is also the memorable moment when the dove returns with a freshly plucked olive leaf, which shows that the waters had subsided. Within the general storyline, this makes perfect sense. But the narrator appears to assume that, when the waters go down, growing things reappear in the same condition they were in before the waters came. The realistic condition of any part of a tree after a year under the sea, even when newly emerged from the waters, would presumably be indistinguishable from flotsam or seaweed. It would not show fresh life, and so it would fail to make the point within the story, that the leaf shows the return of regular conditions for life on earth; thereafter, the dove no longer returns to the ark because, implicitly, it is able to nest in a tree.

In addition to these internal clues as to the nature of the text, the Flood story also raises problems in relation to its wider narrative context. These problems are not dissimilar to those raised by the Cain and Abel story, for again there is a tension between the internal logic of the story and its present narrative setting.

First, we must note that the Flood is unambiguously envisaged as a universal flood, wiping out all life on earth, other than that preserved with Noah in the ark. Although sometimes it has been argued, for apologetic reasons,[18] that the Flood was a local flood within the Middle East, such a reading goes clearly contrary to both the specific detail and the general thrust of the biblical text. The universality of the perishing of animal and human life is explicit in Genesis 7:21–23. Nor would it be imaginable that the floodwaters

---

[18] So, for example, Bernard L. Ramm, *The Christian View of Science and Scripture* (Exeter, UK: Paternoster, 1955), of which there is a sharp discussion by James Barr, *Fundamentalism* (London: SCM, 1977), 94–96.

should cover the highest mountains, as is explicit in 7:19–20, if the Flood was local rather than universal. More generally, within the overall narrative sequence, the Flood represents a reversal of the initial creation. In Genesis 1, as the initially all-covering waters are restrained and removed, dry land appears, and life on earth is created. But in Genesis 7, all is undone, as the waters above and below are let out, land disappears, and life is extinguished by the again all-covering waters.[19] Thus, within the Flood narrative itself, the sole continuity of life between pre-Flood and post-Flood is represented by Noah and the others in the ark.

Beyond the Flood narrative proper, however, there are pointers in a different direction. One issue is the presence of the Nephilim both before the Flood (Gen 6:4) and subsequently in the land of Canaan as reported by Israel's spies (Num 13:33). Indeed, there is a note within the text of Genesis 6:4 that explicitly points to the continuity of Nephilim pre- and post-Flood: "The Nephilim were on the earth in those days – and also afterwards – when . . . " To be sure, the apparent problem can without undue difficulty be circumvented, as is proposed by a thoughtful commentator such as Nahum Sarna:

> It is contrary to the understanding of the biblical narrative that they [the Nephilim] should have survived the Flood. Hence, the reference in Numbers is not to the supposedly continued existence of Nephilim into Israelite times; rather, it is used simply for oratorical effect, much as "Huns" was used to designate Germans during the two world wars.[20]

---

[19] Admittedly, sea life would not be adversely affected by the floodwaters, but this is of no interest to the narrator. In a later context, certain rabbis, in an attempt to rationalize this apparent inconsistency within the logic of the narrative, argued that the fish must have been sinless (cf. Zlotowitz and Scherman, *Bereishis*, 1:257)!

[20] Nahum M. Sarna, *Genesis: The Traditional Hebrew Text with New JPS Translation*, The JPS Torah Commentary (Philadelphia: Jewish Publication Society, 1989), 46.

Some rabbis, with rather less sophistication, sought to account for the continuity by the delightful, even if narratively implausible, expedient of having Og (the king of Bashan), as one of the Nephilim, riding on the roof of the ark and so surviving the Flood![21] But whether the harmonizing instincts of the rabbis, or of Sarna, represent the best kind of explanation should not be decided in isolation from the wider narrative portrayal.

And how should one understand the account of Cain's descendants in Genesis 4:17–24? Some of these descendants are said to be the ancestors of those engaged in certain well-known pursuits: Jabal is the ancestor of those who live in tents and have livestock (4:20), Jubal is the ancestor of those who play the lyre and pipe (4:21). The natural implication of the text is that it refers to peoples known in the time of the narrator: The living in tents and the musical playing are depicted with an active participle; and moreover why bother to mention the ancestors here if the descendants are not familiar? In other words, this account of Cain's descendants seems unaware of a Flood that wiped them all out.[22]

Thus we have another tension between the implication of a particular narrative in its own right (that Cain's descendants endure in the time of the narrator) and the wider narrative context in which that particular story is set (a subsequent Flood in which only Noah and his family, descendants of Seth and not Cain, survived).[23] As with the story of Cain and Abel, a comparable solution suggests itself, in terms of the individual narratives having a history of their

---

[21] See Zlotowitz and Scherman, *Bereishis*, 1:187.

[22] The note in Genesis 2:14 about the river Hiddeqel/Tigris flowing "east of Assyria" likewise presupposes geography familiar to the author and intended audience.

[23] Of course, a harmonizing instinct can "solve" the problem by postulating that daughters of Cain were the wives of Shem, Ham, and Japheth.

own, in the course of which they have been transposed from their original context and relocated in their present context. In this way, one both can do justice to the implications of the particular units in their own right and still appreciate the use to which they have been put in their present narrative setting. But again it indicates that the genre of the text needs careful handling.

An analogy may perhaps help. In certain ways the early chapters of Genesis are rather like many pre-Victorian churches and cathedrals in the United Kingdom. Although each building is a unity as it now stands, careful inspection (and a helpful guidebook) reveals an internal history – differing kinds of stone, and differing architectural styles, from differing periods of history. Sometimes the additions are obvious as additions – most obviously graves in the floor and monuments on the walls; the textual equivalent to these is the note or gloss that has been incorporated into the text.[24] However, one is sometimes confronted by marked differences within the fabric of the building. Almost always the correct way of understanding a marked difference of architectural style is not to hypothesize one architect who changed his mind and his materials, but rather to recognize that the building is composite and has a history. Thus, for example, the present east end of Durham Cathedral (which is a few yards away from where I am writing) has displaced an original east end that no longer remains, since it fell down centuries ago; and even to the untrained eye, the style of the east end, with its narrower multiple columns and greater height, differs from that of the nave, with the massive solidity of its shorter columns.

---

[24] Many notes give currently familiar place names to clarify the older place names contained within the narrative; thus, for example, the place named in the story as Luz is subsequently known as Bethel (Gen 35:6); cf. Genesis 14:2, 3, 7, 17.

Once there was a time when biblical interpreters felt constrained to account for everything in the Genesis text in terms of the sole authorship of Moses as a kind of a priori – even though Genesis as it stands is anonymous and nowhere makes any claim to authorship. But one of the lasting benefits of biblical scholarship is the recognition that traditional ascriptions of authorship do not (and indeed probably were not originally intended to) function as guides to composition in the kind of way that has been of concern to an ancient historian in the modern world. This frees one up to work inductively with the evidence that the text itself provides. In many contexts, the supposition that differences in content and style are best explained in terms of the construction of a whole out of originally diverse parts has widely commended itself. To be sure, such an approach by no means solves all problems. But at least, with regard to the specific problems posed by the texts we have been considering, this approach does enable us to make sense of what otherwise is either inexplicable or can lead to rather forced harmonized readings of the text that look like special pleading.

THE PERSPECTIVE AND CONVENTION EMBODIED
IN THE USE OF HEBREW LANGUAGE

One final indicative feature is the use of the Hebrew language by all the speaking characters throughout the early chapters of Genesis. First and foremost, God, who is the prime speaker in this material, speaks in Hebrew, not only when in conversation with humans such as Adam or Cain (Gen 3:9–19, 4:6–15), but also when making pronouncements inaccessible to the human ear – such as the speaking into being of creation throughout Genesis 1, or the soliloquies that portray the divine will before and after the Flood

(Gen 6:6–7, 8:21–22). Correspondingly, all the human characters speak in Hebrew.

How should this phenomenon be understood? The time-honored premodern approach was to appeal to Genesis 11:1, "Now the whole earth had one language and the same words," and to construe this in a historicizing way: All the early inhabitants of earth, pre-Babel, spoke Hebrew, the language of God Himself.[25] A historical claim, however, that Hebrew is the oldest, indeed original, language on earth runs into a barrage of general historical and philological difficulties.[26] The root of the problem is the assumption that Genesis's portrayal of speech in Hebrew must be historicized. But there is an obvious alternative. One can construe the biblical depiction in terms of the general convention of all storytellers, ancient and modern, which is to depict one's characters as speaking in the language of the storyteller and of the target audience. When Shakespeare depicts all the characters in *Julius Caesar* or *Coriolanus* as speaking Tudor English in the context of ancient Rome, one would be unwise to assume that Shakespeare was making a historical claim about the language of ancient Rome rather than making the scenario accessible to his contemporaries. Or when a film producer, such as Franco Zeffirelli in his *Jesus of Nazareth*, has inhabitants of the Holy Land in antiquity speak in English, one would again be unwise to historicize the linguistic depiction, whatever the historical accuracy of other aspects of the general portrayal (where historical homework has

---

[25] So, for example, Rashi in the eleventh century glosses "one language" in Genesis 11:1 with "the holy tongue," that is, Hebrew (see M. Rosenbaum and A. M. Silbermann, eds., *The Pentateuch with the Commentary of Rashi: Genesis* [Jerusalem: Silbermann, 1972], 44).

[26] This issue was debated extensively in the seventeenth and eighteenth centuries in the context of the emergence of a more sharply focused sense of the nature of ancient history and of appropriate scholarly approaches to such history.

been done to try to ensure verisimilitude of setting).[27] Similarly, when God soliloquizes in Hebrew, or when Adam makes a word-play in Hebrew (2:23), one can make good sense in terms of the imaginative convention of the language being that of the narrator and the implied audience, but no real sense if one feels constrained to argue that these Hebrew words are what was "really" said in a frame of reference of ancient history rather than of dramatic narrative portrayal.

Thus the portrayal of characters speaking in Hebrew poses an issue not dissimilar to our previous examples – the content of the text in an important respect stands in tension with the context at the beginnings of the world in which it is now set. Or, to put it differently, all my examples underline the need to take seriously the biblical text as a crafted literary phenomenon, whose conventions must be understood and respected on their own terms and not prejudged in terms of their conformity (or otherwise) to a modern reader's possible initial expectations.

LITERARY CONVENTIONS AND THEOLOGICAL INTERPRETATION

The recognition that the narrative sequence in the early chapters of Genesis is constructed out of originally disparate material that is not historical in modern terms is, of course, open to be taken in more than one way. Not uncommonly, it has led to a reductive

---

[27] So prevalent and recognized is the convention of accessible language that attempts at linguistic "realism," such as the characters speaking ancient lan-guages in Mel Gibson's *The Passion of the Christ*, do not, I think, always succeed in their purpose. Realism is attained by (a) a quality of acting and filming that so engages the imagination that any kind of self-distancing or suspension of disbelief is removed for the duration of the film and (b) the ability of the film to inform thought and practice subsequent to its viewing.

debunking: The material is, at best, a merely human construct, eloquent of the ancient Hebrew imagination but not of God or the true nature of life in the world; while at worst it is a farrago of misguided stories about the world, myths and legends in the popular pejorative sense, whose only good location is in histories of human error. Polemical rhetoric along these lines featured, for example, in the influential late eighteenth-century writings of Thomas Paine: "Take away from Genesis the belief that Moses was the author, on which only the strange belief that it is the word of God has stood, and there remains nothing of Genesis, but an anonymous book of stories, fables and traditionary or invented absurdities or downright lies."[28] More recently, one of Paine's intellectual descendants, Richard Dawkins, expresses himself in comparable terms:

> To be fair, much of the Bible is not systematically evil but just plain weird, as you would expect of a chaotically cobbled-together anthology of disjointed documents, composed, revised, translated, distorted and "improved" by hundreds of anonymous authors, editors and copyists, unknown to us and mostly unknown to each other.[29]

Such polemic has often produced defensive responses that have too readily accepted the questionable categories within which the critique is articulated. But none of this follows from the basic recognition of the text's constructed nature. For what comes into play at this point is one's understanding of revelation: that is, whether it is theologically responsible to recognize God's self-communication and enduring truth about humanity and the world in variegated texts that bear the hallmarks of regular literary conventions

[28] Thomas Paine, The Age of Reason, Part the Second, Being an Investigation of True and Fabulous Theology (London: H.D. Symonds, 1795), 4.
[29] Richard Dawkins, The God Delusion (London: Bantam Press, 2006), 237.

and historical processes. Thus, for example, over against Paine and Dawkins, one might note the no-less-stringent tones of Karl Barth:

> We must dismiss and resist to the very last any idea of the inferiority or untrustworthiness or even worthlessness of a "non-historical" depiction and narration of history. This is in fact only a ridiculous and middle-class habit of the modern Western mind which is supremely phantastic in its chronic lack of imaginative phantasy, and hopes to rid itself of its complexes through suppression. This habit has really no claim to the dignity and validity which it pretends.[30]

The basic issue for the theological interpreter is the relationship between the human and the divine. The human dimensions of the biblical text have been extensively studied in the modern period; and interpreters sometimes conclude, or at least imply, that to take seriously this human element is somehow to eliminate the divine. But although this might have some force against simplistic views of the text, as though it were some sort of direct transcription of divine discourse,[31] it does not really touch the key issue, which is how the divine is mediated by the human – unless it is assumed

---

[30] Karl Barth, *CD* 3.1:81. Barth is the most notable proponent in recent times of an understanding of biblical revelation in terms of ordinary and fallible human language as the vehicle for God's self-communication. The passage cited is taken from a larger discussion of the genre and significance of the creation narratives in *CD* 3.1:61–94.

[31] For some of the wider issues, see the suggestive discussion in Nicholas Wolterstorff, *Divine Discourse: Philosophical Reflections on the Claim That God Speaks* (Cambridge: Cambridge University Press, 1995); and, among responses to Wolterstorff, Ben C. Ollenburger, "Pursuing the Truth of Scripture: Reflections on Wolterstorff's *Divine Discourse*," in *But Is It All True? The Bible and the Question of Truth*, ed. Alan Padgett and Patrick Keifert (Grand Rapids, MI: Eerdmans, 2006), 44–65.

a priori that the human cannot mediate the divine.[32] Indeed, the potentially problematic dynamics of the depiction of God as an acting and speaking character in a human narrative is in no way a modern recognition. The difficult questions revolve around the nature of the relationship between literary artifact and reality. On what grounds should one really trust the omniscient narrator, rather than just grant imaginative credence for the duration of one's reading?

In literary and historical terms, it is of course true that, for example, the words that God speaks in the early chapters of Genesis (and elsewhere) are human words, part of the Hebrew language of ancient Israel, and that they have been set on God's lips by the author of the text at a time long subsequent to the context within which the words are set. In general terms, however, it is hard to improve on the pithy formulation of Jon D. Levenson: "The relationship of compositional history to religious faith is not a simple one. If Moses is the human author of Genesis, nothing ensures that God is its ultimate Author. If J, E, P, and various equally anonymous redactors are its human authors, nothing ensures that God is not its ultimate Author."[33]

In theological terms, the issue for Jews and Christians is *not* somehow to narrow the range of "acceptable" human mediations of the divine – as though individual authors composing narratives of historical factuality should be acceptable in a way that editors and scribes reworking traditional material preserved by a community are unacceptable. For surely *any* significant mode of human

---

[32] Some of the general issues at stake here are discussed in my *Prophecy and Discernment*, CSCD 14 (Cambridge: Cambridge University Press, 2006), esp. 32–38, 227–29.

[33] Jon D. Levenson, "Genesis," in *The Jewish Study Bible*, ed. Adele Berlin and Marc Zvi Brettler (New York: Oxford University Press, 2004), 8–101 (11).

communication should in principle be acceptable as a vehicle for the divine word, unless and until it can be clearly shown that it is problematic in the kind of way that might disqualify it. Rather, the theological issue revolves around probing the classic understanding that one should conceive the human and the divine roles in creating the biblical text as complementary rather than competitive. One should avoid easy polarities between divine revelation and human imagination, or between that which is divinely given and that which is humanly constructed, or between divine sovereignty and human freedom, when the real challenge is to grasp *how these belong together*. Or, in other terms, it is clear that the early chapters of Genesis – like the Bible as a whole – is a work of human construction. The question becomes whether this human construction is itself a response to antecedent divine initiative, and so mediates a reality beyond itself, and, if so, how fidelity in mediation should be understood, evaluated, and appropriated; or whether it is human construction "all the way down," with no reality beyond itself. Such a question is, of course, not easily answered!

The approach adopted here is what has become known as a "canonical approach" (though the label may or may not be helpful).[34] Among other things, this involves working with the text in its "received form,"[35] while recognizing that this received

[34] Amid the extensive literature, a succinct introduction is Christopher R. Seitz, "Canonical Approach," in *Dictionary for Theological Interpretation of the Bible*, ed. Kevin Vanhoozer et al. (London: SPCK, 2005), 100–2.

[35] There are difficulties over whatever terminology one chooses to use. Early advocates of a canonical approach tended to speak of working with the final form of the text, because the concern was to articulate an alternative to inquiries into the sources and tradition-history behind the text. Yet, of course, in relation to text-critical issues and the ancient versions, final form is a less comprehensible or useful notion. The terminology of received form encounters some of the same difficulties, but remains preferable, I think, because it shifts the focus to the role of the biblical text in relation to Jewish and Christian communities that have received it.

form may be the outcome of a long and complex process of religio-historical development – and so one is *not* trying to put the clock back by arguing for compositional simplicity or straightforward historicity.[36] From Jewish and Christian perspectives, the heart of the matter revolves around a willingness to trust the continuing religious traditions, in their various forms, of which the Genesis narratives form a part. That is, the Genesis parts are to be read in relation to a canonical whole – where what is canonical is not just the biblical corpus but also the continuing frames of reference within which its meaning is probed and appropriated. Such a trust is intrinsically related to a sense of the past and present fruitfulness of those traditions in their various Christian and/or Jewish forms. Within such contexts there is a commitment to *think with* the biblical text and its historic appropriations. Searching and critical questions are put to both text and tradition as a corollary of allowing text and tradition, received as mediators of a divine reality, to put searching and critical questions to the reader. In such a frame of reference, theological interpretation can begin to realize its potential.

---

[36] To be sure, one may still argue either way on any particular text or issue. The point is that there is no in-principle commitment to conservative positions as these have been developed within modern scholarship.

CHAPTER 3

Genesis 1: Picturing the World

The picture of the world in Genesis 1 is sublime, and it remains so despite its detractors.[1] Yet an account of its theological significance is as controverted as anything in the whole Bible. Handling Genesis 1 is not made any easier by the way in which many of the debates that surround it tend to bear either on particular parts of it, such as humanity in the image of God, or on particular issues whose relation to the text is in fact rather oblique, such as the nature of Jewish and Christian understandings of creation ex nihilo or the implications of modern creationism.

In order to try to maintain a focus on Genesis 1 as a whole, I propose to offer several different readings of the text – the difference each time being the context envisaged – in part because differing contexts, for both text and interpreter, bring different readings. My primary concern is to argue that the theological significance of this biblical text is inseparable from the varying ways in which it impacts on the imagination; *how one pictures the world* is the issue at stake. However, the way in which one pictures the world relates to the varying contexts within which that picturing is done.

---

[1] So, e.g., Hermann Gunkel maintained that "[i]t is the exegete's thankless but still necessary task to establish the fact that Gen 1 is not so 'sublime' as it is usually found to be" (*Genesis*, trans. Mark E. Biddle [Macon, GA: Mercer University Press, 1997 (German 3rd ed., 1910)], 119).

A FIRST READING OF GENESIS 1

First, I offer a preliminary reading of the text "in itself."[2] Initially, one overall observation. Although an impressive sequence of divine fiats – "Let there be ... and it was so" – runs through Genesis 1, creation is not through fiat alone, but also substantially through fashioning.[3] The overall picture is that of God as a craftsman fashioning initially shapeless material into something pleasing that evokes his delight in his handiwork – hence the repeated pronouncement that what has been made is "good," and indeed, when taken as a whole, "very good" (Gen 1:31).[4] Elsewhere, the Old Testament not infrequently depicts God as a potter who works with clay, fashioning not only humans but also the course of events.[5] Although this is not the image used in Genesis 1, and other images may implicitly be present,[6] there is nonetheless a real analogy in terms of the fashioning of something of value and delight

---

[2] The scare quotes are to indicate that the notion of reading a text "in itself" is less straightforward than it sounds.

[3] The key verbs for this are *bārāʾ* (create, Gen 1:1, 21, 27, 2:4) and *ʿāśâ* (make, 1:7, 16, 25, 26, 31, 2:2, 3, 4). There is a helpful discussion of the relationship between fiat and fashioning in Robert P. Gordon, "The Week That Made the World: Reflections on the First Pages of the Bible," in *Reading the Law: Studies in Honour of Gordon J. Wenham*, ed. J. G. McConville and Karl Möller, LHBOTS 461 (New York: T & T Clark, 2007), 228–41, esp. 230–34.

[4] Although the use of "good" (*tôb*, whose range in Hebrew is as broad as that of "good" in English) has sometimes been taken to be an ethical term here, depicting the sinless nature of creation prior to the Fall or the moral dimensions integral to creation, such a sense owes more to subsequent theological controversy than to the logic of the text, where "good" expresses the maker's assessment of his handiwork; that is, it concerns aesthetics more than ethics.

[5] See Genesis 2:7 and Jeremiah 18:1–12, both of which depict God's activity with the same verb, *yṣr*.

[6] "Division and separation are priests' business (e.g., Lev 10:10; 11:46–47). So in bringing the world into being, as well as thinking like a planner, speaking like a monarch ... Yhwh was involved in dividing like a priest" (John Goldingay,

out of material that is initially shapeless and barren and lacking in the qualities that the craftsman imparts to it.

Whatever one's decision as to the best construal of the grammar and structure of 1:1–3,[7] the picture of the initial state of the earth in 1:2 is clear: The earth is entirely covered with water in a situation of complete darkness. Not only is there no life on earth, but also there are no conditions for life. However, the mention of the *rûaḥ 'ĕlōhîm*, the "spirit of God,"[8] implies in some way the presence of God within this barren world and so sets the scene for its imminent transformation in 1:3. The transformation comes through the divine pronouncement, "let there be light" – a pronouncement that, in the terms of contemporary linguistic theory, is performative, that is, it brings about that of which it speaks.[9]

Old Testament Theology, vol. 1, *Israel's Gospel* [Downers Grove, IL: InterVarsity Press, 2003], 94).

[7] That is, is Genesis 1:1 a succinct summary sentence in its own right, "In the beginning God created the heavens and the earth," or the beginning of a longer sentence, "In the beginning when God created...," which reaches its culmination either in 1:2, with a depiction of the initial condition of the earth, or in 1:3, with God's pronouncement of light? For the most part, the interpretative heat is generated by bringing postbiblical questions to bear on a reading of the text. To do this is not a problem, though it helps to be aware that that is what one is doing. For example, the reading of the text most congruent with creation ex nihilo is to take 1:1 as the act of creation ex nihilo, distinct from God's subsequent fashioning from 1:2 onwards. This is fine, indeed preferable, grammatically, but there remains the internal difficulty that God only creates the heavens (*šāmayim*) on day two (1:7–8) and the earth on day three (1:9–10).

[8] The precise sense of these words is much contested. I opt here for what I judge to be the most likely construal.

[9] For the classic statement, see J. L. Austin, "Performative Utterances," in Austin, *Philosophical Papers 3* (New York: Oxford University Press, 1979), 220–39; Austin, *How to Do Things with Words*, 2nd ed. (Cambridge, MA: Harvard University Press, 1975). For more recent discussion and debate, see Craig Bartholomew, Colin Greene, and Karl Möller, eds., *After Pentecost: Language and Biblical Interpretation*, Scripture and Hermeneutics 2 (Grand Rapids, MI: Zondervan, 2001).

The power of divine speech – a notion that is variously developed in prophecy (e.g., Isa 55:10–11; Jer 1:9–10, 23:29) – is that it adds to what was there before. Previously, there was only darkness; now there is both light and darkness. The darkness is not abolished, but is intrinsically less significant than the light, for only the light receives the divine approval, and "light" in religious contexts is generally a term of positive resonance and potential.[10] God then orders things through separation and naming in such a way as to introduce time in familiar empirical terms, the alternation of darkness and light that marks the life of the world.

The next step is to diminish the overwhelming presence of water on the earth by removing much of it and holding it back with a kind of barrier (a "firmament" or "dome"), which God names "heavens/sky," which one sees when one looks upward from the earth's surface. What then happens to the waters above this barrier is of no interest in this context. Implicitly, it is where rain comes from. Indeed, in the context of the Flood, the opening of "the windows of the heavens" (Gen 7:11) envisages that large parts of the separating barrier are opened like windows or hatches, so that water can descend in quantities that will return the conditions on earth to its initial watery emptiness; only when these openings in the barrier are closed (8:2) can the watery expanse begin to diminish and familiar conditions on the earth return. Ordinarily, however, the barrier established by God creates a space that makes the conditions of life on earth possible.

---

[10] The Gospel of John, in its profound reworking of Genesis 1 in light of Jesus Christ, reflects on the fact that although darkness is not abolished by light, and thus endures, it does not have the ability to abolish the light: "[T]he light shines in the darkness, and the darkness has not overcome it" (John 1:5). The way in which light overcomes darkness is then expounded in the rest of the gospel as a whole.

On the third day, the waters remaining on the earth are con-tracted so that dry land, named "Earth," appears, and the waters become "Seas"; as the light was added to the darkness, so the land is added to the sea. God then designates the land as a place for vegetation to grow, vegetation containing seeds so that it will be able constantly to renew itself in cycles of dying and new life. On the fourth day, God makes the sun and the moon (though for some reason they are not named as such) and the stars. How their light-giving function relates to the already-existing light is passed over in silence, but these creations of the fourth day will inhabit the light and darkness already established on the first day. The text emphasises their practical significance to mark the alternating days and nights and indicates three further functions. In reverse sequence, "for days and years" indicates that the heavenly bodies enable a calendar to be formed, "for seasons" indicates most likely the calculating of times for festivals, "for signs" indicates probably the significance of heavenly phenomena as portents (as, famously in the New Testament, the star that the magi saw at the birth of Jesus).[11]

On the fifth day, the waters and sky of day two are populated with fish and other sea creatures and birds. On the sixth day, the land of day three is populated with animals of every kind, culminating in God's making of human beings "in his image." This phrase, one of the weightiest and most influential in the whole Bible, is not explained, but is closely conjoined with God's telling male and female to multiply – like vegetation, humans contain their own seed – and God's giving humans rule over all other living creatures and ordaining that the vegetation of day three shall be the food of these creatures of the land of day six.

[11] Matthew 2:1–2; cf. Luke 21:11b.

Finally, on day seven God ceases from his labors and marks the day as blessed and hallowed. Thereby the pattern of a seven-day week is established – one of the most enduring and least contested legacies of the Bible – with a time of rest and refreshment that is specially privileged within it.[12] Is this seventh day the climax of creation? The intrinsic seven-day pattern of the text would surely seem to suggest so. Yet for many readers, the creation of human beings on the sixth day is the real climax. The interpretative issue is nicely posed by the familiar chapter and verse divisions (courtesy of medieval Christians),[13] whereby day six now concludes Genesis 1, and day seven is separated off into Genesis 2. It is doubtful that the author of this seven-day creation would have approved, and yet this structural division, which in a certain way changes the logic of the text, has been incorporated into its standard form.

What should one make of the overall picture of Genesis 1? First, the basic pattern of the text seems clear. On the first three days, God transforms the dark and barren watery expanse into a setting fit for life, and then on days four to six fills it with life appropriate to its various elements. God entirely approves of his handiwork and rests on day seven. God is the archetypal craftsman in the archetypal week. This is a God who is active with and in the world he makes, a world that owes its existence to him, and whose humans have a responsible mandate from God.

Second, this is a picture of the world as the writer knew it. This is not a picture of a world that ceased in the next couple of chapters, when humans sinned, but a picture of the world familiar

---

[12] Exodus 31:17 strikingly depicts even God as "refreshed" through rest on the seventh day. For the sense of the verb *npš* (in the Niphal) as "refresh," cf. Exodus 23:12; 2 Samuel 16:14.

[13] See *The Cambridge History of the Bible*, ed. Peter Ackroyd et al., 3 vols. (Cambridge: Cambridge University Press, 1963–70), 2:147.

to the writer and his intended audience. As such, it incorporates the writer's understanding of the way the world is – as is most obvious in the depiction of the waters and the barrier that holds much of them back. Nonetheless, the purpose of all this is to focus on portraying the world, the known world with life in it, as the result of God's work and the object of his delight.[14]

Third, despite the lack of a formal hymnic structure, as in Psalm 104, there is nevertheless a natural sense in which Genesis 1 can function to evoke worship. This is, of course, strengthened by the text's use in liturgical contexts from ancient times through to the present. For its focus on the majestic nature of the God who makes the world, who gives such dignity and responsibility to humans, and who purposes ultimate rest, can readily evoke the response of Psalm 8:1, 9 (Heb. vv. 2,10), "O LORD, our sovereign, how majestic is your name in all the earth."

GENESIS 1 IN RELATION TO ITS POSSIBLE COMPOSITIONAL CONTEXT

Genesis 1 mentions no author, nor does it hint at a context for an author. The reader is invited to share the perspective of the omniscient narrator who tells of God's actions and words from the very beginning, and the mundane setting of the author is ignored. Nonetheless, interpreters have asked about the likely date and context of composition of the text and reflected on the difference that such information could make to its reading.

---

[14] "Without doubt, there is to be found here a great deal of the knowledge of the origin of the world that had been worked out and taught at the time, and as knowledge it is largely obsolete today. But this knowledge does not come under discussion here for its own sake; it is there, rather, as an aid towards making detailed statements about God's creation" (Gerhard von Rad, *Genesis: A Commentary*, trans. John H. Marks, rev. ed., OTL [London: SCM, 1972 (German 9th ed., 1972)], 48).

Although there is little consensus about pentateuchal criticism any more, one of the few contentions that still does command consensus is that Genesis 1 is to be ascribed to "P," the Priestly author in the context of Judah's exile to Babylon in the sixth century BCE.[15] Discussions presupposing this consensus tend to focus on likely implications for Israel's religious development and self-understanding, and a conventional account tends to draw on certain sociological and psychological principles along lines such as this:

> Life in exile compelled Israel more and more to emphasize the exclusiveness of its faith. If it did not wish to disappear abroad, it had to reflect upon its own distinctiveness; it preserved the tradition and let its distinctive features come to the fore. Old cultic uses which were formerly not fundamental came to have a new and exclusive sense: circumcision, which was probably customary in Egypt and among Israel's eastern neighbours . . . but not in Mesopotamia, became now a distinguishing feature and "sign of the covenant" (Gen. 17P). The strict observance of the sabbath commandment too became constitutive for adherence to the Yahwistic faith (the work of seven days in Gen. 1 . . .).[16]

The discussion can, of course, be focused differently, for example in terms of Genesis 1's possible existential significance for the Judahites in exile:

> The experience of the people of God may be not so much fragmentation as disintegration. The fall of Jerusalem was one such moment, both for people deported to Babylon and for people left behind in Judah. When the creation story portrays God definitively bringing order out of unrelated pieces, this particularly encourages people whose life world has fallen apart in the way it had for Judah in

---

[15] Because of the nature of the evidence, the arguments cannot be conclusive, and so it is unsurprising that there are some dissenting voices (quite apart from those who affirm Mosaic authorship on confessional grounds).

[16] Werner H. Schmidt, *The Faith of the Old Testament*, trans. John Sturdy (Oxford, UK: Blackwell, 1983 [German 4th ed., 1982]), 254.

the sixth century. God's project from the beginning involved bringing order, and it promises that disintegration will not have the last
word.[17]

Either way, these citations demonstrate how scholarly focus has
tended to be on the possible function of the text in its putative
context of composition, and on the light this might shed on the
mentality of its composers. This concern to use the text to construct
a certain kind of historical picture tends to displace the imaginative
picture within the text itself from the mind of the reader. The
reader moves from sharing the stance of the omniscient narrator
in imaginatively using the text as a lens for seeing the natural world
to a stance of considering the text in relation to the thought world of
its authors in historical conjecture. These stances can, of course, be
combined. Nonetheless, the nature of the theological thinking that
characterizes each stance, not surprisingly, differs rather markedly.

GENESIS 1 IN RELATION TO ALTERNATIVE
ANCIENT PICTURES

One of the fruits of nineteenth-century explorations of the Middle
East was the rediscovery of a number of creation accounts from
the wider world within which ancient Israel was situated. The
best known of these is the Babylonian account *Enuma Elish*. One
consequence of reading this comparative material is that the reader
asks afresh what the issues were within the ancient world that were
addressed within such accounts; one is thereby reminded that the
questions that tend to arise for moderns did not necessarily arise
for the ancients, and vice versa. Although this issue is often treated
as part and parcel of reading Genesis 1 as composed during the

---

[17] Goldingay, *Theology*, 96.

Judahites' exile in Babylon, it is in principle distinct and may usefully be discussed on its own terms.

What is the interpretative significance of these other ancient accounts for reading Genesis 1? Whether or not one supposes the Genesis writer to be reworking these ancient accounts, or at least motifs drawn from them, the tenor of the Genesis account suggests an oppositional, or contrastive, construal of the relationship when they are set alongside each other. So, for example, Hermann Gunkel, who emphasized the indebtedness of the Genesis account to earlier non-Israelite accounts and considered that its distinctive tone only arose as the end result of a long process of reworking, could still say of the end product,

> The pagan myths tell of gods whose relationships in reproduction and battle give rise to the world. Gen 1, however, knows of a sole God, not begotten and not begetting, at whose feet lies the world. There is no greater contrast, then, than between the colorful, fantastic mythology of these peoples and the intellectually clear, prosaic supernaturalism of Gen 1.[18]

This basic stance has been articulated by numerous other scholars. Yehezkel Kaufmann, for example, says,

> The basic idea of Israelite religion is that God is supreme over all. There is no realm above or beside him to limit his absolute sovereignty. He is utterly distinct from, and other than, the world; he is subject to no laws, no compulsions, or powers that transcend him. He is, in short, non-mythological. This is the essence of Israelite religion, and that which sets it apart from all forms of paganism . . .
>
> Nor is Yhwh ever portrayed as world conqueror in the cosmogonic legends of the Bible. There is no biblical parallel to pagan myths relating the defeat of older gods (or demonic powers) by younger; no other gods are present in primordial times. Yhwh's battles with

---

[18] Gunkel, *Genesis*, 127.

primeval monsters, to which poetical allusion is occasionally made, are not struggles between gods for world dominion.[19]

Various aspects of Genesis 1 come to the fore in such a comparison. For example, there is only one deity, not many; creation comes from sovereign word and action, not from triumphing over others in combat; and there is no account of God, for example in battle or performing other actions, other than in relationship with the world – that is, there is a "demythologizing" in relation to other ancient Near Eastern accounts. Although of course the sovereignty of the one God is present in Genesis 1 on any reckoning, it is an aspect of the text that receives particular emphasis in this kind of comparative reading.

Other particular aspects of Genesis 1 can also be illuminatingly reread in a comparative framework. It is commonplace, for example, to construe Genesis 1's account of the sun, moon, and stars *against* the kind of significance the celestial bodies were widely held to have within Israel's ancient Near Eastern context. As Gordon J. Wenham puts it,

> The most obvious reason for the detail in the fourth day's description is the importance of the astral bodies in ancient Near Eastern thought. In neighbouring cultures, the sun and the moon were some of the most important gods in the pantheon, and the stars were often credited with controlling human destiny. . . . So there is probably a polemic thrust behind Genesis' treatment of the theme . . . the sun, moon, and stars are created by God: they are creatures, not gods.[20]

---

[19] Yehezkel Kaufmann, *The Religion of Israel*, trans. and abridged by Moshe Greenberg (New York: Schocken, 1972 [7-volume Hebrew original, 1937–56]), 60, 62. Although Kaufmann is portraying Israelite religion generally, it is clear that Genesis 1 plays a key role within his portrayal.

[20] Gordon J. Wenham, *Genesis 1–15*, WBC 1 (Waco, TX: Word, 1987), 21.

Alternatively, J. Richard Middleton strikingly shows how the creation of humanity "in the image of God" can take on wider resonance when compared with other ancient accounts:

> It is my judgment that the description of ancient Near Eastern kings as the image of a god, when understood as an integral component of Egyptian and/or Mesopotamian royal ideology, provides the most plausible set of parallels for interpreting the *imago Dei* in Genesis 1. If such texts – or the ideology behind them – influenced the biblical *imago Dei*, this suggests that humanity is dignified with a status and role vis-à-vis the nonhuman creation that is analogous to the status and role of kings in the ancient Near East vis-à-vis their subjects. Genesis 1 . . . thus constitutes a genuine democratization of ancient Near Eastern royal ideology. As *imago Dei*, then, humanity in Genesis 1 is called to be representative and intermediary of God's power and blessing on earth.[21]

Although the considerations arising from these two examples can be angled primarily toward a history of ancient religious thought (e.g., Judahite ideological resistance to Mesopotamian hegemony), they can equally be valuable for a renewed imaginative appreciation of Genesis 1 in itself, whose perspective on the world, when seen to have a strong implicit "this and not that" dimension, can have deeper intrinsic resonance.

One cautionary note, however, should be sounded. It is all too easy for comparative discussions of the Old Testament in relation to ancient Near Eastern parallels to acquire a tacit dimension either

[21] J. Richard Middleton, *The Liberating Image: The* Imago Dei *in Genesis 1* (Grand Rapids, MI: Brazos, 2005), 121. Compare Jon D. Levenson's observation that "[t]he entire race collectively stands vis-à-vis God in the same relationship of chosenness and protection that characterizes the god-king relationship in the more ancient civilizations of the Near East. . . . Genesis 1:26–27 . . . appoints the entire human race as God's royal stand-in" (*Creation and the Persistence of Evil: The Jewish Drama of Divine Omnipotence* [Princeton, NJ: Princeton University Press, 1988], 114, 116).

of complacent superiority or of apologetic. Jews and Christians inherit ancient and still-living traditions of life and thought of which the biblical texts remain constitutive, and they speak (in many and varied ways) from within these frames of reference, while other traditions from the biblical world have not proved similarly enduring and so do not have comparable contemporary "insider" accounts. To be sure, Jews and Christians alike would say that the enduring fruitfulness of the biblical texts is a prime factor in privileging them above other ancient texts. Nonetheless, where the stance is not shared, as increasingly it is not in the contemporary Western world, it is important to recognize that what may feel to the "insider" like an objective and dispassionate comparison may look rather different to those whose frame of reference differs and so do not take the same things for granted. A judgment about the "superiority" of Genesis 1 in relation to its ancient Near Eastern counterparts is a rational judgment, but a judgment not separable from a broader set of understandings and life commitments.

JON D. LEVENSON'S READING OF GENESIS 1

Genesis 1, as a narrative set at the beginning of Israel's scriptures, has by virtue of its form and location an obvious primacy for theological thinking about creation in relation to the Old Testament. But in perhaps the most thought-provoking recent biblical study of creation, Jon D. Levenson's *Creation and the Persistence of Evil*, the significance of Genesis 1 is interestingly reconceived. Levenson appeals to poetic fragments elsewhere in the canon, fragments that depict a conflict between YHWH and powerful creatures. Although the instinct of Gunkel or Kaufmann was to see these as interesting historical relics, hints of Israel's sharing in common ancient traditions that its developing religious outlook largely superseded and transformed, Levenson wishes to give them greater continuing significance. He argues that they correspond to the continuance of evil and resistance to God's good purposes within the world: "[I]n Israel the combat myth of creation increasingly tended to appear in moments in which Yhwh and his promises to the nation seemed discredited."[22] Moreover, although Levenson clearly places a value on Genesis 1 that he does not place on *Enuma Elish*, his account of the relationship between them is more subtle than that of Gunkel or Kaufmann; Levenson finds deep correspondence between the assumptions embodied in *Enuma Elish* and in Genesis 1, not least in the understanding that cosmogony culminates in temple building.

Among other texts, Levenson appeals to Psalm 74:12–17, which

> attests eloquently to an Israelite myth of combat between God and aquatic beasts, followed by his triumphant act of world ordering. This is a myth that speaks of God's total mastery not as something self-evident, unthreatened, and extant from all eternity, but as something won, as something dramatic and exciting.[23]

Or, more generally,

> Yhwh's kingship in Israel, like his kingship in the pantheon and his mastery over creation, remained vulnerable and in continual need of reaffirmation, reratification, reacclamation.[24]

Levenson further observes that

> [t]wo and a half millennia of Western theology have made it easy to forget that throughout the ancient Near Eastern world, including Israel, the point of creation is not the production of matter out of nothing, but rather the emergence of a stable community in a benevolent and life-sustaining order. The defeat by Yhwh of the forces

---

[22] Levenson, *Creation and the Persistence of Evil*, 132.
[23] Ibid., 9.
[24] Ibid., 138.

that have interrupted that order is intrinsically an act of creation. The fact that order is being restored rather than instituted was not a difference of great consequence in ancient Hebrew culture.[25]

The potency of Levenson's argument is that he ties in the poetic fragments about combat and divine victory not only to the ancient Near Eastern context of the biblical writers but also to larger religious frames of reference, both the covenant theology of the Hebrew Bible and also the appropriation of biblical theology within rabbinic Judaism:

> Leviathan is to creation as Amalek is to history and as the Evil Impulse is to the Good in Rabbinic psychology. Each is an ancient or even innate impediment to reality as God, the potentially omnipotent, wishes it to be. Each can be suppressed for the nonce, but will disappear only in the eschatological reversal.[26]

As part of his thesis, Levenson develops links between Genesis 1 and the significance of tabernacle and temple elsewhere in the Hebrew Bible[27] – for the Jerusalem temple is to be seen as a microcosm of the world as macrocosm, and this implies a particular role for Israel in its worship:

> My point is that the idea of creation in the Hebrew Bible often has a more specific life setting than a disembodied, ahistorical theological analysis would lead us to believe. Cosmogony is not fully grasped until it has been related to the microcosm and to the rites that took place there and were thought to allow human participation in the divine ordering of the world.[28]

[25] Ibid., 12.

[26] Ibid., 41.

[27] "Our examination of the two sets of Priestly texts, one at the beginning of Genesis and the other at the end of Exodus, has developed powerful evidence that, as in many cultures, the Temple was conceived as a microcosm, a miniature world" (ibid., 86).

[28] Ibid., 91.

Or, as he later puts it,

> Gen 1:1–2:3, the Priestly creation story, is not about the banishment of evil, but about its control.... [I]n building the new structure that is creation, God functions like an Israelite priest, making distinctions, assigning things to their proper category and assessing their fitness, and hallowing the Sabbath.... As a result, the creative ordering of the world has become something that humanity can not only witness and celebrate, but something in which it can also take part. Among the many messages of Genesis 1:1–2:3 is this: it is through the cult that we are enabled to cope with evil, for it is the cult that builds and maintains order, transforms chaos into creation, ennobles humanity, and realizes the kingship of the God who has ordained the cult and commanded that it be guarded and practiced. It is through obedience to the directives of the divine master that his good world comes into existence.[29]

This is not the place to critique Levenson's thesis.[30] My concern rather is with the difference it makes to a reading of Genesis 1 and the imaginative picture it encourages. Levenson invites readers of Genesis 1 into a rich resonance chamber, where the text's significance only becomes clear when it is read in relation to three contexts – wider assumptions characteristic of its world of origin, the theological thinking of the Hebrew Bible, and the appropriation of the Bible by rabbinic Judaism. He leaves the reader with a sense of the role of human obedience and worship in maintaining Genesis 1's vision of the world, which one would not have otherwise.

GENESIS 1 AND EVOLUTIONARY BIOLOGY

I propose now to move into a different register, so as to touch on (though no more than touch on) some of the issues at stake in the

---

[29] Ibid., 127.
[30] For a thoughtful interaction, see Middleton, *Liberating Image*, 235–69.

modern debates about "science and religion." If one is looking
at the theological significance of Genesis 1 not just in relation
to academic biblical scholarship but in relation to its actual use
in wider culture, one can hardly ignore "science and religion"
concerns. For simplicity, however, I will confine myself to a brief
look at a post-Darwinian view of the world in the words of one of
its most robust and polemical, but unfailingly lucid and engaging,
exponents, Richard Dawkins.

In his *River Out of Eden: A Darwinian View of Life*,[31] Dawkins
sets out an imaginatively powerful scenario, which he neatly links
with Darwin himself and his religious beliefs:

> Charles Darwin lost his [faith] with the help of [a wasp]: "I cannot
> persuade myself," Darwin wrote, "that a beneficent and omnipo-
> tent God would have designedly created the Ichneumonidae with the
> express intention of their feeding with the living bodies of Caterpil-
> lars." Actually Darwin's gradual loss of faith, which he downplayed
> for fear of upsetting his devout wife Emma, had more complex
> causes. His reference to the Ichneumonidae was aphoristic. The
> macabre habits to which he referred are shared by their cousins the
> digger wasps.... A female digger wasp not only lays her egg in a
> caterpillar (or grasshopper or bee) so that her larva can feed on it
> but, according to Fabre and others, she carefully guides her sting
> into each ganglion of the prey's central nervous system, so as to
> paralyze it *but not kill it.* This way, the meat keeps fresh. It is not
> known whether the paralysis acts as a general anaesthetic, or if it is
> like curare in just freezing the victim's ability to move. If the latter,
> the prey might be aware of being eaten alive from inside but unable
> to move a muscle to do anything about it. This sounds savagely cruel
> but as we shall see, nature is not cruel, only pitilessly indifferent.
> This is one of the hardest lessons for humans to learn. We cannot

---

[31] Richard Dawkins, *River Out of Eden: A Darwinian View of Life* (London:
Weidenfeld and Nicholson, 1995).

admit that things might be neither good nor evil, neither cruel nor kind, but simply callous – indifferent to all suffering, lacking all purpose.

We humans have purpose on the brain. We find it hard to look at anything without wondering what it is "for," what the motive for it is, or the purpose behind it. When the obsession becomes pathological it is called paranoia – reading malevolent purpose into what is actually random bad luck. But this is just an exaggerated form of a nearly universal delusion. Show us almost any object or process, and it is hard for us to resist the "Why" question – the "What is it for?" question.[32]

There are, of course, important underlying issues of historical context in relation to which Dawkins frames his argument. He has in mind the eighteenth-century argument for the existence of God, an argument that appealed to the inherent, and without God apparently inexplicable, complexity of "design" within the world. The most famous exponent of the argument from design was William Paley in his 1802 *Natural Theology*, a work that made a huge impact on the nineteenth-century cultural imagination. Paley helped frame the theological categories within which Darwin himself thought, within which Darwin's work was perceived by others, and in more distant relation to which Dawkins still articulates his own account. Dawkins highlights Paley's work and explicitly admires Paley – even though he considers him to be fundamentally mistaken – because he considers Paley's argument from design "the most influential of the arguments for the existence of a God."[33] Indeed, Dawkins makes the remarkable claim that "I could not

---

[32] Ibid., 95–96.

[33] Richard Dawkins, *The Blind Watchmaker: Why the Evidence of Evolution Reveals a Universe Without Design* (New York: W. W. Norton, 1986), 4.

imagine being an atheist at any time before 1859, when Darwin's
Origin of Species was published" – for only with Darwin's work did
it become clear that what Paley explained by "God" could be better
explained in terms of natural selection.[34]

Dawkins' key move is to reframe the theological argument from
design in the scientific categories of "utility function" and then to
destroy it thus:

> Let us return to living bodies and try to extract their utility function.
> There could be many but, revealingly, it will eventually turn out
> that they all reduce to one. A good way to dramatize our task is
> to imagine that living creatures were made by a Divine Engineer
> and try to work out, by reverse engineering, what the Engineer was
> trying to maximize: What was God's Utility Function?
>
> Cheetahs give every indication of being superbly designed for
> something, and it should be easy enough to reverse-engineer them
> and work out their utility function. They appear to be well designed
> to kill antelopes. The teeth, claws, eyes, nose, leg muscles, backbone
> and brain of a cheetah are all precisely what we should expect
> if God's purpose in designing cheetahs was to maximize deaths
> among antelopes. Conversely, if we reverse-engineer an antelope we
> find equally impressive evidence of design for precisely the opposite
> end: the survival of antelopes and starvation among cheetahs. It is
> as though cheetahs had been designed by one deity and antelopes by
> a rival deity. Alternatively, if there is only one Creator who made the
> tiger and the lamb, the cheetah and the gazelle, what is He playing
> at? Is He a sadist who enjoys spectator blood sports? Is He trying to
> avoid overpopulation in the mammals of Africa? Is He maneuvering
> to maximize David Attenborough's television ratings? These are all
> intelligible utility functions that might have turned out to be true. In
> fact, of course, they are all completely wrong. We now understand
> the single Utility Function of life in great detail, and it is nothing
> like any of those.[35]

[34] Ibid., 5.
[35] Dawkins, *River Out of Eden*, 104–5.

Having thus disposed of the design argument by a droll reductio ad absurdum, Dawkins goes on to state his positive alternative:

[T]he true utility function of life, that which is being maximized in the natural world, is DNA survival. But DNA is not floating free; it is locked up in living bodies and it has to make the most of the levers of power at its disposal. DNA sequences that find themselves in cheetah bodies maximize their survival by causing those bodies to kill gazelles. Sequences that find themselves in gazelle bodies maximize their survival by promoting opposite ends. But it is DNA survival that is being maximized in both cases.[36]

After providing further examples, Dawkins comes to his peroration in which one potent imaginative picture, the world as the wondrous creation of a good God, is displaced by another – the world as the place of unending and pointless suffering, or rather suffering whose sole point is the survival of entirely uncaring DNA:

If Nature were kind, she would at least make the minor concession of anesthetizing caterpillars before they are eaten alive from within. But Nature is neither kind nor unkind. She is neither against suffering nor for it. Nature is not interested one way or the other in suffering, unless it affects the survival of DNA.... The total amount of suffering per year in the natural world is beyond all decent contemplation. During the minute it takes me to compose this sentence, thousands of animals are being eaten alive; others are running for their lives, whimpering with fear; others are being slowly devoured from within by rasping parasites; thousands of all kinds are dying of starvation, thirst and disease. It must be so. If there is ever a time of plenty, this very fact will automatically lead to an increase in population until the natural state of starvation and misery is restored...

... In a universe of blind physical forces and genetic replication, some people are going to get hurt, other people are going to get lucky, and you won't find any rhyme or reason in it, nor any justice.

[36] Ibid., 105–6.

The universe we observe has precisely the properties we should expect if there is, at bottom, no design, no purpose, no evil and no good, nothing but blind, pitiless indifference.... DNA neither knows nor cares. DNA just is. And we dance to its music.[37]

The strength of Dawkins' position comes from its smooth and rhetorically potent combination of science (post-Darwinian biology, reformulated in the light of the discovery of DNA), theology (the incompatibility of endless and destructive suffering with a good God), and imagination (the construction of a compelling scenario of life in the world that can displace traditional Jewish and Christian scenarios rooted ultimately in Genesis 1). This is not the place to discuss the science, but three comments on the general frame of reference may be apposite.

First, it is important to recognize that at least some of Dawkins' conceptual points are well taken. For example, his critique of an undue prepossession with certain "Why?" questions may be fully justified, as when he says, "Questions can be simply inappropriate, however heartfelt their framing."[38] Precisely this point will be basic to my reading of the Cain and Abel story.[39] To find the right question to ask, and the right way of asking it, is of fundamental importance within theology as within science.

Second, it is almost impossible to overemphasize the intellectual damage done by the seventeenth- and eighteenth-century mutation, indeed corruption, of a doctrine of creation into an argument from design. This tried to make "God" into an "explanation" of the world in a way analogous to the scientific concern to explain the world. Yet any attempt to speak thus of God inevitably produces what is popularly, and not inaccurately, called "the god of the gaps."

[37] Ibid., 131, 132, 133.
[38] Ibid., 97.
[39] See Chapter 5.

For when God is invoked to explain what science cannot explain, it is the present state of science that is envisaged as incapable of offering an explanation – which in no way means that science in the future will not succeed where the present fails. As scientific knowledge advances, God becomes superfluous, as in the famous and paradigmatic encounter between Laplace and Napoleon in 1802: "I have no need of that hypothesis."[40] Dawkins' remarkable claim, noted previously, that "I could not imagine being an atheist at any time before 1859, when Darwin's *Origin of Species* was published," clearly shows that Dawkins thinks that God language and talk is meant to function in the same kind of way that science functions: Darwin's scientific account of natural selection means that the complexity and apparent design of the world no longer needs Paley's theological hypothesis of God for its explanation.

However, unless one is willing to abandon the whole frame of reference in which God functions as an explanation analogous to the explanations of science, one will be sucked down steadily and inescapably into a theological bog. It is a matter of the two entirely different senses in which the word "mystery" can be used. There is the common use of mystery as a puzzle, where a situation is only mysterious because insufficiently little is known about it, and the mystery disappears when enough is known: The mystery in detective stories is an enigma awaiting resolution by the ingenious investigator with the result that by the end of the story, there is no longer a mystery because one now knows "whodunit." Mystery in this sense, if appealed to ("we can explain no more, for we are dealing with a mystery"), is, of course, the god of the gaps; and no doubt the suspicion that theologians appeal to mystery because

---

[40] For a discussion, see Michael J. Buckley, *At the Origins of Modern Atheism* (New Haven, CT: Yale University Press, 1987), 325.

they do not understand the issues and are not undertaking the necessary hard intellectual work is sometimes justified.[41]

Yet the proper theological sense of mystery is to express an inherently deep reality, the grasp and understanding of which intrinsically becomes ever more demanding the more fully one engages with it – in the convenient tag, "the more you know, the more you know you don't know." God is not demystified by accurate knowledge: quite the opposite; and to appeal to God as the cause of the world is not to offer the kind of cause for which scientists look. One might put it by saying that in place of *explanation*, which scientists properly provide, theology is concerned with *understanding*, a way of thinking, and relatedly living, that is always open to further development and deepening. Or, in the terminology of the Old Testament, theological thinking is in pursuit of *wisdom*, whose presence makes all the difference to how someone lives in the world, as distinct from an accurate intellectual grasp of affairs that does not include the existential resources for living well that are intrinsic to wisdom.

Third, something of the distinctive grammar of theological thinking about creation can become apparent through reflection on a simple example. A characteristic Christian (or Jewish or Muslim) affirmation that complements "God made the world" is "God has made me." What does, and does not, such an affirmation mean? Negatively, it does not mean that one's presence in the world is the result of something like a magician's trick, a sudden appearance without obvious explanation ("one moment I wasn't there, next moment I was"). That is, the claim to be made by God is not a denial of regular biological processes of conception

---

[41] This is a basic line of argument in, for example, Robert Oden, Jr., *The Bible Without Theology: The Theological Tradition and Alternatives to It* (San Francisco: Harper & Row, 1987).

from sperm and ovum, maturation within a womb, and birth after some nine months. Positively, the affirmation entails an understanding of both origin and destiny, in terms of coming from God and going to God. Its primary significance is in terms of what it means for a present existential understanding in the here and now. The affirmation seeks to express such existential realities as trust, accountability, dependence, contingency, the sense of oneself as a creature in relation to a creator.

If one transposes the frame of reference from "God made me" to "God made the world" and a consideration of Genesis 1, certain strong resonances with the aforementioned readings, especially the initial reading and Levenson's reading, become apparent. Such resonances become entirely obscured in the frame of reference variously utilized by both Paley and Dawkins.

GENESIS 1 AND ALTERNATIVE PICTURES OF THE WORLD: A PROPOSAL

The problem of suffering is a well-known existential issue within theology and philosophy. Dawkins seeks to make it into a decisive argument against God, within theological as well as scientific categories, by simultaneously emphasizing its ubiquity, its necessity, and its amorality. The imaginative picture of a God who in sovereign goodness makes a world that is "very good," and who wondrously brings good even out of evil, is displaced by the imaginative picture of a world of overwhelming amounts of suffering whose only explanation is the maximizing of the survival of DNA in its "blind, pitiless indifference."

But why should one accept an either-or dichotomy, when both-and may be nearer to the truth? Most people simultaneously hold a number of imaginative pictures of the world. Which comes to the fore depends to some extent on context. A walk in a green and sunny countryside or in the mountains encourages one kind of picture; looking at photographs of what the Allies found when they arrived in Nazi death camps or reading accounts of the Holocaust/Shoah encourages a different kind of picture. But both pictures must be held.

Genesis 1 is by no means the only picture of the world in the Bible. We have already noted Levenson's proposals to highlight certain poetic fragments, which picture God's triumph over unruly monsters, as a way of giving weight to the persistence of evil alongside the sovereign power of Yhwh. For Levenson, these do not displace Genesis 1, but are to be held alongside it in order to give greater existential depth to the engagement with God that is part of Israel's creation faith. So, instead of having to choose between Genesis 1, with its picture of the world as an object of delight, and a picture of the world as full of incomprehensible suffering and evil, why should one not hold these in dialectical tension as both true, with each needing the other to give a fuller picture of the truth of the world?

One biblical analogy to this can be found in Psalms 44 and 89, two psalms that seem explicitly constructed to pose the tension between, on the one hand, Israel's trust in God's faithfulness, power, and good purposes and, on the other hand, events that seem fundamentally to call these into question.[42]

In brief, Psalm 44:1–3 offers a "credal" affirmation with regard to Israel's past, God's actions on behalf of Israel's ancestors;[43] 44:4–6 continues in the credal vein, only with respect to the present; Israel

---

[42] Other readings of these psalms are, of course, possible and are well represented in the standard literature.

[43] For convenience, I use the familiar English numeration of the verses of both Psalms 44 and 89.

trusts in God in the here and now. These two sections affirm Israel's recognized allegiance and self-understanding in relation to God. But the third section, 44:9–16, calls this into question with its contention that God has done the opposite of what their creed affirms: God has debased Israel and given victory to its enemies, so much so that Israel was a pushover (44:12). The fourth section, 44:17–22, explores one possible reason for this. If Israel had been faithless, then they could understand this as an act of divine judgment. Yet the psalmist affirms that Israel has been faithful, indeed that it is their very faithfulness that is the reason for their calamitous situation (44:22). The final section, 44:23–26, appeals to God in strong language to *do* something and offers no resolution whatever of the preceding conflict and tension within the psalm, other than to end on a note of appeal to God's "steadfast love" (*ḥesed*).

Psalm 89 poses the problem even more sharply than Psalm 44. Psalm 89:1–18 is an introductory hymn of praise to YHWH, with two repeated keynote emphases, YHWH's faithfulness and his sovereign power. The second section, 89:19–37, rehearses, in glowing terms, God's promises to David and his descendants: "I will establish his line for ever, and his throne as long as the heavens endure" (89:28). The text raises the possibility that David's descendants may be faithless, but although this brings deserved chastisement, it cannot nullify God's promise (89:30–33). Indeed, the section ends with the strongest commitment on the lips of God in the whole Bible, that God absolutely will not be false to his promise to the house of David (89:34–37). Yet the third section, 89:38–45, accuses God of doing the very thing that he had so solemnly promised not to do: "You have renounced the covenant with your servant, you have defiled his crown in the dust" (89:39). The fourth section, 89:46–51, ends, like Psalm 44, with an appeal to YHWH and his "steadfast love" (*ḥesed*), but offers no resolution of the preceding contradiction between God's promise and what has actually happened to the Davidic king. The very buildup of the psalm – the praise of the God of faithfulness and sovereign power (89:1–18), who has made a promise to the house of David (89:19–37), a promise formulated in the strongest possible terms (89:34–37), so that if ever there was a divine promise that could be trusted, this is surely it – all seems designed to prepare for and highlight the conflict with the situation of defeat and shame whose face value denies all that has previously been affirmed, and for which there is anguished appeal to God but no resolution. Thus Psalm 89, like Psalm 44, is designed to confront the reader/hearer/singer/user with as stark a conflict as possible. If there is a problem of "contradictions" in the Bible, it is surely here, with the psalms put together for this very purpose.

The point of these psalms depends on refusing premature or facile resolution of the conflict they present. For some people, trust in God can be taken to mean that one must somehow deny or qualify the pain and awfulness of what can happen ("things aren't really so bad"). For others, if circumstances conflict with credal affirmations of faith, then it is the credal affirmations that must give way ("faith is a nice idea; but it's not real"). The psalmists, however, insist on maintaining both poles of the conflict in their fullness and are willing to live without resolution – though not without renewed appeal to God's steadfast love, even though it is precisely the apparent failure of this that has caused their problems. Implicitly, the psalms are to lead not to abandoning trust in God but to renewed and deeper engagement with God, even while it is left open how this will work out.

By analogy, theological use of Genesis 1 must surely hold its picture of the world as an object of delight in tension with other pictures, those elsewhere in the Bible and those of modern science, which in various ways highlight evil, suffering, and randomness within the world. The positive understanding of the world remains more fundamental than any negative understanding – that is, good is somehow more basic than suffering and evil, for otherwise the vision of God is deformed, hope fades, and the personality becomes liable to disintegration. Even so, any mature understanding of the world as God's world – any affirmation of the enduring truth and value of Genesis 1 – must embrace complexity and conflict whose only good resolution will lie in hard-won existential ability to live with deeper trust in God whose ways are mysterious, in the proper theological sense of that term.

CHAPTER 4

Genesis 2–3: Adam and Eve and "the Fall"

Few, if any, portions of the Old Testament have been more influential on historic Christian theology than the story of Adam and Eve in the Garden of Eden in Genesis 2–3. Although in recent years the story has received any number of readings of a remarkably diverse kind (which I cannot begin to enumerate or analyze here), the classic construal of the story in terms of "the Fall" of humanity retains a certain primacy in Christian thinking. So, this will be the focus here.

It is sometimes pointed out, usually in implicit or explicit critique of the classic significance of the narrative, that the Old Testament itself appears to make no use of the story – with the implication that therefore it could not really be that important within the Old Testament, and therefore perhaps should not really feature in theological use of the Old Testament in the way it often has. Such an observation, however, is largely beside the point and tends to confuse the task of a history of religious thought with the task of constructive theological interpretation of scripture. Internal cross-reference within the Old Testament is not necessarily a good guide to intrinsic significance.[1] The oneness of God as proclaimed in the

---

[1] Little within the Pentateuch as a whole receives mention elsewhere in the Old Testament.

Shema (Deut 6:4) appears to be cited within the Old Testament only once (Zech 14:9), yet the instincts of historic Judaism to fix on the Shema as a keynote text are surely entirely sound.[2] Similarly, the location of Genesis 2–3 at the very outset of the Old Testament, with the first interactions between God and humanity, gives a contextual weight to the narrative that is as great as could be.

JAMES BARR ON GENESIS 2–3

A useful starting point will be the thoroughly argued denial that Genesis 2–3 should be understood as "the Fall" found in James Barr's *The Garden of Eden and the Hope of Immortality.*[3] Barr was an eminent late twentieth-century interpreter of the Old Testament and, on this particular issue, is representative of a significant consensus of Old Testament interpreters.

Barr's positive proposal is that Genesis 2–3 is "a story of how immortality was almost gained, but in fact was lost" (4). However, his initial exposition is predominantly given to arguing against "the interpretation that has been more dominant and familiar, according to which the story tells of the 'Fall of Man,' a sudden, drastic and catastrophic change by which the human relationship with God was ruined" (4). He appeals to a range of considerations to support this contention.

---

[2] Deuteronomy is a book whose theological perspectives are influential within much of the Old Testament; the Shema represents the keynote of Moses' address to Israel in his role as prophet par excellence (in Moses' telling, this is the beginning of his account of the covenant subsequent to his appointment as prophet, 5:22–33); and the prescriptions for reciting, teaching, and displaying the words of the Shema (6:6–9) all draw attention to its intrinsic importance.

[3] James Barr, *The Garden of Eden and the Hope of Immortality* (Minneapolis, MN: Fortress, 1993); subsequent references will be parenthetical. In what follows I draw on my "Did the Interpreters Get It Right? Genesis 2–3 Reconsidered," *JTS* 59 (2008): 22–40.

Initially Barr fixes on the interpretation of Genesis 2–3 by Paul. He points out that "this [i.e., the 'Fall of Man'] understanding derives essentially from St Paul" and "is a peculiarity of St Paul"; that is, it has only a "narrow basis within the New Testament itself" (4):

> Jesus himself, though he noted some features of the early Genesis story in other respects, shows no interest in Adam or Eve as the persons who brought sin and death into the world. Apart from Paul, Adam is mentioned little in the entire New Testament and only incidentally. And even in Paul the Adam-Christ typology is not so very widespread.... Powerful, then, as the Adam-Christ comparison was to prove, it was not an essential structure of the earliest Christian faith but was part of a typology which one particular person or tradition found helpful for the expressing of an understanding of Christ. (5)

Further, there are significant elements of the story that "did not easily fit with the Pauline exploitation of it. Of these the most obvious and important lay in the place of *death*." Despite the assumption of "most traditional Christianity" that prior to Adam and Eve's disobedience, "humans were sinless and free from all threat or reality of death," this in fact runs counter to the story if "read for itself," which "nowhere says that Adam, before his disobedience, was immortal, was never going to die" (5). Rather, "the problem that Adam's disobedience created... was not that he brought death into the world, but that he brought near to himself the distant possibility of immortality. This alone is the reason why he and his wife have to be expelled from the Garden of Eden" (5–6). Beyond these initial considerations, whose purpose is to marginalize Paul's construal from being *the* Christian theological reading of the story to being *one among other* readings of it,[4] Barr next appeals to factors internal to the Old Testament itself.

---

[4] Barr is specifically targeting Paul's use in Romans 5:12–21; cf. also 1 Corinthians 15:21–22.

On the one hand, "it is not without importance that the term 'sin' is not used anywhere in the story ... nor do we find any of the terms usually understood as 'evil,' 'rebellion,' 'transgression' or 'guilt'" (6). On the other hand, the Old Testament, though "deeply conscious of the actuality and pervasiveness of sin and evil," nevertheless has no "theological principle" that sin is "something that belonged of necessity to all human life," nor does it appeal to the Adam and Eve story to account for sin and evil in the world:

> Of course, the Old Testament has page after page of evil deeds, and disasters that follow failure to pursue the will of God are practically normal within it. But these are *actual* evils, not evils that are necessitated by a given inheritance, a propensity towards evil which humans cannot of themselves overcome.[5]

Barr next looks at the internal logic of the story in relation to death. "The centrality of death is emphasized from the beginning" with a warning of death by God (2:17), which is denied by the serpent (3:5). Here, "[t]he serpent was the one who was right" for "[t]hey did not die" (8):

> [I]t is not death in itself that is God's response to the disobedience: rather the punishment lies in the area of *work*. . . . The death to which Adam will fall victim ... is not in itself a punishment. . . . [Eve] is certainly to have a bad time ... but coming far short of being put to death. . . . [Adam's] returning to dust is part of the picture of his bitter agricultural life; in the end, after all his struggle with the unrewarding land, he would himself be swallowed up in it and become part of it. (9–10)

---

[5] Barr, *The Garden of Eden and the Hope of Immortality*, 8. At this point in his exposition, Barr leaves this statement unqualified. Later, when discussing the Flood narrative, he recognizes with reference to Genesis 6:5 that "[i]t is here, and nowhere else in the Bible, that we find a statement coming close to the idea of 'total depravity'" (75). However, he nowhere discusses the recurrence of the wording and thought of 6:5 on the lips of Yʜwʜ at 8:21 in a post-Flood context – on which, see the discussion in Chapter 6.

Barr raises the objection "that, though Adam and Eve did not actually die immediately after their disobedience, they were nevertheless 'condemned to death' and thus God's original warning that they would die in the day that they ate of the tree was indeed fulfilled"; but he rebuts this as "an evasion of the text and its evidence." For the text does not say that Adam was initially immortal, and God's initial warning makes sense "only if the punishment for disobedience is speedy"; and since Adam lives on to the age of 930 years, "this necessarily means that the threatened punishment is not carried out" (10–11).

Finally, Barr judges that the overall tenor and tone of the narrative tell against the traditional interpretation. He observes,

> [n]ot only... is the vocabulary of guilt and revolt lacking, but the atmosphere of catastrophe is also absent... there is no breakdown of relationship between God and them [i.e., the humans]. They continue to talk on normal, if irritated, terms. It simply is not true that relations between God and the human pair have broken down. (11)

Eve's motivation in taking the fruit is not some traditional Augustinian or Protestant conception of "the will to be more than human, the desire to transcend the limitations of humanity and be like God," for in fact, "[t]he motivation is sketched with a noticeably light touch" and "is less that of aspiration to divine status, still less that of rebellion against God; it is more a mixture of physical attraction, curiosity and insouciance or inadvertence" (13–14). Not unrelatedly, God's initial prohibition does not involve "any very central ethical principle," but rather displays "sheer irrationality" (12).

Thus one should note "the somewhat unserious aspect of the whole thing." This is "well exemplified by those critics who complained 'What a fuss about a mere apple!'" There is no sense of "a totally catastrophic sin which would estrange from God not only the immediate offender but also all future descendants and indeed all future humanity." Rather, "the story has a mildly ironic and comic character rather than one of unrelieved tragedy and catastrophe" (11–12).

Barr's positive thesis that immortality is the concern of the narrative is developed much more briefly (while drawing on the points already made). The biblical examples of Enoch and Elijah, post-biblical Jewish interpretation of the death of Moses, and to some extent the interest in immortality in the Wisdom of Solomon (which also influenced Paul's views on sin and death) all show the prima facie likelihood within the context of Genesis of the central theme of the narrative being immortality, which might have been gained but was in fact missed. This immortality, moreover, should not be understood as life after death, but as "the continuance of life without death" (19).

A REFORMULATED VERSION OF THE "TRADITIONAL" INTERPRETATION

Anyone whose primary frame of reference for reading Genesis 2–3 is a classic Christian understanding of "the Fall" can hardly fail to be stimulated – and perhaps provoked? – by Barr's reading. On any reckoning, he points to various features in the text that tend to receive insufficient attention in many a rendering of the narrative as "the Fall." Moreover, it is intrinsically doubtful that any one reading can do full justice to all the features of the text; whichever construal one proposes, it is likely that certain details of the text will be less well accounted for than others and will remain to tease the imagination. Nonetheless, I wish to propose an alternative reading that, while by no means identical with a Pauline-Augustinian interpretation, stands in a certain continuity with it.

Is a Gnostic Precedent a Good Precedent?

By way of introduction, I observe that there is one aspect of Barr's account of Genesis 2–3 that seems not to bother him at all but that perhaps should bother him more than it does: the portrayal of God that emerges. As Barr puts it, "[i]t is God who is placed in a rather ambiguous light. He has made an ethically arbitrary prohibition, and backed it up with a threat to kill which, in the event, he does nothing to carry out" (12). On the specific issue of God's initial warning of death, should the forbidden fruit be eaten, a warning that the serpent flatly denies and about which the serpent is apparently right, Barr follows the serpent all the way. Not only was "[t]he serpent . . . the one who was right in such matters" (8) but also the serpent's suspicious account of God's motivation in making the prohibition is given full credence: "Why was it wrong to eat that fruit? In fact, we are left to surmise, because God wants to keep to himself the knowledge of good and evil: he does not want anyone else to have it" (12). What Barr describes as "surmise" is in fact simply a paraphrase of the serpent's ascription of a grudging motivation to God (Gen 3:5).[6]

Barr does not mention that there is an ancient pedigree for reading this narrative in such a way as to find God to be morally

---

[6] One may note that Barr is representative of numerous recent commentators at this point. With regard to YHWH's truthfulness, T. L. Thompson says, "The conflict in the narrative begins because Yahweh has lied to the human being about the nature of the *tree of wisdom,* and has declared that it is rather a *tree of death*" (*The Origin Tradition of Ancient Israel: The Literary Formation of Genesis and Exodus 1–23,* JSOTSup 55 [Sheffield, UK: JSOT Press, 1987], 209); with regard to YHWH's motives, W. Lee Humphreys confidently affirms that "[t]he Snake is correct in what he suggested was really on Yahweh's mind" (*The Character of God in the Book of Genesis: A Narrative Appraisal* [Louisville, KY: Westminster John Knox, 2001], 49).

deficient and the serpent to be reliable – it is found in the ancient Gnostics, who considered the deity of the Old Testament to be other than, and inferior to, the true God, and who found authentic wisdom to be present in the serpent whose speech is superior to that of the Old Testament deity.[7] To be sure, Barr would not have regarded such an observation as a properly critical objection to his reading. For, quite apart from possible appeal to the often-cited principle that "yesterday's heresy is today's orthodoxy," Barr straightforwardly considered any attempt to use Christian theological axioms as guides to Old Testament interpretation to be a mistake; to appeal to the truthfulness of God is to impose on the Old Testament an anachronistic theological frame of reference that only developed in post–Old Testament thought and that skews an attempt to read the Old Testament with historical honesty on its own terms.[8] If the text shows God in a morally doubtful light, then one should face up to it and accept it as a genuine feature of an ancient religious text from a culture other than that of today, rather than indulge in apologetically motivated attempts to deny it: better philological and historical transparency than theological special pleading.

My proposal, however, is not to use the Gnostic precedent for certain central aspects of Barr's reading as a way of dismissing it; rather, I want to use it heuristically, to stimulate a rereading of the biblical text. For when a narrative is open to various readings and resists simple closure – as the history of interpretation of Genesis 2–3 clearly shows – then it can hardly be open to objection to see whether there is an alternative reading that does justice to the

---

[7] See Irenaeus, *Against Heresies* 5:22–23.

[8] This is the central issue that Barr develops in his essay "Is God a Liar? (Genesis 2–3) – and Related Matters," *JTS* 57 (2006): 1–22.

specifics of the text while at the same time standing closer to classic Christian rather than Gnostic instincts. In effect, this is to remind ourselves that theological interpretation, while needing to attend carefully to textual specifics, depends for its overall plausibility on the larger frame of reference to which it appeals and within which it functions.[9]

Identifying the Key Issue

At the heart of the interpretation of this narrative lies a decision about the weight to be given to the discrepancy between what God says about the forbidden fruit, "when you eat it you will die" (2:17), and what the snake says – "you will not die" (3:4). Barr sees it as insignificant; I propose that it should be crucial.

YHWH's setting the human in the garden with responsibility over it (2:15) is conceptually similar to God's gift of dominion over creation to humanity in the overture account of creation (1:26–28); the human is given the dignity of responsibility under God, in a way that has wide resonance for humanity in general, and Israel in particular. The words that YHWH speaks (2:16–17) are the first words of direct, personal address, such that one might reasonably suppose them to have keynote significance: Here are the creator's instructions for his creation, in some way determinative of the relationship between them. What context other than that of creation could be more weighty?[10] In other words, if this is

---

[9] Barr's frame of reference is the self-understanding of "modern biblical scholarship," which validated itself as a discipline through insistence on independence from traditional Christian doctrinal formulations, however much its practitioners may themselves be believers.

[10] Barr hardly reflects on the intrinsic significance of the creation context, nor on its preservation in a structurally crucial position at the beginning of Israel's account of the world.

a foundational portrayal of the God whose people Israel know themselves to be, then high expectations naturally attach to the portrayal of God here. Specifically, if God's warning of death as the penalty for disobedience here (2:17) is an empty warning, then why should other warnings from God elsewhere be taken seriously? The heuristic assumption for the reader must surely be that God's words here are reliable.

It is noteworthy that God does not explain or justify either the permission to eat freely from the trees generally or the prohibition, with warning, of eating from the tree of the knowledge of good and bad. But in context the most natural assumption is that this is because these are the "maker's instructions" – the one who has made both the human and the garden knows what is best for them, and so has no need to explain. That is, alongside an assumption that the words should be reliable is a corresponding working assumption that the speaker is trustworthy.

When the snake appears, depicted only with the relatively mild yet ambiguous epithet "crafty" (3:1),[11] there are two reasons why the implied reader should be suspicious of what it says. First is the simple fact that the serpent "gets wrong" what God had originally said, inverting God's permission into prohibition (3:1), as the woman duly points out (3:2–3). There is an innuendo, in such inversion, to the effect that one might more naturally associate God with restriction rather than generosity; and such a tacit implication about God's character is not necessarily dismissed by pointing out the obvious inaccuracy of the serpent's words. Second, although the enmity and conflict between humans and snakes still lies in the

---

[11] Although the adjective *ʿārûm* always has a positive sense (prudent or shrewd) in Proverbs, elsewhere in the Old Testament the qualities it depicts always appear ambiguous, so that "cunning" or "crafty" seems an appropriate rendering.

future from the perspective of the storyline (3:15), from the reader's perspective, it is already an existing reality, familiarity with which the reader brings to the story. So, although the serpent is clearly not identified with Satan, as in much subsequent construal of the story, the implied reader has good reason to be wary about words from an archetypal ancestor of enmity – indeed, potentially deadly enmity[12] – against humans. Thus when the snake continues by flatly denying God's warning of death, insists that the result will be beneficial, and fills the silence about God's initial motive in a suspicious way – grudging repression, not benefit, was God's concern (3:4–5) – then the reader's working assumption is that the snake will be proved wrong.

When the woman looks again at the prohibited tree, seeing it with fresh eyes in the light of the serpent's words, all she can see is that everything about it looks desirable; so, why should there be a problem with it? Thus she, together with the man, acts on this apparent desirability (3:6). Given the story so far, what would one expect to happen at this point? One would expect that God's words would be proved right, the serpent's wrong. That is, the woman and man would die. Most likely the fruit would prove to be poisonous. Alternatively, one can easily imagine other scenarios – perhaps a lion coming up and attacking them or the ground opening up and swallowing them.[13] But whatever the means, the result would be the same: rapid death.

So, the actual continuation is startling (3:7). The woman and man remain alive, as the serpent had said. Their eyes are opened, as the serpent had said. And, later on, they are said to have "become

---

[12] If snakes in the Middle East do bite a human ankle, the poison can usually be expected to lead to death.

[13] For these, see 1 Kgs 13:24, 20:36; 2 Kgs 17:26; and Num 16:29–33, respectively.

like God" (3:22), as the serpent had said. Heuristic expectations and working assumptions are confounded. How should this be understood? And what does it imply for God's character? Barr in effect shrugs at this point: That's just the way it is. Yet I find myself more sympathetic to the Gnostics, at least insofar as they recognized that if the Old Testament deity is unreliable here, then this is a weighty unreliability.

One possible analogy would be a trusted parent who gives a child a serious warning, and whose warning is contradicted by a shifty and doubtful character. Yet that shifty character then appears to be justified by events. In such a situation, would not the child's trust in the reliability of the parent be to some extent undermined, and the parent's character reevaluated, in favor of some trust in one previously not considered trustworthy? Yet it is basic to the Old Testament that YHWH is to be trusted; the psalmist's "Trust in him at all times, O people" (Ps 62:8) is representative, not exceptional. If this story casts doubt on God's trustworthiness, then why should the compilers of the Old Testament not only have preserved it but also even given it prime position in the collection?[14]

---

[14] David Penchansky's reading of YHWH as a "monster" in this narrative (*What Rough Beast? Images of God in the Hebrew Bible* [Louisville, KY: Westminster John Knox, 1999], 5–20; cf. the Preface, note 3) depends on at least two factors. First, one must "ignore what other parts of the Bible say about God" – though of course such ignoring, together with an invitation to freedom from "forc[ing] it [i.e., Genesis 2–3] to agree with more acceptable theological views" (ibid., 5), may be a licence to recontextualize the story within one's own ideological preconceptions. Second, although Penchansky speculates fascinatingly about who may have been originally responsible for the story – "Anarchists? Revolutionaries? . . . Atheists and cynics?" (ibid., 16) – the question of why the narrative was preserved within Israel's canonical scriptures at their outset, and how it is likely to have been understood by those who preserved it, is passed over in silence.

Moreover, if the issue at stake in the narrative is, in some way, trust in God, then Barr's observation about the lack of "sin" language and his sense of the intrinsically trivial nature of the prohibition of eating one particular fruit ("What a fuss about a mere apple!") may be somewhat beside the point. Although Barr apparently thinks that for an offence against God to be serious, it should be morally obvious – "Eating that fruit is not in the same category of offences as murder, which was Cain's offence, or filling the earth with violence, which was that of the generation before the Flood" (12) – such a judgment is open to question.[15]

As a counterexample, admittedly from the New Testament but nonetheless heuristically suggestive for theological thinking in relation to the Old Testament also, one might consider the testing of Jesus in the Gospel of Matthew.[16] In Matthew's portrayal, Jesus' earthly ministry is framed by invitations to use for his own purposes God's power that he has as Son of God. At the outset (Matt 4:1–11), this takes three forms: first, to turn stone into bread so as to meet his hunger; second, to claim God's promise of protection as specified in scripture; third, through a compromise, to claim a dominion that is already promised to him. At the end (Matt 27:38–44), as Jesus hangs dying on the cross, the same "If you are the Son of God" recurs, now with a proposal that he should come down from the cross so that Israel's leaders would believe in him.

How should all this be evaluated? One might suggest that, whether it be feeding his hunger or saving himself from a cruel death, these seem entirely "reasonable" things for Jesus to do.

---

[15] In Israel's world, food and eating can have great symbolic significance – one thinks most obviously of the kashrut. Barr's dismissiveness may be anachronistic, more indicative of his sense of priorities than of that of the text.

[16] See my The Bible, Theology, and Faith: A Study of Abraham and Jesus, CSCD 5 (Cambridge: Cambridge University Press, 2000), esp. 198–205, 217–20, 223–24.

No great transgression of God's moral will would be involved, no tragedy, no catastrophe. Indeed, nothing very weighty might appear to be at stake, such that one could hardly find fault with Jesus for going along with the suggestions put to him. And yet, of course, to think thus would be seriously to misunderstand Matthew's portrayal of what it means for Jesus to be Son of God, in which his refusal to go along with the enticing suggestions is not marginal but fundamental to the whole meaning of his trusting and obedient sonship.

I think, therefore, that the classic Christian instinct to resist a reading of Genesis 2–3 in which God is untrustworthy and his words unreliable fully deserves to be tried out heuristically. Of course, if there is no way of accommodating it without doing violence to the specifics of the text or producing a reading that is implausible in terms of the Old Testament, then the instinct may indeed need to be overruled. But although the attempt to follow the instinct may be pronounced a failure in the event, it should not be ruled out in principle in advance.

Rereading the Narrative

The usual approach has been to reconsider Yʜwʜ's initial words of warning, in particular to ask whether "you will die" may have a meaning other than its prima facie meaning.[17] Although one common move has been to read the words as meaning "you will become mortal," I agree with Barr that there is insufficient foundation for this in the text. But an alternative is to explore the possible implications of the fact that, in life generally as well as in religious contexts

---

[17] The emphatic wording "you shall die" (*môt tāmût*) is regularly used elsewhere in the Old Testament to depict an imminent termination of life, e.g., Gen 20:7; 1 Sam 14:44; Jer 26:8.

specifically, the language of "life" and "death" is regularly used in metaphorical ways. One thinks, for example, of the response by the father of the prodigal son to the angry elder brother in Jesus' parable: "[T]his brother of yours was dead and is alive, he was lost and has been found" (Luke 15:32). Within the Old Testament, a prime instance comes in the summary challenge of Moses in Deuteronomy 30:15–20: "See, I have set before you today life and prosperity, death and adversity. . . . I call heaven and earth to witness against you today that I have set before you life and death, blessings and curses. Choose life so that you and your descendants may live." The linkage of life with prosperity and blessings, and of death with adversity and curses, makes clear that what is envisaged is metaphorical, to do primarily with *the kind of life* that Israel will live. The meaning of death is explicated particularly by the terrible curses enumerated in Deuteronomy 28:15–68.

If one applies this heuristically to the Eden narrative, after the surprising initial denouement in Genesis 3:7, one finds that the continuing narrative is readily open to a metaphorical construal of death. Although previously God and the man had worked together (2:19, 22), now the sound of God nearby inspires fear so that the man hides (3:8, 10). Although previously the man had delighted in the woman as "bone of my bone and flesh of my flesh" (2:23), now he refers to her as "the woman you gave me" and points the finger at her (3:12). That is, in the primary relationships between the man and God, and between the man and the woman, elements of alienation and estrangement have come in and have, as it were, poisoned the well. Then, in the following divine pronouncements, in addition to hostility between humans and snakes, the primary roles of the woman and the man in their ancient context, as wife and mother and as farmer and food producer, respectively, will become burdensome. Or, to put it differently, what Barr says about work as the form of the divine punishment for the man, and a "bad time" as the form for the woman, remains the case – but these are to be seen as an outworking of death, understood as alienation within human life in its various primary forms.

If this is along the right lines, what does it mean for reading the narrative as a whole? Genesis 2–3 becomes an example of the kind of story in which information disclosed within the sequence of events causes readers to change their perception of what has preceded. One's initial impression concerning the divine warning in 2:17 becomes modified. It is because the prima facie sense of the warning is unrealized in a way that is problematic that one looks again to see whether the words might yet hold true, only in a sense other than that initially imagined. That is, although one might naturally suppose that disobedience to God would result in death (in its obvious sense), the writer's concern is with the fact that, in general, disobedience to God does *not* meet with any such penalty; the relationship between human disobedience and divine judgment is to most appearances ambiguous.

This readily relates to a wider phenomenon in the life of Jewish and Christian (and also Muslim) faith: the discovery that certain moral and theological principles that one holds to be true may not appear to be true in everyday life; the heedless and the ungodly seem generally to do no less well, and often better, than the faithful. Indeed, the experience of stepping outside the realm of obedient trust in God can often appear positive, as it did for Eve – the scenario looks attractive on its own terms, and the immediate result can be a sense of enlargement and liberation ("eyes opened"). It is therefore often the case that, in the terms of the narrative, apparently God is wrong and the serpent is right: What God says can be disregarded and disobeyed with impunity, even enrichment. This can, of course, lead to a person feeling the need to revise, and maybe relinquish, hitherto-held principles – the familiar scenario of moral disillusionment and/or loss of faith in some form or other.

Yet the context of puzzlement and disillusionment may also be the context of moral and spiritual maturing. For one may look again at those principles already held and dig deeper, as it were, so as to ask whether they may indeed be true even if such truth is no longer at a surface level in the kind of way that was initially supposed. This, I propose, is the strategy employed within Genesis 2–3 – to lead the reader into deeper understanding of what is, and is not, meant by "death" as the consequence of disobedience to God. The felt liberation may be misleading, and the sense of impunity illusory, for death may be present metaphorically in a diminution of, and alienation within, the personal and the public life of humanity. If believers have not fully felt the force of the possibility that God's words may not be trustworthy and true – for so much in life seems to contradict them, and the cynic or the doubter is rarely short of evidence to which to appeal – they will not be led into a more searching understanding of the real significance of their beliefs; but such leading is vital to moral and spiritual health.

Such a reading of Genesis 2–3 is fully congruent with my contention that the issue at stake in God's prohibition and the humans' transgression need not be morally obvious to be genuinely serious. The fact that the serpent never tells the woman to transgress but rather undermines God's trustworthiness and truthfulness, leaving her to draw her own conclusions, points to the real core of human alienation from God and the real root of disobedience – not that God and humans can no longer converse, but rather the difficulty that the human heart and mind can have in genuinely trusting God as a wise creator and living accordingly.

CONCLUSION

If, in the light of my proposed reading, one were to try to classify the Eden narrative, one might perhaps appropriately consider it to be a kind of "wisdom" literature. For, its function of provoking hard reflection on the nature of life in the world with a view to moral and spiritual growth is congruent with such a classification.

Alternatively, to put it in other categories, the text provokes a reader into the kind of process that has been well articulated by Paul Ricoeur. An initial "first naiveté," when moral and religious teaching is taken straightforwardly at face value, rightly gives way to a phase of "critical distanciation," when it is realized that life and sacred texts are more complex and problematic than initially seemed to be the case. However, although people can get trapped in critical distanciation, and so become disillusioned, it is possible to move beyond it to a "second naiveté," where one learns to re-appropriate the moral and religious teaching in a deeper and more nuanced way than would have been possible without the problematizing phase.[18]

The narrative strategy presupposed by my reading is certainly bold; for, the point may be missed, and much is asked of readers. But it does have the merit of displaying the kind of depth and penetration suitable to a foundational story about human life under God that was deemed worthy to be placed at the outset of the Bible.

---

[18] See Paul Ricoeur, *The Rule of Metaphor: Multi-disciplinary Studies of the Creation of Meaning in Language,* trans. Robert Czerney with K. McLaughlin and J. Costello (Toronto, ON: University of Toronto Press, 1977 [French orig., 1975]). Note also Mark I. Wallace, *The Second Naiveté: Barth, Ricoeur, and the New Yale Theology,* 2nd ed., SABH 6 (Macon, GA: Mercer University Press, 1995).

CHAPTER 5

Genesis 4: Cain and Abel

The famous story of Cain and Abel is puzzling for most readers. Why does God prefer Abel's sacrifice to Cain's? And what is the story really about? As with all the resonant narratives of Genesis, there are various possible readings, whose theological significance may differ considerably.

One time-honored approach is to see the Cain and Abel narrative as a negative exemplification of the double love commandment, a failure to love God and love neighbor. This reading takes its cue from the context of the story, subsequent to Genesis 3 (traditionally construed): "Gen 4 graphically illustrates how alienation from God produces alienation from one's fellow human beings."[1] Alternatively, one can read the story as exemplifying some of the problems of human free will: "The use that humans make of their freedom to be responsible for themselves is catastrophic: the first deed recounted is a murder, fratricide in fact. . . . We see here what humans are capable of. But we also see, with inescapable clarity, that God will not allow this: Cain is banished from the human community."[2] Or one can read the story as an overture that

---

[1] Charles H. H. Scobie, *The Ways of Our God: An Approach to Biblical Theology* (Grand Rapids, MI: Eerdmans, 2003), 163.

[2] Rolf Rendtorff, *The Canonical Hebrew Bible: A Theology of the Old Testament* (Leiden: Deo, 2005), 15–16.

introduces certain prime moral and theological categories that will be more fully developed elsewhere in the Bible: "Genesis 4 is not only the first narrative about sin and guilt that compresses the action into particular terms, it is also at the same time a narrative of forgiveness that unfolds at least in rudimentary ways."[3]

Interestingly, however, none of these three rather conventional readings gives weight to the divine preference for Abel over Cain, which sets the narrative in motion. A reading that is exegetically attentive and sharply focused theologically will surely need to give an account in the first instance of this surprising divine decision, without which Cain might not have acted as he did. I will come at this issue via one particular reading, which also has the advantage of highlighting one of the prime contemporary anxieties in relation to the Bible and the faiths rooted in it – that belief in one God leads people into brutality toward others, that monotheism entails violence.[4]

EXPOSITION OF REGINA M. SCHWARTZ'S INTERPRETATION

Regina M. Schwartz's book, *The Curse of Cain: The Violent Legacy of Monotheism*,[5] nicely contains its thesis in its title; and, lest the

---

[3] Horst Dietrich Preuss, *Old Testament Theology*, trans. Leo G. Perdue, 2 vols., OTL (Louisville, KY: Westminster John Knox, 1995–96 [German orig., 1992]), 2:172.

[4] Literature along these lines is burgeoning. Note, for example, Mark McEntire, *The Blood of Abel: The Violent Plot in the Hebrew Bible* (Macon, GA: Mercer University Press, 1999), 6: "[T]hat the plot of the Hebrew Bible pivots on acts of violence illustrates that violence is a central, if not the central, issue for the entire text." He goes on to say that the Cain and Abel story "is vital to the understanding of violence in the Bible because it is the initial occurrence" (17).

[5] Regina M. Schwartz, *The Curse of Cain: The Violent Legacy of Monotheism* (Chicago: Chicago University Press, 1997); subsequent citations will be parenthetical. I draw here on my "Is Monotheism Bad for You? Some Reflections on

reader should be in doubt, the cover illustration is a vivid detail from Titian's painting of Cain and Abel, in which Cain is brutally murdering his brother.[6]

Schwartz propounds a thesis about the nature of identity, primarily collective identity, in the ancient and modern worlds. She sees the characteristic modern construal of collective identity as operating with categories inherited from the Bible, categories determined by monotheism and its corollaries, categories that endure even when secularized, and yet are pernicious. Identity, in biblical categories, is at someone else's expense and entails violence and exclusion toward those whose identity is other.

Schwartz develops her thesis around a basic polarity between *scarcity* and *plenitude*, which involve two different visions of life. The vision of scarcity is "[w]hen everything is in short supply, it must all be competed for – land, prosperity, power, favor, even identity itself" (xi), while plenitude is the opposite, a vision that there is "enough for everyone ... the challenge of living with the assumption, despite evidence to the contrary, that each will have his basic needs met" (35). The trouble with biblical monotheism is that it is inseparable from a vision of scarcity, which encourages violence against others in order to make secure both restrictive identity and limited resources.

Schwartz sees the Cain and Abel story as the paradigmatic biblical portrayal of these problematic dynamics:

Why did God condemn Cain's sacrifice? What would have happened if he had accepted both Cain's and Abel's offerings instead of

God, the Bible, and Life in the Light of Regina Schwartz's *The Curse of Cain*," in *The God of Israel*, ed. Robert P. Gordon, University of Cambridge Oriental Publications 64 (Cambridge: Cambridge University Press, 2007), 94–112.

[6] Rubens's comparable depiction of *Cain Slaying Abel* features on the cover of McEntire's book (see note 4).

choosing one, and had thereby promoted cooperation between the sower and the shepherd instead of their competition and violence? What kind of God is this who chooses one sacrifice over the other? This God who excludes some and prefers others, who casts some out, is a monotheistic God – monotheistic not only because he demands allegiance to himself alone but because he confers his favor on one alone. While the biblical God certainly does not always govern his universe this way, the rule presupposed and enforced here, in the story of Cain and Abel, is that there can be no multiple allegiances, neither directed toward the deity nor, apparently, emanating from him. Cain kills in the rage of his exclusion. And the circle is vicious: because Cain is outcast, Abel is murdered and Cain is cast out. We are the descendants of Cain because we too live in a world where some are cast out, a world in which whatever law of scarcity made that ancient story describe only one sacrifice as acceptable – a scarcity of goods, land, labor, or whatever – still prevails to dictate the terms of a ferocious and fatal competition. Some lose. (3–4)

She also sees the important conceptual links (to which we will return) between the story of Cain and Abel and that of Esau and Jacob when she discusses the latter:

That motiveless favoritism [YHWH accepting Abel and his offering, but not Cain and his offering] is precisely the point, for all we know is that, just as some unexplained scarcity makes a human father have only one blessing to confer but two sons to receive it, so some obscure scarcity motivates a divine Father to accept only one offering from two sons. The rejected son inevitably hates his brother. . . . According to the biblical myth, the origins of hatred and violence among brothers is scarcity. If there is not enough to go around, then Jacob must literally impersonate Esau to get what is his, and Cain must destroy his rival to seek the favor that was Abel's. Scarcity, the assumption that someone can only prosper when someone else does not, proliferates murderous brothers and murderous peoples. And it seems that even God, the very source of blessing, does not have enough to go around: "Bless me, me too, my father! . . . Do you have only one blessing, my father?" (82–83; cf. 4)

Moreover, Schwartz has in mind a contemporary, primarily North American, context as she writes, as becomes evident in the conclusion to her preface:

> Scarcity is encoded in the Bible as a principle of Oneness (one land, one people, one nation) and in monotheistic thinking (one Deity), it becomes a demand of exclusive allegiance that threatens with the violence of exclusion. When that thinking is translated into secular formations about peoples, "one nation under God" becomes less comforting than threatening. (xi)

This is a potent reading and use of the biblical text, which makes more conventional readings of the Cain and Abel story seem somewhat tame by comparison. Schwartz operates like a theologian, in moving between biblical text and contemporary world, seeking to draw out the implications of the former for understanding and living in the latter. However, her concern, like that of a significant number of other contemporary voices, is to *disable*, rather than enable, the enduring significance of the Bible; for she considers the biblical vision to be deeply destructive. Nonetheless, she poses the challenge for an explicitly theological reading to eschew comfortable pieties and to be comparably searching.

A THEOLOGICAL READING OF CAIN AND ABEL

An initial point to notice at the outset of the story, in the account of Eve's giving birth to both Cain and Abel, is that there is only one mention of Eve's conceiving (4:1b). It is thus a natural inference, often made in the history of interpretation, that Cain and Abel were twins. This strengthens the similarity between the story of Cain and Abel and that of Esau and Jacob, where Rebekah explicitly bears twins, the birth of one of whom before the other is basic to the narrative that follows (25:21–26). Whether or not one grants that specific parallel, on any reckoning, the narrative analogy between the two pairs of brothers is important within Genesis.

The key to understanding the Cain and Abel story is surely how one construes Yʜwʜ's favoring of Abel and his offering over Cain and his offering (4:4–5). For the decision one makes here will strongly influence one's interpretative decisions at other difficult points.

Put simply: To rationalize, or not to rationalize, that is the question. The great majority of interpreters, from antiquity to the present, have felt a strong urge to rationalize at this point. They feel that there must be some reason, in principle accessible to the interpreter, to explain Yʜwʜ's preference and that this reason is likely to be some kind of defect. The defect could be in Cain himself: The New Testament classically depicts him as "from the evil one" and his deeds as "evil" (1 John 3:12). More commonly, however, Old Testament interpreters locate the defect within Cain's sacrifice: that it was inferior in quality to Abel's (which consisted of "firstlings" with "fat portions"; see 4:4), that it was from the earth that was cursed (3:17), or that there was something faulty in the sacrificial ritual. This last actually appears in the text of the Septuagint, in its rendering of the difficult words spoken by Yʜwʜ to Cain (4:7): "If you offered rightly, but did not divide rightly, did you not sin . . . ?"[7] Once the text thus ascribes fault to Cain (even if of an apparently minor, technical kind), the crucial step has been taken. Subsequent fuller depictions of Cain and his offering as defective, and Abel as correspondingly acceptable, on the part of the New Testament

---

[7] In terms of the consonantal text, the LXX's *Vorlage* may have differed from the MT by only one letter, despite the greatly divergent construal (see John W. Wevers, *Notes on the Greek Text of Genesis*, SBLSCS 35 [Atlanta: Scholars Press, 1993], 55).

writers and the Fathers who mostly read their Old Testament in the Greek are thus simply developing the intrinsic logic of the biblical text when it is read in Greek. Moreover, there is no doubt that this reading of the text can be morally and theologically generative. For example, Cain as the negative counterpart of a David who said, "I will not offer burnt-offerings to the LORD my God that cost me nothing" (2 Sam 24:24), or an Abel who acted "by faith" (Heb 11:4) can, when well handled, have a valence not restricted to their common location in Sunday School curricula.

Even so, there are good reasons to resist rationalizing, reasons that I suggest bring us closer to the heart of the story in its Hebrew form. First, a comparable divine favoring of one sibling over another is pronounced while Jacob and Esau are still in Rebekah's womb (Gen 25:23). The logic of that scenario – that it necessarily excludes any question of merit or just deserts on the part of either Jacob or Esau – is nicely spelled out by Paul (Rom 9:10–12). The narrative analogy of Cain and Abel with Esau and Jacob is resonant.

Second, it is worthwhile to stand back from the biblical text and to reflect more generally on a fundamental and inescapable aspect of the human condition – that many of the factors that most matter to people are unequally distributed in ways that do not relate to people's merits. For many people, one of the things that they are most proud of, or most ashamed of, is bodily appearance and shape; likewise with intelligence. Yet these are factors substantially determined for us in the womb entirely irrespective of our preferences or deserving, and they are distributed in endlessly variant and unequal ways. To be sure, some modifications of appearance are possible (not least with the advent of cosmetic surgery – though this will only ever be an option for a minority), and quality of upbringing and education can make a difference to the development and exercise of intelligence. Nonetheless, one can only modify within certain parameters what one has been given in the womb. It remains a fact of life that some are more attractive than others, some are more intelligent than others; in a nutshell, some are more "favored" than others, for reasons irrespective of what they deserve.

Further, much of what happens in life happens unpredictably and apparently randomly. One person enjoys robust good health; another gets cancer or multiple sclerosis. One person, born in prosperity and/or a time of peace, lives long; another, born in poverty and/or time of war, dies young. One falls in love, and the love is reciprocated; another suffers unrequited love. Deadly accidents, from drunken driver to earthquake, can strike out of the blue. And so on. It is hardly necessary to recount the endless ways in which tragedy strikes to recognize tragedy as a factor of the human condition; that is to say, once again, that some are less favored in life than others, for reasons irrespective of their merits.[8]

In situations of being "unfavored," people often display an instinctive tendency to try to rationalize: "Why me?" "What have I/we/you done to deserve it?" Yet such backward-looking questions are incapable of receiving a good answer, for it is intrinsic to the situation that what has happened to them has not been because they deserved it. The only questions that can be fruitful are questions that look forward rather than back: What is to be made of the situation? What can I/we/you yet hope for?[9] It is this that brings us back to the text of Genesis, for this is precisely the focus of Yhwh's all-important admonition to Cain (Gen 4:6–7).

---

[8] This is not, of course, to deny that sometimes people bring tragedy onto themselves.

[9] Cf. John 9:2–3 where Jesus rejects a backward-looking, rationalizing question in favor of looking to a future transformation.

Unfortunately, the Hebrew of 4:7 is difficult, and the divergent construal of the Septuagint does not help. Nonetheless, it may be that some of the perceived difficulties relate to a failure to see the basic thrust of Yhwh's words. In any case, this is a passage where exegesis and theological interpretation are inseparable, and so we must linger a little.

A common rendering of Yhwh's opening words in v.7 is the following: "If you do well [or do what is right], will you not be accepted?" This tends to direct the reader to thinking that Cain has done something wrong. Schwartz, for example, remarks on this:

> This sounds much like the unhelpful dictum from Exodus, "I will be gracious to whom I will be gracious and I will show mercy to whom I will show mercy." Yet however circular, God's response does suggest that Cain has already done something wrong (even before he has) since he has been rejected. In what follows, Cain earns that judgment retrospectively by murdering his brother. (3)

Yet the interpretation revolves around discerning the Hebrew idiom. Yhwh's opening words are, quite literally, "Is there not if you do well lifting up?" – that is, "If you do well, will there not be a lifting up?" The question then becomes, the "lifting up" of what? This is a matter of the usage of the verb *nāśā'* (lift up). Although *nāśā'* is commonly used with *'āwôn* (guilt, punishment) in the sense of "forgive/accept," and *nāśā'* can be used on its own with this same sense (e.g., Gen 18:24, 26) – hence the common translation here – this is most likely the wrong idiom in context. The sense of *nāśā'* is surely contextually determined by the "falling" of Cain's face in the preceding narrative and the immediately antecedent question (4:5, 6): that which has fallen, that is, the expression on Cain's face (or possibly his drooping head), can be raised again. Thus, Yhwh's words do not have Cain's supposed wrong in view, but rather make the point that the disappointment writ large in his face can be remedied if he handles the situation well.

However, Cain may fail to handle the situation rightly ("if you do not do well"). If so, then sin is at the door like an animal that is "lying down." The image here may be of an animal making its lair, where the point would be constant latent threat; or the image may be of an animal crouching, preparing to leap upon its prey for which it is hungry. Either way, Cain would be at risk from this animal ("its desire is for you"). In context, the animal would seem to be an embodiment of Cain's resentment at being unfavored, a resentment that threatens to consume him. Yet the coming of this threatening beast does not mean a foregone conclusion, for Cain can still resist: "[B]ut you must master it."[10] The challenge is hard, but not impossible.[11]

To be sure, as the storyline resumes, Cain simply rejects Yhwh's words and allows the beast of sinful resentment to have its way with him; he kills Abel. Cain responds bitterly and overreacts to favoring with murder. Indeed, in the following dialogue between Cain and Yhwh, it may be a reputation for overreactive murderousness, as embodied in the saying, "Whoever kills Cain will suffer a sevenfold vengeance," that subsequently constitutes the mark of Cain, which will preserve him and his descendants.[12] Yet in terms of human

---

[10] The precise translation of *timšol bô* is unclear because of Hebrew's general paucity of modal auxiliaries. Is it "will" or "may" or "should" or "must" master it? There is a wonderful probing of the issue in John Steinbeck's *East of Eden.*

[11] Another possible rendering of 4:7a reads, "Is there not, whether you do well in lifting or whether you do not, sin crouching at your door . . . ?" An appropriate idiomatic sense for "lift" is not obvious in this case. However, the thrust of Yhwh's words would still be on the nature of the challenge facing Cain, which would face him whatever he did.

[12] See my "The Mark of Cain – Revealed at Last?" *HTR* 100 (2007): 11–28.

dynamics, it need not have been so; and the possibility within Yнwн's words receives a different outworking in the story of Esau and Jacob.

When Jacob steals Esau's blessing, Esau is overwhelmed with grief (27:38), an instinctive response that is a narrative analogy to the falling of Cain's face. Unsurprisingly, this is closely followed by murderous intent (27:41). So, Jacob leaves home for a long time. Yet many years later (in a part of the story neglected by Schwartz), when he returns home, Jacob remains fearful that Esau may yet wish to settle old scores and makes varying preparations – and also encounters the mysterious figure at Peniel, where the encounter with God appears also to be in some way an encounter with the brother whom he has cheated and whom he fears (Gen 32). Astonishingly, when the brothers meet, Esau tearfully welcomes Jacob (33:4). For the Christian there can be no greater commendation of Esau's welcome than that its terminology and gestures are those with which Jesus depicts the father's welcome of the prodigal son (Luke 15:20). In other words, although the narrative has followed Jacob during his absence from home and said nothing about Esau, Esau, who was in a situation comparable to Cain's, has spectacularly done what Cain failed to do. He has mastered the beast of resentment, which might have devoured him; he has indeed done well – though how he got there we are not told.[13]

CONCLUSION: DOING WELL IN DEMANDING CIRCUMSTANCES

I am proposing that the fundamental issue posed by the story of Cain and Abel is the fact that many of the things that matter most

---

[13] It is a pity that in the history of interpretation, Esau has generally received a bad press.

in God's world are unequally distributed and that being favored or unfavored represents an imponderable element largely beyond human design or deserving; this raises the searching existential issue of how one is to respond when apparently unfavored and tempted to resentment and bitterness. Within Genesis as a whole, this regularly takes the form of God's subverting the "natural" order of things by favoring a younger son over an older.[14] In the paradigmatic narrative of Genesis 4, the issue is focused in God's differing responses to the sacrifices of Cain and Abel, with the younger Abel being favored, and God's challenging Cain about how to respond.

Jon D. Levenson pithily puts the theological issue thus:

> [God's] warning locates the source of the crime in the criminal himself: it is not God's favoring Abel that will bring about the murder, but rather Cain's inability to accept a God who authors these mysterious and inequitable acts of choosing. What Cain cannot bear is a world in which distributive justice is not the highest principle and not every inequity is an iniquity.[15]

One might suggest that Schwartz is a direct descendant of Cain in this matter. For her, apparently, inequity is indeed iniquity. It is in keeping with this that she is simply dismissive of Yhwh's words to Cain ("unhelpful") and does not linger to consider their likely thrust; neither does Esau's momentous response to Jacob receive any attention whatsoever.

---

[14] See the groundbreaking treatment in Jon D. Levenson, *The Death and Resurrection of the Beloved Son: The Transformation of Child Sacrifice in Judaism and Christianity* (New Haven, CT: Yale University Press, 1993); also Joel S. Kaminsky, *Yet I Loved Jacob: Reclaiming the Biblical Concept of Election* (Nashville, TN: Abingdon, 2007), 15–78. Note also Frederick E. Greenspahn, *When Brothers Dwell Together: The Preeminence of Younger Siblings in the Hebrew Bible* (New York: Oxford University Press, 1994).

[15] Levenson, *Death and Resurrection*, 74–75.

The issues here are, of course, difficult to handle well.[16] The fact that the biblical writers, not only in Genesis 4 but also elsewhere, do not shrink from ascribing differential favoring to God can easily be taken (and, in the history of the last two thousand years, often has been taken) to justify complacency on the part of the favored and passive acquiescence in their lot on the part of the unfavored. Yet to think thus would be precisely to fail to grasp the biblical vision. For passive acquiescence is the very thing that is *not* envisioned for the unfavored Cain and Esau – rather, a life and death struggle with a beast that is seeking to devour them. More generally (at the risk of generalizing unduly), the biblical understanding of divine favoring – "election" in various forms – is, I think, best summed up in the axiom of Jesus that "much is expected of those to whom much has been given" (cf. Luke 12:48); the response that God seeks and commends is always in line with what people have initially been given, or not given.

One can readily understand – even sympathize with – Schwartz's dislike of aspects of our world. But whether the remedy is to see them as rooted in the Bible, and escapable if only one could truly break free from the Bible's lingering influence, raises basic issues about one's worldview and how best one forms it. For the reasons given previously, I think Schwartz's strategy is mistaken, not least because so much of that which she finds problematic is intrinsic to life in this world.[17] Getting rid of the Bible and talk of God will not solve the problems.

---

[16] From a wider biblical and theological perspective, one may feel that God's words to Cain in 4:7 say too little about grace, the resources from God for coping with the struggle. But that may simply be a reminder that one story cannot say everything and that responsible use even of foundational stories requires a wide-ranging canonical frame of reference.

[17] An interesting omission in Schwartz's discussion is the struggle for resources in the animal world and its relation to evolution.

If believers ascribe all life in the world to God's providential purposes, then their concern should be neither to rationalize injustice, oppression, and tragedy, nor to deny that the disappointments and resentments that can be felt in response to undeserved misfortune and tragedy often constitute some of the hardest struggles that people ever face. Rather, the concern is to express trust and hope that within a difficult world that has much that is often searingly unwelcome, it indeed remains possible to respond constructively and in life-giving ways.

CHAPTER 6

Genesis 6–9: Cataclysm and Grace

Although the story of Noah and the Flood (Genesis 6:5–9:17) is one of the most famous of biblical stories, an understanding of its theological significance is hardly self-evident or straightforward. Moreover, although it is one of the first biblical stories that many children encounter, through picture books with colorful depictions of paired animals in proximity to a houseboat, it is a story that at the present time is generating high levels of unease as to its nature as a religious text and its suitability even for adults, never mind for children.

Richard Dawkins, for example, says,

> The legend of the animals going into the ark two by two is charming, but the moral of the story of Noah is appalling. God took a dim view of humans, so he (with the exception of one family) drowned the lot of them including children and also, for good measure, the rest of the (presumably blameless) animals as well.[1]

Although, as will be seen, this account of the story's "moral" hardly reflects an attentive reading of the text, Dawkins' attitude is representative of a widespread contemporary sense that the Bible

---

[1] Richard Dawkins, *The God Delusion* (London: Bantam Press, 2006), 237–38.

is a far more problematic and dangerous text than has sometimes been allowed by those who revere it as holy scripture.

Within modern scholarship, although the moral and theological significance of the Flood story has not been neglected, it has usually been considered primarily in conjunction with two other debates about the text: on the one hand, the mode of telling of the Flood story, and, on the other hand, the significance of the nineteenth-century discovery of a strikingly comparable account within the Epic of Gilgamesh. So, it will be appropriate to preface our own discussion with some comments on these debates, as well as on the general problem expressed by Dawkins.[2]

REFLECTIONS ON SOME CHARACTERISTIC MODERN APPROACHES

Pentateuchal Criticism and Reading Strategy

First, are we reading one story or two? The Flood narrative has become a parade example in modern scholarship of a composite narrative, whose internal difficulties are best resolved when it is recognized that the story comprises two originally separate accounts, one Yahwistic (J) and the other Priestly (P). Although this view has sometimes been queried – most recently on the grounds that the story as it stands displays an elaborate chiastic structure that could hardly be the result of the poor editing often hypothesized – no alternative has, I think, generally commended itself. At any rate,

---

[2] I draw here on my "On Interpreting the Mind of God: The Theological Significance of the Flood Narrative (Genesis 6–9)," in *The Word Leaps the Gap: Essays on Scripture and Theology in Honor of Richard B. Hays*, ed. J. Ross Wagner, C. Kavin Rowe, and A. Katherine Grieb (Grand Rapids, MI: Eerdmans, 2008), 44–66.

Ernest W. Nicholson observes, "In spite of many attempts to challenge it, the evidence in favour of the two-source theory of the composition of this narrative remains compelling."[3]

Whatever the nature of the compositional process – about which, to be honest, we will never be certain – Genesis presents the story as one story. If it remains possible, without resorting to special pleading, to read it as one story, it seems to me potentially fruitful to make the attempt. Thus my remarks in the next three paragraphs represent not a hypothesis about composition but a proposed reading strategy.

One of the prime markers of two separate accounts is the apparently pleonastic repetitiveness, with consistent differences of vocabulary, at the beginning and end of the story (and, to a lesser extent, the middle section also).[4] At the beginning, Yhwh's initial recognition of and response to human wickedness (6:5–8) is followed by an account of God (ʾĕlōhîm) seeing and responding to human corruption (6:9–12). At the end, Yhwh's response to Noah's sacrifice that he will never again flood the earth (8:20–22) is followed by an account of God (ʾĕlōhîm) establishing a covenant with Noah never again to flood the earth (9:8–17).

Might one not read this as a kind of narrative equivalent to Hebrew poetic parallelism? Hebrew poetic parallelism in the second line characteristically repeats and extends the thought in the first line. So, here, a preliminary formulation is followed by a repetition and extension; the determinative divine decisions, which Yhwh first resolves in his own mind (6:5–8, 8:21–22), are

---

[3] Ernest W. Nicholson, *The Pentateuch in the Twentieth Century: The Legacy of Julius Wellhausen* (Oxford, UK: Clarendon, 1998), 205.

[4] The case is succinctly set out in Graham Davies, "Introduction to the Pentateuch," in *The Oxford Bible Commentary*, ed. John Barton and John Muddiman (Oxford: Oxford University Press, 2001), 12–38 (17).

subsequently not just resolved on but also communicated in a fuller and slightly different way to a human recipient, Noah (6:11–13, 9:8–17); at both beginning and end, preliminary resolution is followed by reexpressed resolution together with communication.

Alternatively, it is usually reckoned that the story contains two conflicting chronologies. In the one (J), the Flood lasts forty days and forty nights, while in the other (P), the Flood lasts a year, and there are detailed subdivisions of this year as it goes along. Yet this is not straightforward. For the *only* exception to the detailed overall chronological framework is the references to "forty days and forty nights" (7:12) or "forty days" (7:17, 8:6).[5] Yet the fact that "forty days/years" is the Hebrew idiom for an indefinite, long period of time[6] means that this is not the same kind of chronology as the specific count of months and days. Rather the "forty" is a different kind of notation, a generalizing statement – "a long time" – which can belong within the one chronology. In sum, therefore, despite some undoubted internal unevennesses and peculiarities that have been highlighted by modern pentateuchal criticism, I think it remains possible and appropriate to read the text as one story.

The Flood in Genesis and the Epic of Gilgamesh

Another characteristic question within modern debate concerns the interpretative significance of flood narratives from other ancient cultures. The best known of these from the wider world of ancient Israel is Tablet 11 of the Epic of Gilgamesh, which tells of

---

[5] I do not include the "seven days" of 7:4, 10 and 8:10, 12, as these do not in any way appear to compete with the overall chronology. The location of 7:10 and 8:12 within the overall schema is pinpointed by the date that immediately follows.

[6] "Three days/years" is the corresponding expression for an indefinite, short period of time.

Utnapishtim and a flood.[7] This account has sufficient commonality with the Genesis account to make comparison illuminating. Since, however, we do not know the actual relationship between these accounts, their possible relationship can be, and has been, argued any which way. In general terms, however, it is not, I think, greatly controversial to suggest that a good reading strategy is to take the Genesis account as a Hebrew retelling of a common story, whose details are shaped by the concern to set the well-known story in a particular light: Think about it *this* way, and one will understand more truly the situation of the world under God. As Gerhard von Rad put it when concluding a brief comparison of the Genesis story with that in the Epic of Gilgamesh, "[T]he biblical story of the Flood has been made a witness to the judgment and grace of the living God."[8]

A CHARACTERISTIC POSTMODERN ANXIETY

Although these modern questions have played a valuable role in sharpening our reading of the Flood narrative, in our current postmodern context, certain other questions have come to the fore. The recurrent underlying issue appears to be a matter of *assumptions* – those things that the biblical writers and premodern readers were happy to assume, but which have in one way or other become problematic in a contemporary context; one thinks, for example, of extensive recent debate in relation to ancient and contemporary assumptions about gender.

First and foremost, as noted at the outset, is a growing anxiety as to whether the Flood story is a good story to think about and

---

[7] See, e.g., *ANET*, 93–97.

[8] Gerhard von Rad, *Genesis: A Commentary*, trans. John H. Marks, rev. ed., OTL (London: SCM, 1972 [German 9th ed., 1972]), 124.

use at all as part of a religiously authoritative book. For a story that envisages God's wiping out the whole of life on earth (except eight people, and animals in pairs) seems intrinsically unpromising. The story's assumption that it is unproblematic for God to do this has itself become problematic. Does not such a story risk cheapening life, and does such a deity deserve worship?

How might one make progress? Initially, one may observe that the history of interpretation of the Flood narrative is extensive and well documented.[9] One characteristic of this history is that Jews and Christians have *not* used the Flood story as an argument for cheapening life, either human or animal (the history of Noah's curse on Ham/Canaan is a different, but separate, matter). Moreover, it is false to suppose that contemporary readers are the first to have moral and spiritual difficulties with the biblical text. Postmodern ethical anxiety revives a characteristic Enlightenment critique.[10] Nor were the eighteenth-century *philosophes* the first to encounter such problems, as a study of classic interpreters such as Origen and Luther rapidly reveals.[11]

It is worth noting a recurrent minority emphasis within Jewish interpretation that, while not raising a problem about the story as a

---

[9] See Jack P. Lewis, *A Study of the Interpretation of Noah and the Flood in Jewish and Christian Literature* (Leiden, NL: Brill, 1968).

[10] This is rightly stressed by Heikki Räisänen in response to frequent contemporary misrepresentations of historical-critical scholarship as intrinsically nonethical and politically disengaged ("Biblical Critics in the Global Village," in *Reading the Bible in the Global Village: Helsinki*, ed. Heikki Räisänen et al. [Atlanta: Society of Biblical Literature, 2000], 9–28). See Chapter 1, note 6.

[11] An engaging guide to ways in which premodern interpreters showed awareness of, and responded to, difficulties in the content of scripture, especially those identified by feminists, is found in John L. Thompson, *Reading the Bible with the Dead: What You Can Learn from the History of Exegesis That You Can't Learn from Exegesis Alone* (Grand Rapids, MI: Eerdmans, 2007).

whole, nonetheless clearly would have preferred a different story.[12] Thus there are those Jewish interpreters who quite simply find fault with Noah. Either they fix on the phrase (6:9) "righteous . . . in his generation" and suggest that, since that generation was so corrupt, righteousness in that context was, crudely, no big deal.[13] Or they construe Noah's lack of speech throughout the story suspiciously: Noah's failure to warn others, to express compassion for them, or to ask God to spare them shows that his sympathies are too narrow and self-centered.[14] (This is somewhat analogous to those who find fault with Abraham in Genesis 22, the offering of Isaac, for not being the Abraham of Genesis 18, the interaction with God over the fate of Sodom and Gomorrah – why obey God in an extreme situation when one might remonstrate with him instead?) For whatever reasons such moves may be made, they suggest a dissatisfaction with the story's assumption that it is appropriate for Noah to display his integrity and obedience with never a word. It is an interesting precedent for the feeling that a different story would be a better or more usable story.

Second, one of the many implications of other ancient flood stories, in the Epic of Gilgamesh and elsewhere, is surely that, within the ancient world of which Israel was a part, a story of a flood was in some way a *given*. There is thus an intrinsic constraint

---

[12] Since the conventions of ancient Hebrew narrative indicate a spare mode of narrating, there are always opportunities for the interpretative imagination to develop that about which the text is silent. Classic midrash made the most of this, as do many contemporary narrative readings.

[13] See Lewis, *A Study of the Interpretation of Noah*, 133.

[14] Noah's being at fault for not warning his contemporaries is especially found in the *Zohar* (*The Chumash: The Stone Edition*, ed. Nosson Scherman [Brooklyn, NY: Mesorah Publications, 1993], 31); for a modern example, see Morris Adler as cited in W. G. Plaut, ed., *The Torah: A Modern Commentary* (New York: Union of American Hebrew Congregations, 1981), 65.

that the storyline necessarily entails the extensive obliteration of life on earth. Here, some of the characteristic emphases within the Old Testament come into sharper focus when compared with, say, the story in the Epic of Gilgamesh.[15] On the one hand, the Old Testament will not allow that there is any power other than Yhwh who could bring and remove such a flood, which involves unmaking and remaking creation. On the other hand, the reasons for Yhwh's actions are charged with moral concern for the integrity of creation (Gen 6:5, 11–13), and the text strikingly depicts Yhwh at the outset as acting more in sorrow than in anger (Gen 6:6–7).[16] Thus, the Old Testament concern seems to be how to envision the ultimate disaster that the Flood represents, which is a given, within the morally demanding and life-bestowing purposes of Yhwh – or, in von Rad's terms, within "the judgment and grace of the living God."

Third, the story's concept of a small, faithful remnant that survives overwhelming judgment and disaster and is the basis for hope for the future may not instantly be congenial (though it becomes an important motif in prophetic literature). And yet is it so different from a popular scenario of contemporary science fiction? This scenario envisages some general catastrophe overtaking civilization on earth as we know it and focuses on the struggle of a few in the post-catastrophe earth to reestablish worthwhile life in the face of immense obstacles. These are almost always stories of courage and hope against the odds, and the viewer or reader is implicitly meant

---

[15] Compare the reading of Genesis 1 in relation to *Enuma Elish* in Chapter 3.

[16] The portrayal of Yhwh in Genesis 6:6–7 is perhaps the more striking when it is compared with the briefer allusion to the story in Isaiah 54:8–9, which does implicitly depict Yhwh's action in the Flood as marked by "anger" (*qeṣep*). The ethos of the Genesis narrative is thus far removed from, say, Jonathan Edwards's notorious depiction of "sinners in the hand of an angry God."

to focus on those who demonstrate these positive qualities rather than think about the catastrophe as such.

None of these considerations invalidate the postmodern anxiety, but they should tell against its being utilized in any abstract or decontextualized way. However, we must now look more closely at the biblical text itself to try to determine what the story's concerns really are.

TOWARD A THEOLOGICAL INTERPRETATION OF THE FLOOD NARRATIVE

Despite Dawkins's easy affirmation of the "appalling moral" of the story, it is not difficult, if one actually reads the text, to see that its concerns reside less in where it begins than in where it ends. It is in what the story leads up to that its significance is primarily to be found. That is, although the story indeed begins with God's decision to wipe out life on earth because of its corruption, its goal is the divine decision never again to wipe out life on earth (Gen 8:20–22); the rainbow becomes a symbol of this divine commitment to sustain life on earth (9:8–17).

The rainbow is one of the most unusual, beautiful, and moving of all recurrent natural phenomena. Its symbolic resonances are many, and one can imagine it variously: for example, as a bridge between earth and heaven (akin to Jacob's ladder; see Gen 28:10–22), or as the bow of the divine warrior now laid aside. It usually appears after a time of heavy rain when the sun comes out and shines again but while dark clouds are still in the sky; and often the dark clouds are a backdrop for the many colors of the rainbow. Thus, when the rainbow is viewed in the light of the preceding Flood narrative, its appearance at the very moment when one can see both darkness and light in the sky comes to symbolize God's commitment to light over darkness, to beauty over chaos, to life over death.

The Collocation of Genesis 6:5 with 8:21

Within this general frame of reference, it may be helpful to focus on one specific peculiarity of the text as a way of further penetrating the story's significance.

Most commentators have recognized that an important key to understanding the story is provided by the repetition of certain weighty words within the thoughts of Yhwh. At the very outset (Gen 6:5), the reason why Yhwh decides to send a flood is as follows: "The Lord saw that the wickedness of humankind was great in the earth, and that every inclination of the thoughts of their hearts was only evil continually." Yet this evil within human inclinations not only remains unchanged by the Flood but also is explicitly appealed to in the context of Yhwh's subsequent decision never again to send a flood (8:21): "And when the Lord smelt the pleasing odour, the Lord said in his heart, 'I will never again curse the ground because of humankind, for the inclination of the human heart is evil from youth; nor will I ever again destroy every living thing as I have done." The puzzle is why one and the same thing should, apparently, be the reason for (in convenient theological shorthand) both judgment and grace. Is this a deliberate theological paradox? Or what? Interpreters have, of course, long been aware of a difficulty here. Chrysostom, for example, comments on 8:21 that this is "a strange form of loving kindness," while Luther observes that "[i]t seems that God can be accused of inconsistency here," and Calvin states, "This reasoning seems incongruous... God seems to contradict himself."[17] In the twentieth century, Gerhard von Rad sees that something highly significant is at stake:

> This saying of Yahweh [8:21] without doubt designates a profound turning point in the Yahwistic primeval history, in so far as it expresses with surprising directness a will for salvation directed towards the whole of Noachite humanity, "although" (the Hebrew particle can be translated in this way) "the imagination of man's heart is evil from his youth." So far as that is concerned – Calvin says in his exposition of the passage – God would have to punish man with daily floods. In its hard paradox this v. 21 is one of the most remarkable theological statements in the Old Testament: it shows the pointed and concentrated way in which the Yahwist can express himself at decisive points. The same condition which in the prologue is the basis for God's judgment in the epilogue reveals God's grace and providence. The contrast between God's punishing anger and his supporting grace, which pervades the whole Bible, is here presented almost inappropriately, almost as indulgence, an adjustment by God towards man's sinfulness.[18]

Recognition that the collocation of 6:5 and 8:21 is in some way theologically significant is thus well established in interpretations of the Flood narrative.

The Evil-Thought Clause in Genesis 8:21

Within YHWH's climactic words in 8:21, particular importance attaches to its subordinate clause – "for the inclination of the

---

[17] See, respectively, Chrysostom, Homily 27:10 in *Homilies on Genesis 18–45*, trans. Robert C. Hill, The Fathers of the Church (Washington, DC: Catholic University of America, 1990), 170; Martin Luther, *Luther's Works*, vol. 2, *Lectures on Genesis, Chapters 6–14*, ed. Jaroslav Pelikan (Saint Louis, MO: Concordia Publishing House, 1960), 120; and John Calvin, *A Commentary on Genesis*, repr. ed. (London: Banner of Truth, 1965 [Latin orig, 1554]), 283–84.

[18] Von Rad, *Genesis*, 122–23.

human heart is evil from youth" – a clause I will refer to as the evil-thought clause.

First, the specific verbal resonances between Yhwh's resolution for the future and his initial reasons for sending the Flood come *only* in the evil-thought clause, which restates less emphatically, but definitely nonetheless, the opening characterization of humanity:

> ⁶:⁵and that every inclination (*yēṣer*) of the thoughts of their hearts was only evil continually
>
> ⁸:²¹ for (*kî*) the inclination (*yēṣer*) of the human heart is evil from youth

The puzzle or paradox of the text is particularly focused on these few words and their construal.

Second, it is noteworthy that the divine words in 8:21 would read entirely smoothly without the evil-thought clause. While such smoothness in omission by itself shows little, several further factors may encourage a heuristic reading of the divine words without this clause.

Without the clause the divine words of 8:21 appear as poetic, with both parallelism and a clear 3:3 pattern:

lō᾽-᾽ōsîp lĕqallēl ôd	*et-hā᾽ădāmâ ba῾ăbûr hā᾽ādām*
I will never again curse	the ground because of humankind
wĕlō᾽-᾽ōsîp ῾ôd lĕhakkôt	*et-kol-ḥay ka᾽ăšer ῾āśîtî*
nor will I ever again destroy	every living creature as I have done

One of the striking characteristics of the early chapters of Genesis is that most of the significant pronouncements are made in poetry – a heightened mode of speech appropriate to memorable

moments (as in much Hebrew prophecy). In the immediate context of 8:21, the divine words about the seasons that directly follow
are in poetic form (8:22). Without the evil-thought clause, one can
straightforwardly see the divine pronouncement in 8:21 as poetic
in form. (Interestingly, the presence of the evil-thought clause in
8:21 has so effectively obscured this poetic form that no modern
translation of which I am aware sets out 8:21 as poetry, though the
continuation in 8:22 is almost invariably set out thus;[19] translators
have apparently not paused to reflect on the oddity of a short divine
pronouncement half in prose and half in poetry.)

It seems to me, therefore, that there is a case for seeing the
evil-thought clause as a distinct addition to an otherwise already
complete and rounded divine pronouncement in poetic form.[20]

Reading the Story without the Evil-Thought Clause

How, then, would the text read without the evil-thought clause?
Noah is, in effect, the sole representative of the human race, since his
wife, sons, and sons' wives are narratively formulaic (they are only
there "for the ride"). Throughout the Flood Noah has been a model
of obedience to YHWH's instructions. Now he offers a sacrifice
whose pleasingness to YHWH is emphasized (8:20–21a). In response,
therefore, to this sacrifice, YHWH makes two inner resolutions.[21]
YHWH will not increase the curse on the earth pronounced in Eden

---

[19] So, e.g., NEB, REB, JB, NIV, NJPSV. ESV sets out 8:21–22 as prose throughout.

[20] A recent discussion that recognizes the likely redactional role of the
evil-thought clause and its interruption of an otherwise poetic divine
speech is Markus Witte, *Die biblische Urgeschichte: Redaktions- und theolo-
giegeschichtliche Beobachtungen zu Genesis 1,1–11,26*, BZAW 265 (Berlin: de
Gruyter, 1998), 181 (he lists other scholars with a similar proposal in n. 133).

[21] YHWH's responsiveness to sacrifice here is analogous to his responsiveness
elsewhere to prayer and repentance, all of which are understood to *matter* to
YHWH.

(Gen 3:17) and will never again destroy all life, as had happened in the Flood. On this basis the regular conditions of life on earth, its seasons and its harvests, will continue (8:22). This will enable sacrifices such as Noah offers to be offered on a regular basis. The earth has been purified by the Flood so as to be a place of more acceptable worship to Yʜwʜ.

When one reads the text thus, one of the difficulties in the received text disappears – namely, the way in which Yʜwʜ's resolutions in response to Noah's sacrifice seem somehow disproportionate when directly juxtaposed with the reality of continuing evil in the human disposition; as von Rad put it, "his supporting grace . . . is here presented almost inappropriately, almost as indulgence, an adjustment by God towards man's sinfulness."[22] Simply put, if there is no mention of human sinfulness in the evil-thought clause, and righteous Noah who is making an appropriate sacrifice is, in effect, the only human on earth, then Yʜwʜ's pleasure in him and corresponding resolutions about life hereafter do not jar.

Reading the Story with the Evil-Thought Clause

What, then, is the difference made by the presence of the evil-thought clause? It changes the tenor of the whole speech by bringing to the fore two issues that are otherwise at most only implicit in the story at this point. These are weighty issues that, in convenient theological shorthand, can be characterized as divine mutability and human depravity.

The issue of divine mutability is not as such explicit, but rather a natural inference. If, according to the evil-thought clause,

---

[22] Von Rad, *Genesis*, 123. Compare Derek Kidner's "If God seems too lightly propitiated . . ." in Kidner, *Genesis: An Introduction and Commentary*, TOTC (London: Tyndale, 1967), 93.

humanity has not changed and is the same post-Flood as pre-Flood, then what is the reason for the fact that the condition of humanity that brought on the Flood does so no longer? As Anthony F. Campbell and Mark A. O'Brien put it, "because nothing has changed in human nature, the change must be placed in God"; or, as Walter Brueggemann puts it, "humankind is hopeless.... Hope will depend on a move from God."[23] If corrupt humanity will not change, then God will change in not enacting on humanity the judgment that such corruption might be expected to bring onto itself.

Second, there is the clause's explicit statement about enduring evil in human thought. This readily leads into larger theological debates: for Christians, about original sin, and for Jews, about the evil tendency (*yēṣer hārāʿ*). I do not, however, wish to get involved in the well-worn Jewish–Christian debates that can arise here. Rather, I want to consider the logic of the evil-thought clause in relation to the story as a whole.

The logic of the evil-thought clause is hardly straightforward in the context of 8:21. In Genesis 6:5 it is straightforward, in the context of the corruption that had afflicted the world as a whole. But in 8:21 that corrupt humanity has been wiped out. There are only eight representatives of humanity left, and of these only one is significant, that is, Noah; and Noah is righteous, a person of integrity (6:9), who has been obedient to YHWH throughout. That is, Noah is surely the very person of whom it *cannot* be said that "the inclination of his heart/mind is evil from his youth." Yet it is

---

[23] Antony F. Campbell and Mark A. O'Brien, *Sources of the Pentateuch: Texts, Introductions, Annotations* (Minneapolis, MN: Fortress, 1993), 97n17; Walter Brueggemann, *Genesis*, Interp (Atlanta: John Knox, 1982), 80–81.

the humanity represented by Noah that is still characterized as evil in 8:21. How is this to be understood?

If one seeks to remain within the narrative's own frame of reference, the "evil thinkers" would have to be in Noah's family: His sons must surely be the prime suspects. Although they are passive and formulaic within the Flood story proper, they subsequently take an active role, and Ham's voyeurism (or whatever it was) with regard to his father brings a curse (9:18–27). Noah's drunkenness in this later story could also be argued to place Noah in a more ambiguous light than would be evident from the Flood story proper. However, to introduce at this point later developments from a separate narrative episode is surely rather forced.

So, I suggest that the originating context for the evil-thought clause is not the world of the story, but rather the world of the scribe who added the clause. The widespread corruption of human thought surely belongs to the frame of reference of a Hebrew scribe, who is engaging with the question of why the world of his own day – which might well have appeared no less corrupt and heedless of God than the generation of the Flood – is the recipient of divine forbearance rather than judgment. This scribe recognizes that the main point of the existing Flood narrative is to offer an account of divine maintenance of regular human life. Yet he wishes to deepen an understanding of what is at stake in such maintenance. Thus, by adding the evil-thought clause to Yhwh's resolution about future dealings with humanity, he makes explicit that the familiar post-Flood world is no improvement on the notorious pre-Flood world; the humanity that receives the divine forbearance has not changed from the humanity that was swept away. The scribe's work is thus indicative of the use of traditional narrative for articulating a contemporary existential reality. The potent legends are precisely those in which an ancient story can become a renewable resource for better understanding of a problematic present.

To be sure, the introduction of evil-thinking humanity into a context where only Noah, the person of integrity, is significant does indeed stretch the logic of the story. Yet the exemplary role of Noah remains clear. Human responsiveness to God in the manner of Noah remains central to the continuing purpose of life on earth and the appropriate use of the crops that the seasons bring.

The text's overall emphasis remains YHWH's resolution to sustain life on earth in the future. This resolution, however, is a paradoxical expression of merciful divine forbearance in the face of recognition of human life post-Flood as no improvement on human life pre-Flood. Humanity remains undeserving of the gift of life in a regular world order, but the gift will be given nonetheless. The logic of saying this, however, may in certain respects be akin to that of prophetic utterances that seek to engender appropriate responsiveness.[24] That is, YHWH's forbearance, rightly understood, should lead not to complacency or the heedless exercise of evil thinking, but rather to the living of life in a way that recognizes its quality as gift.

ISRAEL AND THE WORLD, SINAI AND THE FLOOD

Finally, the evil-thought clause can direct us to an illuminating intertextual parallel to the Flood story. For the story of Israel's sin with the golden calf and subsequent covenant renewal at Sinai in Exodus 32–34 has a comparable expression of theological paradox.

---

[24] An axiomatic statement is Jeremiah 18:7–10, on which see my *Prophecy and Discernment*, CSCD 14 (Cambridge: Cambridge University Press, 2006), 48–55, esp. 52.

The narrative sequence of Exodus 32–34 is striking.[25] While the people of Israel are still at Sinai, the mountain of God, the place where the covenant with God is ratified (Exod 24), their making of a golden calf is seen as a fundamental act of apostasy – a kind of equivalent to committing adultery on one's wedding night. God proposes to do away with Israel on the grounds that "they are a stiff-necked people" (Exod 32:9; a motivating factor repeated in 33:3, 5), though in doing so leaves a space for Moses to intercede on their behalf, which he duly does. The culmination of a prolonged sequence of intercession by Moses is YHWH's self-revelation as "a God merciful and gracious . . . abounding in steadfast love and faithfulness . . . forgiving iniquity and transgression and sin" (34:6–7a). This mercy is clearly the basis for the renewal of the covenant with Israel. Yet as Moses bows to the ground and worships in response to this divine self-revelation, he asks that YHWH would accompany Israel "although/for [*kî*] this is a stiff-necked people" (34:9). Here we have the same phenomenon as in the Flood narrative – a "stiff-necked people" clause, which is analogous to the "evil-thought clause." The factor that is appealed to as a warrant for God's judgment is cited again in the context of God's mercy, introduced each time by the same particle, *kî*.

This striking analogy leads to a recognition of further strong narrative analogies. At their beginnings, the world in general and the chosen people in particular prove faithless and incur divine judgment (Gen 6:5–13; Exod 32:1–10). Each time, one person – Noah and Moses, respectively – remains faithful and is said (uniquely

---

[25] I draw here on my *At the Mountain of God: Story and Theology in Exodus 32–34*, JSOTSup 22 (Sheffield, UK: JSOT Press, 1983), esp. 84–93; cf. also Terence E. Fretheim, *Exodus*, Interp (Louisville: John Knox, 1991), 301–7; and Rolf Rendtorff, *The Canonical Hebrew Bible: A Theology of the Old Testament*, trans. David Orton (Leiden, NL: Deo, 2005 [German orig., 2001]), 63.

within the Old Testament) "to have found favour with Yʜwʜ" (Gen 6:8; Exod 33:12, 17),[26] on the basis of which they are able to mediate God's grace for the future. Noah and Moses are mentioned at the turning point within each narrative, when there is a shift from judgment for the past to hope for the future (Gen 8:1; Exod 33:11). Noah offers sacrifice, Moses offers intercession (Gen 8:20; Exod 33:12–18), and each of these actions constitutes the context within which divine mercy is pronounced (Gen 8:21; Exod 33:19, 34:6–7).

This narrative analogy suggests a deep theological vision. God deals with the world in general in the same way as with Israel in particular.[27] If both Israel and the world show themselves to be faithless at the outset and to be continuingly faithless ("evil in thought" and "stiff-necked"), then their continued existence is similarly to be understood in terms of the merciful forbearance of God toward those who do not deserve it: Life for both Israel and for the world is a gift of grace – recognition of which should elicit a gratitude that renounces faithlessness.

---

[26] The other person in the Bible of whom this is said is Mary at the Annunciation (Luke 1:30); this collocation is, to say the least, theologically suggestive.

[27] In compositional terms, it is likely that Israel's particular self-understanding before God has been used to portray the standing of the world in general, and so the Flood narrative has been shaped in the light of the Sinai narrative.

CHAPTER 7

On Reading Genesis 12–50

Much that was said about reading Genesis 1–11 in Chapter 2 applies also to reading Genesis 12–50, for there are many continuities of content and convention between these chapters. Indeed, any sharp distinction between chapters 1–11 and 12–50 has no warrant in the biblical text itself. Nonetheless, some distinction remains heuristically useful. Now in Genesis 12–50, the focus is no longer on the world and humanity generically; rather, the prehistory of Israel in the form of its ancestors becomes the center of attention. This raises certain distinct issues that merit separate comment.[1]

THE PATRIARCHS AS A PROBLEM FOR JEWISH OBSERVANCE OF TORAH

From a Jewish perspective, perhaps *the* central issue in understanding Genesis 12–50 is posed by the normative, indeed definitive, nature of God's self-revelation to Moses and Israel at Sinai/Horeb, together with the covenant making and gift of torah. If the norm for life with God is here, then how is Israel to understand those whose life with God is in some way of enduring significance – as

[1] In this chapter I draw on my *The Old Testament of the Old Testament*, OBT (Minneapolis, MN: Fortress, 1992; repr., Eugene, OR: Wipf & Stock, 2001).

Abraham and Sarah's, Isaac and Rebekah's, and Jacob and his twelve children's clearly are – and yet who lived without torah, because torah had not yet been given?

There are various possible approaches to this question. Should one perhaps imagine that torah somehow "must have" been known to the patriarchs and that they really were observant after all?[2] This could take the form of supposing that Genesis's silence about observance need not mean its absence, and so the patriarchs were in fact formally observant. Or one could surmise that perhaps they were intuitively aware of the requirements of torah, perhaps as a kind of natural law, and so realized even without formal observance the essential purpose of torah. Alternatively, if one decides that Genesis really does show that the patriarchs were not observant, what might this imply? Might the patriarchs' acceptability to God in the absence of torah in effect relativize the significance of torah for Israel? All these options can be seen in the classic literature.

The issue is nicely posed at the very outset of the late eleventh-century Genesis commentary by Rashi, the greatest of the medieval Jewish commentators. Rashi begins his commentary on Genesis 1:1 thus:

> Rabbi Isaac said: The Torah *which is the Law book of Israel* should have commenced with *the verse* (Exod. XII.1) "This month shall be unto you the first of the months" which is the first commandment given to Israel. What is the reason, then, that it commences with *the account of* the Creation?[3]

---

[2] See, e.g., James K. Bruckner, *Implied Law in the Abraham Narratives: A Literary and Theological Analysis*, JSOTSup 335 (Sheffield, UK: Sheffield Academic Press, 2001).

[3] M. Rosenbaum and A. M. Silbermann, eds., *The Pentateuch with the Commentary of Rashi: Genesis* (Jerusalem: Silbermann, 1972), 2. The italics are provided by the translators/editors to help make Rashi's terse mode of expression more

If normative torah for Israel begins with the Passover regulations, why should not Israel's scripture begin there? Why include antecedent material that, prima facie, could not be significant in the same way? That the particularity of God's dealings with Israel is uppermost in Rashi's mind even when commenting on Genesis 1:1 is evident from the way (slightly disconcerting to many a contemporary reader) in which Rashi continues, making clear that the bigger picture that Genesis portrays functions as a narrative backdrop to justify God's ways with Israel:

> Because of *the thought expressed in the text* (Ps. CXI. 6) "He declared to His people the strength of His works (i.e. He gave an account of the work of Creation), in order that He might give them the heritage of the nations." For should the peoples of the world say to Israel, "You are robbers, because you took by force the lands of the seven nations *of Canaan*," Israel may reply to them, "All the earth belongs to the Holy One, blessed be He: He created it and gave it to whom He pleased. When He willed He gave it to them, and when He willed He took it from them and gave it to us" (Yalk. Exod. XII.2).[4]

This awareness of an in-principle interpretative issue posed by the pre-torah context of Genesis goes right back to the earliest "commentary" on Genesis that still survives, the pseudepigraphical book of *Jubilees*, dating from, perhaps, the second century BCE. The writer extensively recasts the Genesis narrative, and one of the notable aspects is the way in which explicit torah observance comes to the fore. Its most regular expression is in terms of a liturgical calendar, but there are also keynote passages, such as Abraham's deathbed charge to Isaac, which treats proper sacrificial practice (*Jub.* 21:1–20).

comprehensible to the nonspecialist. For an introduction to Rashi, see Chaim Pearl, *Rashi*, Jewish Thinkers (London: Peter Halban, 1988).
[4] Rosenbaum and Silbermann, eds., *Pentateuch: Genesis*, 2.

The approach of *Jubilees* becomes, in one way or other, characteristic of rabbinic thought generally. As Arthur Green puts it,

> While it is seemingly clear in the biblical narrative that the patriarchs, living before Sinai, had no relationship to the Torah and its commandments, the early Rabbis insist, quite to the contrary, that Torah in all its details was observed and studied in patriarchal times. This claim is unequivocally stated in the well-known talmudic dictum that "Abraham our Father fulfilled the entire Torah before it was given, even *'eruv tavshilin*" (the purely rabbinic device for permitting the preparation of Sabbath food on the preceding festival day). While this seemingly surprising assertion fits the general pattern of the Rabbis' conversion of all the biblical heroes into practicing rabbinic Jews, it also has the specific force of claiming that from the very outset there is no Judaism without the Law.[5]

A different way of articulating Abraham's observance can be found in eighteenth-century Hasidic teachers:

> [T]he claim that Abraham observed the commandments is *spiritualized* in Hasidism by a homiletic attempt to read into the patriarch not the rabbinic insistence on literal conformity with the Torah but rather the Hasidic message of attachment to God through the negation of the corporeal self. . . . [T]he Hasidic theologians . . . are using the figure of Abraham as a locus for discussing their own struggles with the nature of Torah observance and its place within the life of religious devotion.[6]

In short, the existential issues of the present are engaged via scripture. One possible factor in the difference of approach by Hasidism is that in their context there may have been less polemical opposition to observance of torah than there had been in many earlier

---

[5] Arthur Green, *Devotion and Commandment: The Faith of Abraham in the Hasidic Imagination* (Cincinnati, OH: Hebrew Union College Press, 1989), 9.
[6] Ibid., 10.

contexts, and this enabled a perhaps more reflective approach which felt freer to explore and probe possible alternatives – for polemics tend to narrow theological thinking, making it more black and white than might be the case otherwise.

In one way or other, it is clear that the classic Jewish instinct is to handle the problem of the patriarchs' pre-torah context by assimilating them to a torah context. However, the alternative (and opposite) approach, to relativize torah on the basis of patriarchal nonobservance, is adopted by Paul as he rereads Israel's scriptures in the light of Christ's death and resurrection. In Galatians 3 and Romans 4, we find Paul probing the significance of two texts in particular: Genesis 12:3, where God promises Abraham that "all the nations shall be blessed in you," and Genesis 15:6, where the narrator tells how "Abraham believed God and it was reckoned to him as righteousness." Paul makes much both of the intrinsic implications of these texts and of their narrative setting, which is not only antecedent to the giving of the law at Sinai by some 430 years but also still antecedent to the one formal and ritual obligation that is laid on Abraham in Genesis 17, that his descendants should be circumcised. If Abraham can be righteous in a context that specifies faith but not torah observance, and if this same Abraham can be the channel for a promise of blessing to the nations of the earth, then this correlates with and anticipates what God has done in the death and resurrection of Jesus and fundamentally relativizes the significance of torah – which is not thereby deprived of all significance, but no longer has its classic Jewish significance. Paul's perception that the Abraham narrative is open to be read in a way that can challenge the normativity of torah is not at root different from the perception of the writer of *Jubilees* – it is simply that they develop this perception in diametrically opposed ways.

GENESIS AS A COMPOSITIONAL AND
RELIGIO-HISTORICAL PROBLEM

Interestingly, this classic theological problem in approaching Genesis 12–50 has hardly featured in modern scholarship. This is, in essence, because it has been transposed into different categories.

The pre-Moses context of Genesis became interesting to early-modern European interpreters not because of issues of religious observance, but because of historical questions about the composition of the book. For most of the premodern period, the ascription of the whole Pentateuch to Moses functioned primarily as a symbol of its religiously authoritative character. Specific questions about how Moses wrote it were never rigorously raised or pursued; discussion tended to get no further than pondering certain puzzles – most obviously, how Moses could have written of his own death (Deut 34), as well as the periodic recognition that certain texts seem to presuppose a context subsequent to that of Moses (for example, Genesis 13:7b, whose mention of Canaanites and Perizzites "at that time" living in the land seems to presuppose that for the writer they were there no longer, which would appear to be the case only after Israel's conquest under Joshua).

However, in the modern period, historical questions about actual composition began to be raised as never before. For if Moses lived some four hundred years after the patriarchs (Gen 15:13), then how could he have written about the patriarchs without access to earlier sources? It is thus unsurprising that one of the first works of modern pentateuchal criticism was Jean Astruc's 1753 book entitled *Conjectures about the original documents which it would appear that Moses used to compose the book of Genesis.*[7] The history of research

[7] Jean Astruc, *Conjectures sur les memoires originaux: Dont il paroit que Moyse s'est servi pour composer le livre de la Genese: Avec des remarques qui appuient*

from here on has often been rehearsed, and there is no need to give details. Suffice it to say that as awareness grew of apparent complexities within Genesis – differing terms for God, differences of vocabulary, apparently duplicate narratives, apparently composite narratives, chronological tensions, differences of perspective and presupposition seemingly indicative of different historical periods – the assumption of Moses as author steadily faded in favor of a likely plurality of authors from different periods within Israel's history.

A corollary of this was that the picture of pre-Moses religion was replaced by a complex picture of differing religious practices that were substantially, or perhaps entirely, post-Moses, certainly in their composition and perhaps also in their origin. Thus the issue ceases to be one of successive "dispensations," patriarchal and Mosaic, and becomes instead one of diverse movements and developments within Israel's history. In place of the Mosaic norm raising questions about the status of pre-Mosaic religion, the issue tends to become how the norms of Josiah's reform in the seventh century, as represented by Deuteronomy, relate to other patterns of Israelite religion. If one holds to a relatively early date within the time of the monarchy for the Genesis narratives (as scholars generally did until recently), then "patriarchal religion" becomes exemplary of Israelite religion prior to Josiah's changes. Alternatively, some have suggested that what characterizes the patriarchal narratives is essentially family religion, which might well lie beyond the sphere of Josiah's public reform, and thus their content could be contemporary with Josiah's reform or even subsequent to it. It

ou qui éclaircissent ces conjectures (A Bruxelles: Chez Fricx, 1753). For a contextualization of Astruc's work, see Rudolf Smend, *From Astruc to Zimmerli: Old Testament Scholarship in Three Centuries*, trans. Margaret Kohl (Tübingen: Mohr Siebeck, 2007), 1–14.

is currently fashionable to see the patriarchal stories as a whole as an "invention" from the postexilic period, which refracts the relations between those who returned from exile and those who had remained in the land.[8] However, particularly on these latter views, it is hard to see why the material should have been transmogrified so that it could be preserved in its received form as the illustrious and venerable antecedent to Israel and Mosaic torah.

Whatever be the precise details of one's historical account, the point is that a certain kind of conceptual transition has taken place, one that is characteristic of much biblical study in the modern period. It is, in a sense, a transition from theology, as an engagement with issues arising out of a commitment to life and thought within certain norms and parameters, to a religio-historical treatment of Israel's scriptures, in which the term theology is retained primarily to designate a history of religious thought and practice.

One illuminating example of methodological and conceptual shift relates to the identity of the God of the patriarchs in relation to YHWH, the God of Israel. Menachem Haran, in opening a discussion of patriarchal religion, observes,

> The Bible assumes that the Patriarchal God was identical with the God of Israel in the post-Mosaic era, although He made himself mostly known to the Patriarchs under names other than Yahweh. This view has become deeply rooted in Judaism . . . [and] was passed on to Christianity. . . . This view evolved into an incontestable principle in medieval thought, sometimes influencing, albeit indirectly, even modern research. Yet, it cannot serve as a starting-point today,

---

[8] So, e.g., Mario Liverani, *Israel's History and the History of Israel*, trans. Chiara Peri and Philip Davies (London: Equinox, 2005 [Italian orig, 2003]), 250–69. Liverani, however, gives no consideration to the distinctive character of patriarchal religion.

all the more so as it has become obvious that the biblical tradition itself contains decisive evidence against such a view.[9]

Haran, who is not unsympathetic to traditional Jewish perspectives, feels able to assert categorically that the traditional understanding of one deity "cannot serve as a starting-point today" (presumably for scholarly work on the Genesis text). Indeed, he regards this as so self-evident that it does not need to be argued. That is, the diversity of religious beliefs and practices within the historical realm of ancient Israel that has become apparent to modern religio-historical research – one thinks, for example, of modern discoveries of Ugaritic texts at Ras Shamra in northern Syria where the supreme deity is El (as in Israel; later in this section) – self-evidently invalidates the traditional theological understanding, clearly already shared by the pentateuchal editors, that there is one God who was known and related to in different ways. *How* the traditional view is invalidated, and *why* it cannot incorporate newly discovered evidence within its conceptuality, is not at any point explained by Haran. Perhaps one is meant simply to assume that there is something of a gulf fixed between traditional theology and modern religio-historical inquiry, to the detriment of the former.

To be sure, the religious history articulated in modern study of Genesis is still amenable to positive use and appropriation by those who remain sympathetic to theology in a more traditional sense. Among the most obvious examples of this in the twentieth century is work by those German scholars who lived through the Nazi era as members of the Confessing Church and whose interpretations of the Old Testament combined arguments in historical-critical form with an existential edge that expressed a sophisticated Christian

---

[9] Menachem Haran, "The Religion of the Patriarchs," *ASTI* 4 (1965): 30–55 (30).

theological awareness. Examples that retain enduring value even though they contain unresolved tensions in their use of religio-historical categories – about some of whose premises one may for various reasons be doubtful – include Hans Walter Wolff's essays, "The Kerygma of the Yahwist"[10] and "The Elohistic Fragments in the Pentateuch";[11] Claus Westermann's massive three-volume Genesis commentary (where one sometimes has to dig a little to mine the gold);[12] and Gerhard von Rad's *Genesis: A Commentary*,[13] some of whose interpretations are also in his *Biblical Interpretations in Preaching*.[14]

A THIRD WAY: A CANONICAL APPROACH

Where does one go from here? The most fruitful approach for theology, I suggest, is to try to recapture the traditional premodern issue, which relates to the role of Genesis as it has been preserved within the Pentateuch, in a way that also takes seriously the religio-historical insights of characteristic modern scholarship, which relates to the possible origins, development, and ancient

[10] In Walter Brueggemann and Hans Walter Wolff, *The Vitality of Old Testament Traditions*, 2nd ed. (Atlanta: John Knox, 1982), 41–66.

[11] In ibid., 67–82.

[12] Claus Westermann, *Genesis 1–11: A Commentary*, trans. John J. Scullion, CC (Minneapolis, MN: Augsburg Press, 1984); Claus Westermann, *Genesis 12–36: A Commentary*, trans. John J. Scullion, CC (Minneapolis, MN: Augsburg Press, 1985); Claus Westermann, *Genesis 37–50: A Commentary*, trans. John J. Scullion, CC (Minneapolis: Augsburg Press, 1986). There is also a boiled-down version: Claus Westermann, *Genesis: A Practical Commentary, Text and Interpretation* (Grand Rapids, MI: Eerdmans, 1987), though the "practical" within the title is, I think, a little euphemistic.

[13] Gerhard von Rad, *Genesis: A Commentary*, trans. John H. Marks, rev. ed., OTL (London: SCM, 1972 [German 9th ed., 1972]).

[14] Gerhard von Rad, *Biblical Interpretations in Preaching*, trans. John E. Steely (Nashville, IN: Abingdon, 1977 [German orig., 1973]), esp. 11–48.

function of the Genesis text. As already set out in Chapter 2, this is what is involved in a canonical approach to the biblical text.

The in-principle strengths of this approach are at least twofold. On the one hand, if rightly practiced, it should be able to demonstrate the key strengths of both premodern and modern approaches to the biblical text, even though each will look somewhat different in this new contextualization. On the other hand, it offers the prospect of being able to develop a conceptuality that will do better justice – more than was generally possible in either premodern or modern work – to that remarkable phenomenon, unprecedented within antiquity, of particular and selected texts of ancient Israel being collated and interwoven as a distinct and religiously authoritative collection of writings for ongoing generations.

Genesis as "The Old Testament of the Old Testament"

One example of the potential fruitfulness of this approach lies in its ability to re-appropriate the classic Jewish problem with Genesis 12–50 and, then, to extend its implications.

The problem that Genesis poses for Jewish thinking is surely closely analogous to the problem posed by the Old Testament as a whole for Christian thinking. For those whose norms of faith and life focus on the knowledge of God in and through Jesus Christ, the Old Testament poses the same issues as does Genesis 12–50 for Mosaic torah: How does one relate continuity and identity to real and major difference? Christians down the ages have made the same kinds of moves in relation to the Old Testament that Jews have made in relation to Genesis. The predominant instinct has been to assimilate – more or less subtly – the unfamiliar to the familiar, the divergent to the normative.

At a popular level, this has often taken the form of regarding the key figures in the Old Testament as believing Christians (that is, as the Christian counterpart to "practicing rabbinic Jews"). At a more reflective level, this has taken, among other things, the form of typological or figural reading, finding a patterning that imaginatively converges the antecedent to the norm – Israel's crossing the Red Sea becomes a type of baptism, their wandering in the wilderness becomes a type of the testing demands of discipleship, and so on. However, the perception of differences between Old Testament and New Testament has sometimes led to the sense that the Old Testament can pose a threat for the norms of the New Testament. The most extreme form of this was expressed by Marcion in the second century, whose antithetical reading of the Old Testament has generally been marginalized by Christians, rather as observant Jews have marginalized Paul's reading of Abraham as antithetical to torah. But less extreme versions of this general tendency have been given more space in a Christian frame of reference, such as in the work of Martin Luther with his particular polarity of law and grace, or his famous twentieth-century theological descendant, Rudolf Bultmann, for whom (unlike Luther) there was not much that was positive to be said about the Old Testament.

On Interpreting the Revelation of the Divine Name
The way in which a canonical approach has the potential to engage with, and reconceptualize, the insights of modern biblical scholarship can be seen if one sets out a key issue in the development of pentateuchal criticism: If Exodus 3:13–15 implies, and Exodus 6:2–3 states explicitly, that the name of God, YHWH, is first given to Moses and was not known to the patriarchs, who instead knew God as El Shaddai (traditionally rendered "God Almighty"), how then is one to account for the extensive use of the divine name within Genesis, twice even on the lips of God himself (Gen 15:7, 28:13)?

The characteristic traditional approach, which was further developed by conservative scholars in the modern period who felt that alternatives impugned the integrity of the biblical text, was to argue for essential continuity between Genesis and Exodus. Despite the apparent prima facie meaning of Exodus 6:2–3, the Genesis uses of YHWH show that God must in fact have been known to the patriarchs as YHWH. Thus what is new in Exodus cannot be the name as such but rather its meaning and significance; Israel is given a new content for an already-familiar name, in such a way as to convey a sense of fulfilment of the promises made to the patriarchs.

The predominant modern approach has been to insist that both Exodus 6:2–3 and uses of the divine name in Genesis should be taken at face value. This entails that the Pentateuch contains divergent accounts of the beginnings of Israel's knowledge of God as YHWH. There is the source/author who uses the divine name in Genesis and explicitly traces its origins to the earliest period of human civilization (Gen 4:26), usage that identifies this strand as the "Yahwist" (J). Exodus 6:2–3 is then ascribed to those responsible for the other most distinctive strand in Genesis, the "Priestly" writer(s) (P); while Exodus 3:13–15 is yet a third strand, where a preference for referring to God by the generic *'ĕlōhîm* acquires the name "Elohist" (E). The compilers of the Old Testament were apparently happy to preserve divergent accounts and simply live with the difficulties posed when they are combined together. For the scholar, however, the difficulties become a window into the complexity of Israel's religious and literary history.

A third approach, a minority view in the history of interpretation, is that the divine name is indeed to be understood as first made known to Moses, as in Exodus 3 and 6. The corollary is that all the occurrences in Genesis are examples of using a familiar name in a surprising context: God is called YHWH in Genesis because that is how Israel knows God. In other words, the usage is technically anachronistic, but is in keeping with the common practice of storytellers in most ages. Interestingly, this view was propounded by the seventeenth-century scholar who first articulated a historical-critical approach to the Bible in a programmatic way, Benedict de Spinoza:

> I ought to explain how it comes that we are often told in Genesis that the patriarchs preached in the name of Jehovah, this being in plain contradiction to the text above quoted [Exod 6:2–3].... [T]he writer of the Pentateuch did not always speak of things and places by the names they bore in the times of which he was writing, but by the names best known to his contemporaries. God is thus said in the Pentateuch to have been preached by the patriarchs under the name of Jehovah, not because such was the name by which the Patriarchs knew Him, but because this name was the one most reverenced by the Jews.[15]

It is a puzzle of modern biblical criticism that Spinoza's proposal was entirely sidelined by developing pentateuchal criticism, even though his basic point of principle seems self-evidently correct – as when the narrator uses the familiar place name, Bethel (Gen 13:3), even though a later episode makes clear that in Abraham's time the place's name was Luz and it was only subsequently renamed Bethel by Jacob (Gen 28:19). It is likewise uncontroversial to observe that the names that people and places are given in Genesis as a result of encounter with God, even when the particular narrative identifies the deity as YHWH, are all compounded with "El" rather than with some form of the tetragrammaton – thus Ishmael

---

[15] Benedict de Spinoza, *A Theologico-Political Treatise*, trans. R. M. H. Elwes (New York: Dover, 1951 [Latin orig., 1670]), 178–79 (chap. 13).

(Gen 16:11), Bethel (Gen 28:16–19), and Israel (Gen 32:28), not Ishmayah, Bethyah, Israyah, and so on.[16]

The Distinctive Patterns of Patriarchal Religion

This historical-critical insight into the likely processes of textual composition, as instanced by the anachronistic placement of the divine name, can be seen to relate to a wider, and generally consistent, pattern of difference of religious assumption and practice between the narrative of Genesis and the rest of the Pentateuch.[17]

In brief, patriarchal religion lacks the concept of holiness; although Jacob's encounter with God at Bethel is often characterized as typical of "the holy," Jacob's own term for the place is "fearful," not "holy" (Gen 28:17); intermarriage with Canaanite women, though discouraged, is not discouraged on grounds that the women would encourage faithlessness to YHWH, as consistently claimed elsewhere in the Old Testament (Exod 34:11–16; 1 Kgs 11:1–10; Ezra 9–10); the patriarchs do not speak or act for God toward others in the mode of a prophet; no one particular site or sanctuary is privileged over others; the patriarchs are not aggressive toward the inhabitants of Canaan or their territory, of which the Canaanites are recognized as legitimate owners – Abraham or Jacob buy territory (Gen 23, 33:19), rather than seeking to take it forcibly; particular distinctives of Israel's identity, such as the dietary laws and Sabbath observance, are nowhere mentioned (apart from the mention of

---

[16] It seems to me a serious weakness in the fashionable placing of the patriarchal narratives in the postexilic period that this clear evidence of Yahwistic appropriation of originally non-Yahwistic traditions is generally ignored (so, e.g., Liverani, *Israel's History and the History of Israel*, 250–69).

[17] There are, to be sure, a number of exceptions to the generalizations in the next paragraph, all of which I have tried to gather and weigh in *The Old Testament of the Old Testament*, 79–104.

Egyptians eating their food in separation from Hebrews, rather than vice versa, Gen 43:32). The overall "ecumenical" ethos of the storyline is exemplified in the way that the Egyptian Pharaoh and the Hebrew Joseph respectively dream dreams whose content is given by one and the same God – consistently, the generic term for deity, 'ĕlōhîm, is used in this context (Gen 41). The main religious difference between the Pharaoh and Joseph is the quality of their insight into their dreams.

By contrast, when God appears to Moses at the burning bush as YHWH, the concept of holiness is present at the outset (Exod 3:5) and consistently thereafter; the relationship between YHWH and Israel is mediated by Moses, who speaks and acts on God's behalf in a way that has no precedent in Genesis; this relationship is morally and ritually demanding through covenantal torah; it is exclusive – "you shall have no other gods before me" (Exod 20:2); and it becomes consistently focused on a sanctuary, Sinai/Horeb initially, and then the tabernacle as Israel moves on. Unlike Joseph and Pharaoh alike receiving dreams from 'ĕlōhîm, YHWH is now God of Israel and not of Egypt; the Pharaoh neither knows nor acknowledges YHWH (Exod 5:2), and the Egyptians worship gods over whom YHWH shows his power (Exod 12:12). Alternatively, while it was apparently unproblematic for Jacob to erect a pillar (Gen 28:18), such practice becomes prohibited (Deut 16:22).

The possible significance of this consistent contrast between patriarchal religion and Mosaic Yahwism in the rest of the Pentateuch has been underexplored in modern scholarship partly because much of what is portrayed in Joshua, Judges, Samuel, and Kings also does not correspond to Mosaic regulation and is sometimes closer in ethos to Genesis than to Mosaic legislation. Hence the tendency to assimilate the religion of the patriarchs to Israelite religion more generally prior to Josiah's reform. Prescinding, however, from this familiar religio-historical problem,[18] I wish here to maintain a focus on the received form of the Pentateuch and the theological issues it poses.

Theological Issues in a Canonical Approach to the
Patriarchal Narratives

First, we can return to Haran's issue, the diversity of religious assumption and practice in Genesis in relation to the assumptions and practices of Exodus to Deuteronomy. As noted, the Pentateuch is emphatic that Yhwh, the God of Israel, is none other than the God of Abraham, Isaac, and Jacob. How can the text's contention, that the one God can apparently be known in markedly different ways, be related to a recognition that the people depicted within the texts would not have conceived themselves as doing what the tradition says they were doing – serving the God whom Israel knows as Yhwh?

At the very least, this shows that the validity of a theological judgment – if one stays with the classic tradition – need not be dependent on a religio-historical account of what was thought and understood at the time; its logic and justification operate according to different priorities and criteria. Further, one is pushed to reengage the fundamental theological issue of revelation – that God is known by Israel (and Jews and Christians, subsequently) because God has revealed himself. To be sure, one also needs critical tools appropriate to recognizing and analyzing the human mediation of the divine initiative, and here modern religio-historical approaches can enrich the traditional resources. But the point remains that the

---

[18] It is worth mentioning that the consistency of patriarchal ethos as just outlined is not shared by Joshua-Kings, and so even within a religio-historical frame of reference, the issues are complex.

theological issue intrinsically has dimensions that can be opaque to the familiar categories of religio-historical scholarship.

We return also to the ancient Jewish problem with Genesis: How should one recognize material as religiously authoritative that is full of religious practices different from, and sometimes forbidden by, Mosaic torah? As already noted, the mainstream instinct is to assimilate the unfamiliar to the familiar. It is now possible to give greater precision to this, in terms of the editorial shaping and appropriation of the patriarchal material. What seems to have happened is that the editors of the Pentateuch (unlike the author of *Jubilees*) were willing to let much of Genesis stand in its strangeness in relation to torah, most obviously in the figures of Jacob and Joseph. Yet they also molded the Abraham material in certain ways so as to make it more accessible for Israel to appropriate. Thus Abraham becomes a type/figure of Israel: Abraham's descent to Egypt in time of famine and departure from the Pharaoh with wealth after plagues (Gen 12:10–20) now anticipate the subsequent story of Israel; likewise, God's words to Abraham, "I am YHWH who brought you from Ur of the Chaldeans," are so resonant with the opening of the Decalogue, "I am YHWH your God who brought you out of the land of Egypt," that one naturally reads YHWH's dealings with Abraham as patterning YHWH's dealings with Israel (Gen 15:7; Exod 20:2). The language by which Abraham's offering of Isaac is construed – that it is a "test" (Gen 22:1) to establish that Abraham is one who "fears God" (22:12) – is also the language that Moses uses to interpret God's giving Israel the Ten Commandments (Exod 20:20); and it is likely that the Abraham story has been deliberately shaped so as to make Abraham's obedience and offering into a type of Israel's appropriate response to YHWH through torah. Finally, the Abraham who lives before the giving of torah is once explicitly – and notably – said to be obedient in the kind of way that torah prescribes (Gen 26:5).

In all this, one sees an interesting blurring of historical differences in the interests of appropriating the figure of Abraham within
the context of Israel. It is the case neither that historical differences
are eradicated nor that they are preserved for their own sake. What
appears to be going on, as best as we can see, is a *recontextualiz-
ing* of the Abraham material so that it can function as religiously
authoritative for Israel.

This appropriation of Abraham has, as already noted, striking
similarities to what Christians have traditionally done with the
Old Testament as a whole. There is the same conviction that one
God is at work in the differing contexts and that this one God
gives himself to be known in different ways. The issue that Haran
poses concerning the patriarchs in relation to Israel's normative
religion can equally well be posed – again, by Christians – of
Israel's normative knowledge of God focused on torah in relation
to the new norms established around the person of Jesus Christ.
The coming of Jesus in his life, death, and resurrection in relation to
what precedes is in important ways analogous to the self-revelation
of God to Moses at the burning bush and in the Sinai covenant in
relation to what precedes. Christians traditionally follow the lead
of the New Testament, that the God and Father of the Lord Jesus
Christ is none other than Yhwh, the God of Israel; and it can be
theologically fruitful to compare the considerations appropriate
to understanding and justifying this move to those that might be
made with reference to the God of the patriarchs as the God of
Israel.

Moreover, a typological or figural reading of the Old Testament
is one of the prime ways in which Christians have sought to appropriate its distinctive content within a Christian frame of reference.
To be sure, this has not been incorporated into the text of the
Old Testament in the same way that the Mosaic appropriation of
the patriarchs has been incorporated into the Genesis text. Yet the

instincts and conceptualities are closely comparable. The recognition of the editorial shaping and appropriation that has been incorporated into the Abraham material is part of what makes a canonical approach, as articulated here, distinct from a premodern approach that was innocent of the likely compositional processes within the Genesis text.

In sum, it can be seen that some of the classic hermeneutical concerns and moves represented within Christian debate about the relationship between the testaments are already present within the heart of Israel's scriptures, in the relationship between Genesis and the rest of the Pentateuch. The recovery of the classic Jewish "problem" of the patriarchs in Genesis can inform reflection on the nature and interpretation of the Christian Bible as a whole.

CHAPTER 8

Genesis 12:1–3: A Key to Interpreting the Old Testament?

It is perhaps unusual for a book within the Old Testament to have one particular text that can be regarded as a possible interpretative key to the book as a whole, and even to the Old Testament as a whole. Yet such a case has been made in relation to God's call of Abraham in Genesis 12:1–3:

> Now the LORD said to Abram, "Go from your country and your kindred and your father's house to the land that I will show you. I will make of you a great nation, and I will bless you, and make your name great, so that you will be a blessing. I will bless those who bless you, and the one who curses you I will curse; and in you all the families of the earth shall be blessed [or: by you all the families of the earth shall bless themselves]."

The intrinsic significance of this passage is not in doubt. For its context makes it a bridge between God's dealings with the world in general in Genesis 1–11 and his dealings with the patriarchs in particular in Genesis 12–50. These are also words on the lips of God, which clearly introduce and frame the story of Abraham that follows.

Enormous significance is attached to this passage by Paul, who cites part of it, together with Genesis 15:6, in Galatians 3:6–9:

> Just as Abraham "believed God, and it was reckoned to him as righteousness," so, you see, those who believe are the descendants

of Abraham. And the scripture, foreseeing that God would justify the Gentiles by faith, declared the gospel beforehand to Abraham, saying, "All the Gentiles shall be blessed in you." For this reason, those who believe are blessed with Abraham who believed.

Paul's reading of God's promise as constituting, in effect, the gospel to the nations, and his correlative linkage of "blessing" with "justification" and "faith" in the light of Genesis 15:6, are perhaps bold, but "can justly claim to realize something of the semantic potential of a complex and polysemic text."[1] It is unarguably a weighty reading of Genesis 12:3.

A CONTEMPORARY CHRISTIAN APPROACH
TO GENESIS 12:1–3

In the general history of Christian interpretation, my sense is that little special attention has been given to Genesis 12:1–3, though one finds, of course, the expected reaffirmations and reworkings of Paul's construal.[2] In the twentieth century, however, the passage comes to have renewed significance, especially through the work of Gerhard von Rad, who takes it as a key to the theological work of the Yahwist. Von Rad gives great weight to its narrative context in Genesis 1–11:

> The Yahwistic narrator has told the story of God and man from the time mankind began, and this story is characterized on the

---

[1] So claims Francis Watson in his important analysis of Paul's reading of Genesis 12:3, *Paul and the Hermeneutics of Faith* (London: T & T Clark, 2004), 183–93 (183).

[2] So, for example, the Fathers seem primarily to have been interested in Genesis 12:1–3 in terms of its implications for a moral and spiritual journey from sin toward virtue (Mark Sheridan, ed., *Genesis 12–50*, ACCS:OT 2 [Downers Grove, IL: InterVarsity, 2002], 1–4).

human side by an increase in sin to avalanche proportions. . . . This succession of narratives, therefore, points out a continually widening chasm between man and God. But God reacts to these outbreaks of human sin with severe judgments. . . . Thus at the end of the primeval history a difficult question is raised: God's future relationship to his rebellious humanity, which is now scattered in fragments. Is the catastrophe of ch. 11.1–9 final? . . . The Yahwistic narrator shows something else along with the consequences of divine judgment . . . in all the hardship of punishment, God's activity of succor and preservation was revealed. . . . We see, therefore (already in primeval history!), that each time, in and after the judgment, God's preserving, forgiving will to save is revealed, and "where sin increased, grace abounded all the more" (Rom. 5.20). . . .

This consoling preservation, that revelation of God's hidden gracious will, is missing, however, at one place, namely, at the end of the primeval history. The story about the Tower of Babel concludes with God's judgment on mankind; there is no word of grace. The whole primeval history, therefore, seems to break off in shrill dissonance, and the question we formulated above now arises even more urgently: Is God's relationship to the nations now finally broken; is God's gracious forbearance now exhausted; has God rejected the nations in wrath forever? . . .

Our narrator *does* give an answer, namely, at the point where sacred history begins. Here in the promise that is given concerning Abraham something is again said about God's saving will and indeed about a salvation extending far beyond the limits of the covenant people to "all the families of the earth" (ch. 12.3). . . .

From the multitude of nations God chooses a man, looses him from tribal ties, and makes him the beginner of a new nation and the recipient of great promises of salvation. What is promised to Abraham reaches far beyond Israel; indeed, it has universal meaning for all generations on earth. Thus that difficult question about God's relationship to the nations is answered, and precisely where one least expects it. At the beginning of the way into an emphatically exclusive covenant-relation there is already a word about the end of this way, namely, an allusion to a final, universal unchaining of the salvation promised to Abraham. Truly flesh and blood did not inspire this view beyond Israel and its saving relation to God! With this firm linking of primeval history and sacred history the Yahwist indicates something of the final meaning and purpose of the saving relation that God has vouchsafed to Israel.[3]

In von Rad's reading, Genesis 12:3 becomes a key to both Genesis and the Old Testament as a whole. His choice of language ("truly flesh and blood did not inspire this view beyond Israel"), with its clear implication of the rightness of what is said as a result of divine inspiration (cf. Jesus' words to Peter in Matt 16:17), suggests that, for him, this sense of God's purposes extending beyond Israel could only have been articulated by Israel at some higher prompting that overcame instinctive human tendencies to appropriate the divine selfishly. His language about the universality of salvation envisioned in God's words to Abraham shows clearly that he is reading Genesis in the light of Paul. Indeed, part of the potency of von Rad's reading is that it can give one renewed appreciation for Paul's construal.

In his specific discussion of Genesis 12:3, von Rad naturally reaffirms this larger horizon of significance and offers detailed exegetical discussion of a possible difficulty: Is universal salvation really the meaning of the divine promise of blessing?

> The question has been raised at vs. 2b and 3b whether the meaning is only that Abraham is to become a formula for blessing, that his blessing is to become far and wide proverbial (cf. Gen. 48.20). In favor of this conception (which reckons with a remnant of the magical-dynamic notion of blessing) one can refer to Zech. 8.13. It is, however, hermeneutically wrong to limit such a programmatic saying, circulating in such exalted style, to only *one* meaning (restrictively).... In Gen. 12.1–3 its effect is trivial in God's

---

[3] Gerhard von Rad, *Genesis: A Commentary*, trans. John H. Marks, rev. ed. OTL (London: SCM, 1972 [German 9th ed., 1972]), 152–54.

address which is solemnly augmented – completely so in the final strophe! The accepted interpretation must therefore remain. It is like a "command to history".... Abraham is assigned the role of a mediator of blessing in God's saving plan, for "all the families of the earth." The extent of the promise now becomes equal to that of the unhappy international world . . . an idea that occurs more than once in the Old Testament. Both Isaiah (ch. 2.2–4) and Deutero-Isaiah have prophesied about this universal destiny of Israel. The unusual *nibrᵉkū*, to which the Yahwist gives preference against the *hithpael* for this promise, can be translated reflexively ("bless oneself"); but the passive is also possible....

This prophecy, which points to a fulfilment lying beyond the old covenant, was especially important to the retrospective glance of the New Testament witnesses. We find it cited in Acts 3.25f.; Rom. 4.13; Gal. 3.8,16.[4]

Although von Rad's interpretation has not been without its critics, it has, unsurprisingly, been widely received as a model for Christian theological appropriation of the Old Testament.[5]

Claus Westermann, for example, differs from von Rad over various points of detail, but agrees about the general thrust of the text: "In any case, what 12:3b is saying is this: God's action proclaimed in the promise to Abraham is not limited to him and his posterity, but reaches its goal only when it includes all the families of the earth."[6] With regard to the classic crux of the verbal form in 12:3b, *nibrĕkû*, the Niphal of *brk*, used here and also in other forms of the divine promise (Gen 18:18, 28:14), and its relation to those places

---

[4] Ibid., 160–61.

[5] Equally unsurprisingly, Jewish scholars have tended to be less impressed: most notably, in terms of general hermeneutics, Jon D. Levenson, "Why Jews Are Not Interested in Biblical Theology," in his *The Hebrew Bible, the Old Testament, and Historical Criticism: Jews and Christians in Biblical Studies* (Louisville, KY: Westminster/John Knox, 1993), 33–61.

[6] Claus Westermann, *Genesis 12–36: A Commentary*, trans. John J. Scullion, CC (Minneapolis, MN: Augsburg, 1985 [German orig., 1981]), 152.

where the divine promise employs the Hithpael (Gen 22:18, 26:4) – hence, "be blessed" or "bless themselves"? – Westermann thinks that there is no real problem anyway:

> In fact, the reflexive translation is saying no less than the passive. . . . When "the families of the earth bless" themselves "in Abraham," i.e. call a blessing on themselves under the invocation of his name (as in Ps. 72:17, and even more clearly in Gen. 48:20), then the obvious presupposition is that they receive the blessing. Where one blesses oneself with the name of Abraham, blessing is actually bestowed and received. . . . There is then no opposition in content between the passive and reflexive translation.[7]

Alternatively, Brevard S. Childs, when discussing the meaning of Israel's election, more than once alludes to Genesis 12:1–3. He never lingers to analyze or discuss in detail, presumably because the interpretation is not considered controversial: "Israel was indeed chosen 'from all the families of the earth' (Amos 3.2), but with the explicit purpose that all the nations of the world would be blessed (Gen. 12.3)"; "the theme of Israel's redemptive role to the nations, first sounded in Gen. 12.1ff. . . .";[8] "this relationship was toward the purpose of shaping this people into a holy and righteous vehicle by which to reconcile himself to the world (Gen. 12.1ff)"; "When the apostle Paul extended the promise to Abraham (Gen. 12.1ff.) to include the inheritance of the world (Rom. 4.13), he was only exploiting an interpretative direction which had long been represented in the canonical construal of the tradition."[9]

In recent years many Christians have made von Rad's construal their own, especially in relation to mission. Richard Bauckham, in

---

[7] Ibid.

[8] Brevard S. Childs, *Old Testament Theology in a Canonical Context* (London: SCM, 1985), 92, 239.

[9] Brevard S. Childs, *Biblical Theology of the Old and New Testaments: Theological Reflection on the Christian Bible* (London: SCM, 1992), 139, 445.

his *Bible and Mission*, speaks of "the blessing of the nations as the ultimate purpose of God's call of Abraham"[10] and draws out the wider significance of God's call of Abraham (in conjunction with the call of Israel and of David):

> Abraham, Israel and David are not sent out to evangelize the world. But . . . [they] make the church's mission intelligible as a necessary and coherent part of the whole biblical metanarrative. They establish the movement from the particular to the universal that the church is called in its mission to embody in a particular form. They establish the purpose of God for the world that, again, the church is called to serve in mission to the world.[11]

Comparable is Christopher J. H. Wright in his substantial book *The Mission of God*. Wright prefaces an extended discussion of Genesis 12:1–3, in which he draws heavily on von Rad and Westermann, with a look at Paul and Galatians 3:6–9 from which he concludes the following:

> So the Gentile mission, Paul argued, far from being a betrayal of the Scriptures, was rather the fulfilment of them. The ingathering of the nations was the very thing Israel existed for in the purpose of God; it was the fulfilment of the bottom line of God's promise to Abraham. Since Jesus was the Messiah of Israel and since the Messiah embodied in his own person the identity and mission of Israel, then to belong to the Messiah through faith was to belong to Israel.[12]

Indeed, Wright strikingly contends that

> [t]he words of Jesus to his disciples in Matthew 28:18–20, the so-called Great Commission, could be seen as a christological

---

[10] Richard Bauckham, *Bible and Mission: Christian Witness in a Postmodern World* (Grand Rapids, MN: Baker Academic, 2003), 28.

[11] Ibid., 46–47.

[12] Christopher J. H. Wright, *The Mission of God: Unlocking the Bible's Grand Narrative* (Nottingham, UK: InterVarsity, 2006), 194.

mutation of the original Abraham commission – "Go...and be a blessing...and all the nations on earth will be blessed through you."[13]

AN ALTERNATIVE READING OF GENESIS 12:1–3

So congenial is this interpretation to a Christian appropriation of the Old Testament and to furthering that sense of mission that is in any case intrinsic to Christian self-understanding, and so impressive is the roster of scholars who advance it, that it may seem churlish to query it. Nonetheless, for reasons of integrity, it is important to ask whether this is the only, or indeed the best, construal of the Genesis text. The relationship between exegetical precision and canonical frame of reference is finely balanced here.

Von Rad, Westermann, and Wright do to some extent, to be sure, acknowledge possible alternative construals of the idioms of blessing that are used. But in their judgment, these alternatives do not amount to much of a challenge, and the time-honored crux concerning *nibrĕkû* in fact has nothing hanging on it. This is mainly because of their strong sense of the overall thrust of the text, which is God's concern for the needy world of Genesis 1–11. If the purpose of God's call of Abraham is to bless the nations, then the best construal of the idioms of blessing is that which most contributes to this overall tenor of the divine words.

One reason for the absence of any significant alternative reading must surely be not just the attractiveness of von Rad's construal but also the influence of his rhetoric, which is dismissive of an alternative. In the passage already cited, von Rad depicts an alternative construal of blessing as "trivial," with the clear implication that the only way to give the divine words the interpretative weight that

[13] Ibid., 213.

their context demands is to follow what he regards as "the accepted interpretation" that "must therefore remain." In this he develops the rhetoric in his famous essay, "The Form-Critical Problem of the Hexateuch," which first advanced this construal of the Yahwist.[14] There, von Rad raises the issue that Genesis 12:3b might "imply no more than that the name of Abraham will become a token used by non-Israelites with which to bless themselves," and he indeed considers the issue insoluble "on the grounds of linguistic consideration alone." He appeals confidently, however, to the context: "The main objection to so limited an interpretation of this text arises from the fact that it breaks the continuity between the primeval history . . . and the promise of redemption. The entire primeval history would at once sink to the level of a purely decorative addition to the work." Indeed, the alternative is a "pale, attenuated meaning" that "detract[s] . . . from the whole point of the work."[15]

Despite von Rad's rhetoric, there is a readily available alternative reading. The critical question is, May the real concern of the divine speech be not the benefit of the nations but rather the benefit of Abraham? May the nations constitute the backdrop *in spite of whom* Abraham will become a great nation, rather than *for the sake of whom* Abraham will become a great nation?

God initially summons Abraham to leave his existing home and the security and identity of his family and clan to go to a land that he does not yet know (Gen 12:1). This could sound like a venture into danger and oblivion. So, God immediately follows up with

---

[14] Gerhard von Rad, "The Form-Critical Problem of the Hexateuch," recently edited and reprinted in von Rad, *From Genesis to Chronicles: Explorations in Old Testament Theology*, ed. K. C. Hanson (Minneapolis, MN: Fortress, 2005), 1–58, 243–49.

[15] Ibid., 248n101 (for the first English edition see von Rad, *The Problem of the Hexateuch and Other Essays*, trans. E. W. Trueman Dicken [London: SCM, 1984], 166n107).

promises that take the form of a reassurance that, far from oblivion, Abraham will become a great and recognized nation (12:2). This reassurance is further developed through the promise that God will be with Abraham, so that others will experience blessing and curse according to their response to Abraham (12:3a). Indeed, this divine favoring of Abraham will be so great that it will be acknowledged by everyone everywhere (12:3b). Thus, if Abraham will but trust God, he can leave current security and identity behind in the confidence that greater security and identity lie ahead; if Abraham will relinquish now (12:1), he will receive in the future more than he has relinquished (12:2–3).

If one reads the text not from the perspective of Christian faith seeking Old Testament warrant for Christian universalism or mission, but from the imagined perspective of Abraham, and implicitly of the nation that descends from him, then it looks different. Those who respond to the costly call of God to leave behind what they have, and whose subsequent way of living will set them apart from their neighbors and perhaps provoke antagonism, do not regard a divine reassurance that God will bless them and give them positive recognition as in any way trivial. Rather, it engenders a hope that will sustain them through difficult times.

The Idiomatic Meaning of "Blessing"

Various idiomatic features support this reading in which the concern is assurance to Abraham. In the first place, one should hear a classic Jewish construal of Genesis 12:3b from Rashi's commentary:

> There are many Agadoth *concerning this* but the plain sense of the text is as follows: A man says to his son, "Mayest thou become as Abraham." This, too, is the meaning wherever the phrase *wenibreku beka* "And in thee shall be blessed" occurs in Scripture, and the following example proves this: (Gen. XLVIII.20) *beka yebarek* "By

thee shall Israel bless their children saying, 'May God make thee as Ephraim and Manasseh.' "[16]

That is, Abraham will become an object of admiration for others, a model of how people will want those whom they favor to become. The question of the "right" translation of the Niphal verb *nibrĕkû* remains probably insoluble on philological grounds.[17] Nonetheless, it remains likely that the Niphal and Hithpael forms of blessing in the various divine promises do have the same meaning, primarily because the varying contexts of promise do not sufficiently indicate a reason for finding a different meaning, but also because elsewhere in Genesis one can find verbs whose Niphal and Hithpael look to be interchangeable.[18] If this is so, then some form of reflexive sense is indicated, probably "pronounce blessings upon one another."

Before discussing Genesis 12:3b any further, however, I should first note the likely sense of Genesis 12:2b, which concludes with Abraham's becoming "a blessing." Wright, for example, assumes the kind of sense that characterizes the English idiom of someone "being a blessing," in that others are benefitted by them: Blessing here is a "command," a "task," and "the object of this blessing is at first unspecified."[19] Yet such a sense is rarely, if at all, attested in

---

[16] M. Rosenbaum and A. M. Silbermann, eds., *The Pentateuch with the Commentary of Rashi: Genesis* (Jerusalem: Silbermann, 1972), 49.

[17] The most thorough recent study of Genesis 12:3, which also probes the meanings of both Niphal and Hithpael stems, is Keith N. Grüneberg, *Abraham, Blessing and the Nations: A Philological and Exegetical Study of Genesis 12:3 in Its Narrative Context*, BZAW 332 (New York: de Gruyter, 2003). Grüneberg makes the best possible case, I think, for finding a different meaning in the Niphal and Hithpael forms of the divine promise and for construing *nibrĕkû* in 12:3 as passive (176–90).

[18] A prime example is *ḥbʾ* (hide), whose Hithpael in Genesis 3:8 appears to be interchangeable with its Niphal in 3:10.

[19] Wright, *The Mission of God*, 211, 201.

the Old Testament.[20] Rather, the regular idiom is that someone is a blessing or curse if something happens to them such that when people formulate blessings and curses, their name is regularly used as an example of the desired outcome. A clear example is Jeremiah 29:21–23:

> Thus says the LORD of hosts, the God of Israel, concerning Ahab son of Kolaiah and Zedekiah son of Maaseiah, who are prophesying a lie to you in my name: I am going to deliver them into the hand of King Nebuchadrezzar of Babylon, and he shall kill them before your eyes. And on account of them this curse shall be used by all the exiles from Judah in Babylon: "The LORD make you like Zedekiah and Ahab, whom the king of Babylon roasted in the fire."

Comparable is Jeremiah 24:8–9:

> But thus says the LORD: Like the bad figs that are so bad that they cannot be eaten, so will I treat King Zedekiah of Judah, his officials, the remnant of Jerusalem who remain in this land, and those who live in the land of Egypt. I will make them a horror, an evil thing, to all the kingdoms of the earth – a disgrace, a byword, a taunt, and a curse in all the places where I shall drive them.

Here, "all the kingdoms of the earth" – which idiomatically has a force comparable to "all the families of the earth" in Genesis 12:3b – will regard Zedekiah and the Judahites as exemplifying the kind of proverbial extremity that may be invoked on enemies: "May you become like Zedekiah/be a Zedekiah," the converse of "may you become like Abraham." Moreover, although in Jeremiah 29:21–23 the Judahites are envisaged as invoking YHWH to enact the curse, because YHWH is their God, there is no implication in Jeremiah 24:8–9 that all the kingdoms of the earth would likewise invoke

[20] Grüneberg concludes a discussion of this issue: "Thus *brkh* is not used to describe a person as a source of blessings" (*Abraham, Blessing and the Nations*, 121).

Yнwн, because the biblical writers are well aware that nations other than Israel have allegiances to other deities and so should be presumed to invoke those deities in their pronouncements. That is, even if these other nations might recognize the fate of Zedekiah and the Judahites as brought about by Yнwн, the Judahite deity, who had been offended, this recognition would not extend to substantive acknowledgement of Yнwн as the deity to whom they were accountable and in whose name they should make their own pronouncements.

The sense of blessing in Genesis 12:2b, therefore, is surely the opposite of curse as just outlined, a sense precisely captured by Zechariah 8:13: "Just as you have been a cursing among the nations, O house of Judah and house of Israel, so I will save you and you shall be a blessing. Do not be afraid, but let your hands be strong." Von Rad's depiction of the conceptuality here as "reckon[ing] with a remnant of the magical-dynamic notion of blessing" seems designed tacitly to downplay the significance of the text in a way that surely misrepresents the sense of a common idiom.[21] And even if one agrees that "it is . . . hermeneutically wrong to limit such a programmatic saying, circulating in such exalted style, to only *one* meaning (restrictively)," it remains important to try to set out the likely sense within the Genesis context and to hear it in its own right.

In the light of this idiomatic usage, one can see that Westermann (explicitly followed by Wright)[22] surely overinterprets the

---

[21] Von Rad's "magical-dynamic notion of blessing," even in remnant form, is unwarranted in the light of speech-act theory, which shows that recognized social convention is what makes blessings valid. See Anthony C. Thiselton, "The Supposed Power of Words in the Biblical Writings," *JTS* 25 (1974): 283–99; reprinted in Thiselton, *Thiselton on Hermeneutics: The Collected Works and New Essays of Anthony Thiselton* (Aldershot, UK: Ashgate, 2006), 53–67.

[22] Wright, *The Mission of God*, 217–18.

implications of people pronouncing blessings whose sense is "Mayest thou become as Abraham." Westermann says,

> When "the families of the earth bless" themselves "in Abraham," i.e. call a blessing on themselves under the invocation of his name (as in Ps. 72:17, and even more clearly in Gen. 48:20), then the obvious presupposition is that they receive the blessing. Where one blesses oneself with the name of Abraham, blessing is actually bestowed and received.

But *why* is it an "obvious presupposition... that they receive the blessing"? The idiomatic analogy to Genesis 12:3b is Jeremiah 24:8–9, where the invoking of the name of Zedekiah and the Judahites as a curse says nothing about either the efficacy of that invocation or the relationship of those invoking their name to the deity responsible for their condition; the point is entirely the paradigmatic condition of the one whose name is invoked. Moreover, any acknowledgment of Zedekiah's and Judah's deity on the part of all the kingdoms of the earth could be limited to recognizing that, within Israel's frame of reference, what has happened to them should be ascribed to their deity, with no necessary implication that others who invoke the fate of Zedekiah and the Judahites appropriate that frame of reference for themselves. Correspondingly, if all the families of the earth pronounce blessings by Abraham, then they recognize and invoke Abraham as a model of desirable existence. Insofar as the identity of the deity responsible for Abraham's condition comes into view, which the use of the blessing need not imply, then it would remain fully possible that what in Israel's frame of reference is ascribed to Yhwh could be expressed otherwise in a different frame of reference (e.g., "May Chemosh make you like Abraham"). In any case, the point, when Jeremiah envisions all the kingdoms of the earth invoking Zedekiah and the Judahites, is that their fate is paradigmatically awful, and the focus is strongly on Zedekiah and the Judahites in that fate rather than on theological implications concerning the deity responsible.

Thus the supposition that those who invoke Abraham in blessing actually receive the blessing invoked is a non sequitur that goes well beyond the meaning of the Genesis text. The textual concern is to assure Abraham that he really will be a great nation, and the measure of that greatness is that he will be invoked on the lips of others as a model of desirability. The condition of other nations in their own right is not in view, beyond their having reason not to be hostile to Abraham.

The Significance of the Proposed Reading

It must be acknowledged that much in this reading is not novel. The distinctive element, if such there be, lies in the attempt to enter imaginatively into the possible significance of the divine speech for Abraham himself within the text. A comparable interpretation of the Abrahamic blessing is succinctly formulated by (among others) Gunkel in the famous third edition of his Genesis commentary.[23] Gunkel, however, offers an overall reading only in terms of the narrator's supposed historical location as a time when that of which the text speaks was considered to have been realized – a reading that is tacitly reductive, with a pejorative evaluation:

> In the narrator's opinion these promises [viz., Gen 12:2–3] are also fulfilled in the present: Israel is now a very great, widely famed people . . . Israel considers itself to be very numerous, blessed and protected by God, very famous and praised among the nations. Fame-loving Israel often overvalued its reputation among the nations.[24]

[23] Hermann Gunkel, *Genesis*, trans. Mark E. Biddle (Macon, GA: Mercer University Press, 1997 [3rd German ed., 1910]), 164.
[24] Ibid., 164–65.

Moreover, the proposed reading would in no way diminish the biblical mandate for Christian mission, which remains clear even if Genesis 12:1–3 is not part of it. Rather, the role for Genesis 12:1–3 in contemporary Christian appropriation would surely relate to the church's self-understanding in a post-Christian Western culture that has largely become either indifferent or hostile to the biblical vision of God and life with God. God's call to a lifestyle and understanding that may often be sharply countercultural can be costly, and temptations and pressures to assimilate are considerable. So, assurance of God's sustaining and enabling of what he calls people to be and do remains necessary; and faithfulness within such a vocation may become attractive and desirable to those outside the church. I suggest that the New Testament counterpart to Genesis 12:1–3 is not the Great Commission, but rather Jesus' assuring promise to Peter whose recognition of Jesus as Messiah constitutes the basis for the church: "And I tell you, you are Peter, and on this rock I will build my church, and the gates of Hades will not prevail against it" (Matt 16:18).

THEOLOGICAL INTERPRETATION AS A CONTINUING TASK

Exegesis and Theology

If the argument for this alternative reading of Genesis 12:1–3 carries any weight, then what follows? Is this an example of a "right" interpretation that should replace a "wrong" interpretation? Indeed, is this a possible paradigmatic example of the dominant concern of modern biblical interpretation in historical-critical mode – the separating out of philology and history from ecclesial concerns or canonical context, the need to free exegesis from predetermining theological preconceptions so that the voice of the text may be heard in its own right?

For better or worse, life is not so simple. First and foremost, it is not so simple because it is fundamentally unhelpful to polarize philology/exegesis/the text in itself over against theology/presuppositions/ecclesial priorities, because all substantive interpretation involves an interplay between the biblical text and the questions one brings to it, questions that necessarily reflect the interpreter's own preconceptions and frame of reference.[25] On any reckoning it can often be a fine line between anachronistically imposing a mistaken sense on a biblical text in the light of later developments and being enabled by later developments to discern nuances and incipient tendencies in biblical texts that otherwise might have gone unnoticed.

Second, Paul's construal of Genesis 12:3, although informed by many factors, follows the Septuagint. Here, the Niphal verb *nibrĕkû* is rendered by a passive *eneulogēthēsontai* ("they shall be blessed"), as are the other Niphal and Hithpael formulations of God's promise of blessing in Genesis. The precise sense of "in/by you" is unclear, but appears to be instrumental. So, Francis Watson comments, "For the [LXX] translator [of Gen 12:3], the calling and destiny of Israel is to bring blessing to the entire world, and his rendering seeks to bring this out as clearly as possible."[26] If Paul's biblical text already depicted Abraham as a *source* rather than a *model* of blessing, then the decisive move in terms of seeing Abraham's vocation as being for the sake of the nations had probably already been made prior to Paul. Since the Old Testament is read by the writers of the New Testament and by the Fathers for the most part in Greek, the Septuagint's rendering must be taken seriously by subsequent theology; and the relative merits of the Hebrew and

[25] See the discussion in Chapter 1.
[26] Watson, *Paul and the Hermeneutics of Faith*, 184–85.

the Greek, where they differ, becomes an interesting and difficult question that is probably best approached on a case-by-case basis.

On Evaluating Gerhard von Rad's Interpretation

Third, even if I am unpersuaded by von Rad, this does not deny value to his work. Von Rad's original formulation of the significance of the Yahwist and Genesis 12:1–3 was in the context of 1930s Nazi Germany, and his specific situation was as a member of the Confessing Church working at the University of Jena, where National Socialist policies were strongly promoted.[27] In such a context, where the authorities degraded the Old Testament and denied any positive enduring significance to it, von Rad's work was a profound and imaginatively serious contribution; his argument for strong continuity between the Old and New Testaments is an argument that is intrinsic to Christian faith and was particularly timely as a Christian Old Testament scholar's response to Nazi ideology. By contrast, Gunkel's reading of God's call and promises as an example of Israel's rather inflated sense of self-importance would in no way have made any (would-be) Nazi or anti-Semite think twice. Good theological interpretation of the Old Testament is not

[27] See the eye-opening essay of Bernard M. Levinson and Douglas Dance, "The Metamorphosis of Law into Gospel: Gerhard von Rad's Attempt to Reclaim the Old Testament for the Church," in *Recht und Ethik im Alten Testament: Beiträge des Symposiums "Das Alte Testament und die Kultur der Moderne" anlässlich des 100. Geburtstags Gerhard von Rads (1901–1971) Heidelberg, 18.–21. Oktober 2001*, ed. Bernard M. Levinson and Eckart Otto, ATM 13 (Münster, Ger.: Lit Verlag, 2004), 83–110. Although Levinson and Dance focus on von Rad's work on Deuteronomy and do not discuss his work on the Yahwist and Genesis 12:1–3, their comment on the one may apply also to the other: "His analysis says less about Deuteronomy than it says about the situation in which he wrote" (85). See also Bernard M. Levinson "Reading the Bible in Nazi Germany: Gerhard von Rad's Attempt to Reclaim the Old Testament for the Church," *Int* 62 (2008): 238–54.

necessarily that which might aspire to be recognized as correct in any time or any place; rather, part of its rightness may be *specific and contextual,* in its ability to articulate biblical priorities in relation to particular situations of need. To say this is not to prioritize relevance over accuracy, but rather to recognize, with the sociology of knowledge, that human understanding and insight depend on many factors other than pure reason and do not achieve finality in any one situation.

A Jewish–Christian Dimension

Fourth, one facet of the contemporary theological context that was not equally a facet of von Rad's context is the renewal of Jewish–Christian dialogue, together with a far more substantive presence of Jewish scholars within academic biblical study than was the case in von Rad's time. This should, at the very least, make for a greater sensitivity on the part of Christian interpreters to Jewish readings of Israel's scriptures. To be sure, the question of precisely how such sensitivity should operate, and what difference it should make, is still a matter of lively debate. Nonetheless, even if one wishes, as I do, to resist a neat bifurcation between the historical meaning of the ancient Israelite text in its own right and its theological appropriation in differing ways by differing contemporary Jewish and Christian communities – for the dialectics of understanding are more complex than such a model implies – it remains important that Christians should not inappropriately impose their preferred meanings on these ancient texts.

Interestingly, however, a concern to read Abraham's call by God as being for the sake of the nations is not simply a peculiarity of Christian Old Testament interpretation, courtesy of Paul, from which Jews simply disengage. A construal of Abraham as mediator of divine blessing to the nations is in fact also attested in Jewish interpretation down the ages, as is Abraham as a model.[28] Nahum M. Sarna, in the Jewish Publication Society Torah commentary on Genesis, comments on the NJPSV translation of Genesis 12:3b ("and all the families of the earth shall bless themselves by you") as follows:

> This rendering understands Hebrew *ve-nivrekhu* as reflexive. People will take your own good fortune as the desired measure when invoking a blessing on themselves. A more likely translation of the verb is as a passive: "shall be blessed through – because of – you." God's promises to Abram would then proceed in three stages from the particular to the universal: a blessing on Abram personally, a blessing (or curse) on those with whom he interacts, a blessing on the entire human race.[29]

Von Rad would hardly disagree! Prior to Sarna, the other two major twentieth-century Jewish commentators on Genesis, Benno Jacob and Umberto Cassuto, come out with not dissimilar renderings, which seems to be because each explicitly reads the text as anticipating the "universalism" of the Hebrew prophets.

Jacob, for example, construes the verb in 12:3b as reflexive, not passive, but still considers the text to depict a divine concern for the whole world:

> It is a second world, which with Abraham is called into existence: the world of the blessing through people for people. Therein the most magnificent religious universalism comes to expression, which no prophet was able to exceed and which one (for example, Holzinger,

---

[28] See Moshe Greenberg, "To Whom and for What Should a Biblical Commentator Be Responsible?" in Greenberg, *Studies in the Bible and Jewish Thought* (Philadelphia: Jewish Publication Society, 1995), 235–43, esp. 240.

[29] Nahum M. Sarna, *Genesis: The Traditional Hebrew Text with New JPS Translation*, The JPS Torah Commentary (Philadelphia: Jewish Publication Society, 1989), 89.

Gunkel) seeks in vain to diminish. Standing at the beginning of the history of Israel the Torah is completely aware of the end towards which it should proceed.[30]

The idea that the culminating promise to Abraham is restricted in its concern to Abraham is, apparently, uncongenial. This appears to be so because of the wider context of scripture and Jewish tradition within which these commentators are operating. For even if Judaism has not characteristically understood itself in the kind of missionary terms that are intrinsic to Christianity, it has nonetheless regularly wanted to affirm that God's call of Israel not only is an end in itself that needs no further justification than the love of a parent for a child, but also is of potential moral and spiritual benefit to other nations. As Christians can feel constrained to reread Genesis 12:3 in the light of Christ and Christian faith, so Jews can feel a similar constraint in the light of full-orbed Jewish faith. Both in the dynamics of biblical interpretation, and in an understanding of their faith as being for the benefit of others, Jews and Christians can find that, for all their real differences, they have more common ground than has sometimes been supposed in the past.

---

[30] Benno Jacob, *Das Erste Buch der Tora: Genesis* (repr., New York: Ktav, 1974; orig., Berlin: Schocken, 1934), 339 (my translation). An English translation of Jacob's work was recently released: Benno Jacob, *Genesis: The First Book of the Bible*, trans. Ernest I. Jacob and Walter Jacob (New York: Ktav, 2007). For Umberto Cassuto's construal, see his *A Commentary on the Book of Genesis*, trans. Israel Abrahams, 2 vols. (Jerusalem: Magnes, 1964 [Hebrew orig., 1949]), 2:315.

CHAPTER 9

Genesis 12:3a: A Biblical Basis for Christian Zionism?

In the previous chapter, we saw that the extensive scholarly interest that has been directed to Genesis 12:1–3 has tended to focus on v. 3b. By contrast, little scholarly attention has been given to v. 3a, where YHWH says to Abram, "I will bless those who bless you, and the one who curses you I will curse." To be sure, there is some passing comment, but it tends to be little more than routine.[1] Beyond scholarly circles, however, things look different, and at the present time, at least within some Christian groupings within the United States of America, there is great interest in 12:3a, which is taken to mandate U.S. support for the state of Israel, support that is practical, both financial and military, and not solely idealistic.[2] Since I do not think it wise for biblical scholars to ignore the actual use that the Bible receives beyond the academy, and since the appeal to Genesis 12:3a raises interesting issues about what constitutes good interpretation and use of Genesis, it will be appropriate here to consider briefly this particular appeal to this text.

---

[1] An exception is Patrick D. Miller, "Syntax and Theology in Gen XII 3a," *VT* 34 (1984): 472–76; reprinted in Miller, *Israelite Religion and Biblical Theology: Collected Essays*, JSOTSup 267 (Sheffield, UK: Sheffield Academic Press, 2000), 492–96.

[2] The relationship between the United States of America and Israel is, of course, an immensely complex issue, where many divergent influences bear on the United States' policy making. I focus here on one strand.

WHY CHRISTIANS SHOULD SUPPORT ISRAEL

The phenomenon of Christian Zionism is complex and takes many forms, both distinct from and overlapping with the numerous Jewish forms. My impression, however, is that appeal to Genesis 12:3a has been promoted especially by Christians operating within a premillennial dispensationalist frame of reference and that this particular form of Zionism has had significant public impact and influence.[3] So this will be my focus here.

The essential reason for the support is concisely articulated by Jerry Falwell, well known as the founder of the Moral Majority, who has played a key role in the movement:

> Basically God promised to bless those who blessed the children of Abraham and curse those who cursed Israel. I think history supports the fact that he has been true to his word. When you go back to the pharaohs, the Caesars, Adolf Hitler and the Soviet Union, all those who dared to touch the apple of God's eye – Israel – have been punished by God. America has been blessed because she has blessed Israel.[4]

Recently, Jerry Falwell's leading role has been taken over by Pastor John Hagee, the founder of Christians United for Israel. On his Web site, Hagee offers "seven solid Bible reasons why Christians should support Israel." Underneath a heading drawn from Zechariah 2:8, in which Yhwh speaks of Judah as "the apple of his

---

[3] Amid the voluminous literature, a good overview is Timothy P. Weber, *On the Road to Armageddon: How Evangelicals Became Israel's Best Friend* (Grand Rapids, MN: Baker Academic, 2004). Victoria Clark, *Allies for Armageddon: The Rise of Christian Zionism* (New Haven, CT: Yale University Press, 2007) is a highly readable account, in which Clark presents Christian Zionist appeal to Genesis 12:3a as a leitmotif throughout.

[4] Cited in Weber, *On the Road to Armageddon*, 296. I was unable to access the weblink that Weber draws on.

eye", the first reason given starts with a quotation of Genesis 12:3 and continues,

> God has promised to bless the man or nation that blesses the Chosen People. History has proved beyond reasonable doubt that the nations that have blessed the Jewish people have had the blessing of God; the nations that have cursed the Jewish people have experienced the curse of God.

Some of the other seven reasons are little more than reworkings of this first reason. Thus, for example, the fifth reason is as follows:

> Why did Jesus Christ go to the house of Cornelius [sic] in Capernaum and heal his servant, which [sic] was ready to die? What logic did the Jewish elders use with Jesus to convince Him to come into the house of a Gentile and perform a miracle?
>
> The logic they used is recorded in Luke 7:5; "For He [sic] loveth our nation, and He [sic] hath built us a synagogue." The message? This Gentile deserves the blessing of God because he loves our nation and has done something practical to bless the Jewish people.[5]

Elsewhere on the Web site, under "Frequently Asked Questions," there is a section on "Israel and the Jewish People," which begins thus:

> The support of Israel is a biblically based mandate for every Christian. All other nations were created by an act of men, but God Himself established the boundaries of the nation of Israel. God gave to Abraham, Isaac, and Jacob a covenant of land that was eternally binding, and it's recorded in the book of Genesis. God also told Abraham that He would make Abraham's descendants into a great nation and through them He would bless all the families of the earth. In the same passage, God said He would "bless those who bless you" (Abraham), and "curse him who curses you" (Gen. 12:3). That gets my attention. I want to be blessed, not cursed, by God.

[5] www.jhm.org/support-israel.asp (accessed September 19, 2007).

The Bible shows God as the protector and defender of Israel. . . . The prophet Zechariah said that the Jewish people are "the apple of God's eye" (2:8). Any nation that comes against Israel is, in effect, poking God in the eye – not a very wise thing to do! If God created Israel, if God considers Israel the apple of His eye, then it is logical to say that those who stand with Israel are standing with God.[6]

Although Hagee offers other reasons for supporting Israel, such as Christian indebtedness to the Jewish people and the democratic nature of Israel, it is clear that the biblical mandate in Genesis 12:3 takes pride of place.

To be sure, the appeal can take different emphases and can have different implications. Charles ("Chuck") Colson, well known for his Prison Fellowship ministry, combines appeal to Genesis 12:3 with a rather more differentiated political stance than Falwell or Hagee demonstrate:

> Somehow God's covenant with Abraham in Genesis 12:3 has become a *carte blanche* for Ariel Sharon and his government. . . .
>
> As a Christian and believer in the Abrahamic covenant, I'm a strong supporter of Israel and the Jewish people. I take Genesis 12:3 literally. I also believe that Jesus will return and rule the earth for one thousand years from Jerusalem – a pre-millennial perspective on the second coming. I believe that God has a special plan for the Jewish people and the land of Israel.
>
> But I think it is problematic to relate prophecy to current events unfolding in the nation-state of Israel. There may be some relationship, of course. Only God knows. But the secular state of Israel created in 1948 is not, in my understanding, identical with the Jewish people as God's chosen and called-out covenant people.
>
> God clearly has a distinct plan for the Jewish people that the secular state of Israel helps carry out. I don't rule that out, of course. And I strongly support Israel because it is a haven for persecuted Jews – not because I think it fulfils biblical prophecy.

[6] www.jhm.org/faq.asp#israel (accessed September 19, 2007).

I also support a Palestinian state both from historical and pru-
dential considerations. Given the state of affairs in the Middle East,
a Palestinian state is the only practicable solution for peace.[7]

In one way or other, however, it is clear that Genesis 12:3a
plays a fundamental role in significant strands of contemporary
American Christian thinking and foreign-policy advocacy. Victoria Clark sums it up thus:

> This single line of Genesis is the vital insurance policy that goes
> as far towards explaining the appeal of Christian Zionism as any
> thrillingly apocalyptic narrative or Rapture get-out clause. On the
> strength of that endlessly reiterated one-line promise to Abraham,
> millions of Americans have come to believe that if they "bless"
> Israel morally, financially and politically, God will reward them
> by favoring America. "Blessing" Israel for America's sake has been
> motivating Christian Zionists to combat anti-Semitism, donate to
> Jewish charities, and invest in and visit Israel. But it has also involved
> many in opposing any peace process, in supporting the continued
> building of Jewish settlements in the West Bank, in funding those
> internationally outlawed settlements and in backing an extreme
> right-wing Israeli plan to "transfer" the Palestinians to neighbouring
> Arab states.[8]

This appeal to Genesis 12:3a did not originate with Falwell and
his fellow Christian Zionists. In one form or other, it is trace-
able to some of the earliest expressions of a Protestant reading of
the Bible in the sixteenth and seventeenth centuries,[9] though an
understanding of its current use is inseparable from some knowledge of the development of premillenial dispensationalism in the

---

[7] From "Israel's Place in the World Today" – February 18, 2003, on www.
breakpoint.org/listingarticle.asp?ID=5069 (accessed September 19, 2007).

[8] Clark, *Allies for Armageddon*, 12.

[9] See Donald Wagner, "Christians and Zion: British Stirrings" at www.
informationclearinghouse.info/article4959.htm (accessed September 19,
2007).

nineteenth and twentieth centuries.[10] Interesting though it would be to trace and reflect on the circumstances that have encouraged the contemporary widespread adoption of initially marginal views, that will not be my concern here. Nor will I discuss the overall stance of dispensationalism or scrutinize the constantly repeated assertion that the record of history clearly illustrates the outworking of the blessing-and-cursing principle with relation to the Jewish people.[11] Nor will I linger with the not very helpful typology of "liberal and historical" vs. "fundamentalist and literal" approaches to the biblical text, which tends to characterize references to Genesis 12:3 in much of the literature.[12] Rather, my concern is to reflect on what may be learned from this particular appeal to Genesis 12:3a in relation to contemporary theological understanding and use of Genesis more generally.

SOME FACTORS IN THE USE OF SCRIPTURE

The issues at stake are complex, because the appeal to Genesis 12:3a has taken shape within the wider framework of a premillennial dispensationalist frame of reference, which envisages a particular construal of the Bible as a whole. I will concentrate mostly on more limited and specific issues of interpretation, though these

---

[10] Both Weber, *On the Road to Armageddon*; and Clark, *Allies for Armageddon*, are illuminating on this history.

[11] In the *New Scofield Reference Bible* (New York: Oxford University Press, 1970), one of the key works of dispensationalism, we read in the comment on Genesis 12:3a, "It has invariably fared ill with the people who have persecuted the Jew – well with those who have protected him. For a nation to commit the sin of anti-Semitism brings inevitable judgment" (19–20).

[12] E.g., Irvine H. Anderson, *Biblical Interpretation and Middle East Policy: The Promised Land, America and Israel, 1917–2002* (Gainesville: University Press of Florida, 2005), 7–31.

will inevitably interrelate with understandings of an overall biblical hermeneutic.

An Appeal to the "Plain Sense" of the Text

Perhaps the first thing to say is that it seems to me that there is a prima facie case to be made for this use of the biblical text, insofar as it does fix on something genuinely present in the text: YHWH's commitment to Abraham and his descendants, God's being in some sense on their side. The sense of Genesis 12:3a is well illustrated by the Balaam narrative (Num 22–24), where closely similar wording recurs in the last of Balaam's solicited oracles that he pronounces over Israel. The climax of this third oracle is "Blessed is everyone who blesses you, and cursed is everyone who curses you" (Num 24:9b).[13] In the narrative context, Balak's hostility toward Israel is epitomized precisely by his desire to get Balaam to curse them. God's resolve to bless Israel is shown not only by his delight in them, which is the emphasis of Balaam's first oracle (Num 23:7–10); God's blessing is also shown by his giving Israel victory against their enemies – victory over enemies generally being the prime emphasis in Balaam's second and third oracles (Num 23:21–24, 24:7–9a), and victory specifically over Balak and Moab being the sting in the unsolicited fourth oracle (Num 24:17).

Moreover, although the prime thrust of Genesis 12:3a is assurance to Abraham, to give Abraham confidence in God's protection as he sets out into the unknown,[14] it would have obvious implications for a non-Israelite and/or potential enemy who might read it or hear about it. The clear message would be that it was in their

---

[13] Here, as also in Genesis 27:29b, the formulation is impersonal ("blessed be those who bless you . . . ") probably for the simple contextual reason that the speaker is not God as in Genesis 12:3a but a human.

[14] See Chapter 8.

interests to be favorable rather than hostile toward Abraham and his descendants.

There is thus a "plain sense" of the text within a pentateuchal frame of reference that can be taken to warrant the contemporary appeal to it. However, this is a good example of the fact that recognition of the plain sense of a biblical text does not settle the question of its enduring theological significance or its responsible use by either Jews or Christians. For, theological significance and responsible use both relate to the wider frame of reference (the canonical context) of the faiths that seek to appropriate the Bible as enduring truth for today.

Merely Human Words?

Before going any further, I should note that one possible response to the typical contemporary appeal to Genesis 12:3a is simply to dismiss it altogether. These are human words, specifically the words of some ancient Israelite(s), which are set in the mouth of Israel's deity; they are eloquent of Israel's hopes and fears, but not of any greater reality. To suppose that the all-too-human partisan aspirations of an ancient Israelite perspective, whether or not ascribed to a deity, has any enduring significance for the policies of a contemporary state is mistaken, stupid, and dangerous.

The trouble with such an approach is that it is a blunt instrument, which would apply equally to everything ascribed to God in Genesis, or indeed the Bible as a whole – with which, of course, some advocates of this kind of approach would be entirely happy. In this context, however, for better or worse, I do not wish to enter into the kind of argumentation that would be necessary to do justice to such a position, for that would take us too far afield into a general discussion of the nature and reception of revelation in relation to the Bible. Rather, I refer to my general observations about the issue at the end of Chapter 2 and hope that it might be inferred from that, together with the subsequent discussion in this chapter, how best I think a response should be articulated.

Some Observations on Unconditional Divine Promises

Much tends to be made by interpreters of the form of the divine address in Genesis 12:1–3. Although Abraham is commanded to go as Yhwh directs him, the divine promises that follow do not specify Abraham's obedience as a condition of their realization. This *unconditional* form may then be contrasted with the *conditional* form in which divine promises of blessing are frequently expressed elsewhere, as in Deuteronomy 28: "If you will obey Yhwh your God . . . then all these blessings shall come upon you" (28:1–2). If one is to take this unconditional form seriously and argue that the fulfilment of God's promise is not dependent on the obedience of Abraham (or, by implication, that of his descendants after him), then one can argue that this promise is implicitly "forever," *lĕʿôlām* or *ʿad ʿôlām* – as is indeed made explicit in Yhwh's subsequent fuller promise to give the land of Canaan to Abraham (Gen 13:15). Thus the form of the divine promise can encourage the reader to see it as an open-ended divine commitment – and if thus open ended, then also enduring, even to the time of the contemporary reader who approaches the text as scripture.

The distinction between unconditional and conditional promises is valid and is used by scholars in many contexts. Nonetheless, there are a number of constraining factors that should be borne in mind if one is pondering the possibly enduring signficance of Genesis 12:3a.

One such factor concerns the nature of religious language. In a nutshell, language that is unconditional in form may be conditional in function, because of the response-seeking nature of the language. This is set out in axiomatic form with relation to Jeremiah's speaking the word of YHWH in Jeremiah 18:7–10:[15]

> At one moment I may declare concerning a nation or a kingdom, that I will pluck up and break down and destroy it, but if that nation, concerning which I have spoken, turns from its evil, I will change my mind about the disaster that I intended to bring on it. And at another moment I may declare concerning a nation or a kingdom that I will build and plant it, but if it does evil in my sight, not listening to my voice, then I will change my mind about the good that I had intended to do to it.

Both aspects of this axiom are well illustrated elsewhere in the Old Testament.[16] That an unconditional pronouncement of judgment may be averted through repentance is most famously exemplified through Jonah's message to the Ninevites and its aftermath (Jonah 3:4–10); while an unconditional promise of good is forfeited in the case of the priesthood promised to the house of Eli, where the corruption of Eli's sons and Eli's own complacency lead to an annulment of the divine promise (1 Sam 2:27–36). Particularly important is 1 Samuel 2:30:

> Therefore the LORD the God of Israel declares: "I promised that your family and the family of your ancestor should go in and out before me forever [ʿad-ʿôlām]"; but now the LORD declares: "Far be it from me; for those who honor me I will honor, and those who despise me shall be treated with contempt."

---

[15] I discuss the dynamics of this text more fully in my *Prophecy and Discernment*, CSCD 14 (Cambridge: Cambridge University Press, 2006), 48–53.

[16] It is a moot point whether Jeremiah is innovating with this account of the conditionality of prophetic language or is rather making explicit what previously had been implicit; in religio-historical terms, the case can be argued either way, though I am inclined to the latter view. For present purposes, however, my concern is with the significance of such an axiom for possible reading strategies of the Old Testament as a canonical collection.

Here we see that even a promise made "forever" – or perhaps, more precisely, "in perpetuity," for the situation is that of a bequest or disposition whose termination is not envisioned – can be rescinded by the one who made it, God.

In relation to this general point about religious language and divine promises, I should also note the prophetic critique of Israel that relativizes all complacent assurance of God's protection and/or gift of the land. A classic example is Jeremiah's temple address (Jer 7:1–15). People were clearly appealing to Yʜwʜ's presence in the temple as some kind of guarantee of their safety in time of invasion (see esp. Jer 7:4, 10). Yet Jeremiah denounces such an appeal as invalidated by their heedlessness of God's moral requirements; it is a self-contradiction to ignore God's will and yet expect God's protection. The people's corruption means that God's presence will entail not their protection from their enemies but their defeat by their enemies and deportation into exile (Jer 7:15).

In other words, we see in Jeremiah that the language of divine promise is intrinsically *response seeking*. An announcement of disaster is not only a prediction but also a warning, a summons to a different course of action that might enable the disaster to be averted. A promise of blessing likewise seeks to engender a response of gratitude and faithfulness, in the kind of way that if such a response is not forthcoming, then what the promise envisaged may not be forthcoming either. To recognize this does not mean that there is no distinction between unconditional and conditional promises in the Old Testament, nor that the dynamics that are highlighted in Jeremiah are necessarily applicable to Genesis 12:3a. But the responsible reader of the Old Testament is at the very least obliged to recognize that to appeal to divine promises implies an appropriate disposition and practice on the part of the one who makes the appeal.

The Bearing of the New Testament on Christian Appropriation of the Old Testament

Another factor concerns the reception of the Old Testament in the New Testament and the difference that Jesus makes to God's dealings with Israel. An obvious example is the fact that God's covenant of circumcision with Abraham is explicitly "everlasting" (*bĕrît ʿôlām*; see Gen 17:7, 13), again in the sense that it is an arrangement "in perpetuity" whose termination is not envisioned. Yet in the New Testament, this arrangement is terminated (as, already within the Old Testament, God's promise to the house of Eli is terminated). According to Paul – whom mainstream Christian theology has followed – circumcision is no longer necessary; rather, it becomes at best optional and may be problematic. Three times Paul formulates an axiom that relativizes circumcision on the grounds that "neither circumcision nor uncircumcision counts for anything" and stipulates a better alternative (in interestingly different terms each time; 1 Cor 7:19; Gal 5:6, 6:15). Although Paul never explains as such why the divine stipulation concerning circumcision no longer applies (although of course he says much about the Mosaic law more generally), part of the underlying logic may be that the covenant of circumcision implies a hereditary and national basis to being a descendant of Abraham and a member of God's covenant people, while the relationship with God brought about by Christ is otherwise constituted, open to Jew and Gentile alike.[17]

Conditionality and Christian Attitudes toward Jews

The recognition that apparently unconditional divine promises may be conditional, and that divine arrangements made in

---

[17] The distinctions here are difficult to formulate, not least because certain Old Testament voices, and subsequent rabbinic tradition, are emphatic that circumcision is a ritual with a symbolic meaning that must be existentially appropriated (see, e.g., Deut 10:16; Jer 4:4).

perpetuity may be terminated, needs careful handling. Poor handling of it has regularly characterized Christian approaches toward Jews, which have often been marked, at best, by ambivalence or, at worst, by downright and often murderous hostility. On this broader issue, I simply offer two observations.

First, it would be unwise for Christians to appeal to Israel's disobedience and faithlessness as that which has nullified God's promises when it is obvious that the church's record of disobedience and faithlessness is no less than Israel's; to disparage Israel on this basis is to saw off the branch on which the church sits. If God's call and mercy are the bottom line for Christians, so are they for Jews also.

Second, it is the thesis of this book that any responsible use of a text such as Genesis 12:3a cannot be made in isolation from a larger theological frame of reference. This is not to say that exegesis does not matter, or that one frame of reference is as good as another – but rather that the use of any particular part of scripture is intrinsically dependent on a rule of faith. Of course, premillennial dispensationalism functions as such a rule of faith; the question is whether it is a good rule.

Who Are the Children of Abraham?

One of the oddest features of the Christian Zionist use of Genesis 12:3a is the assumption that the implied descendants of Abraham who are included in the promise are Jews. This oddity nicely focuses some of the wider hermeneutical issues, especially since the Zionist reading appears to be in line with the likely sense of the text in its pentateuchal context.

Within Genesis one needs to remember that Abraham's first son, by Hagar, is Ishmael. In terms of the Genesis narrative, Hagar and Ishmael leave the main flow of God's purposes for Abraham and his descendants and go into a sidestream whose progress is not followed. Nonetheless, they receive a divine promise of numerous offspring who will be a great nation (Gen 16:10, 21:13). In the light of the historic Arab and Muslim appeal to Ishmael as ancestor – an appeal that is in various ways both historically and theologically problematic, but that is widely granted in one way or other – there is a certain irony in the divine promise to Abraham being used by Christian Zionists against those whose claim to be Abraham's descendants could be seen as not without warrant in the Genesis text.

More important, however, from the perspective of Christian theology is the way the New Testament treats the question of who should be regarded as a descendant of Abraham. The general thrust is to relativize genealogical descent, on the grounds that only those who show the kind of responsiveness to God that Abraham displayed should be considered children of Abraham; thus, with variations on the theme, say, John the Baptist (Matt 3:8–9; Luke 3:8), Jesus in John's portrayal (John 8:39–40), and Paul (Rom 4; Gal 3). Paul's summary statement, "If you belong to Christ, then you are Abraham's offspring" (Gal 3:29), has been taken down the ages to represent the tenor of the New Testament in ways that have been deeply influential on Christian theology (and sometimes problematic for Jews).

If, then, the divine promise to Abraham is taken to include Abraham's descendants, who qualifies as Abraham's descendants – Jews, Muslims, or Christians? And on what basis does one decide? For present purposes I would simply make two points, which are irrespective of one's precise position on the difficult question of the relationship between Israel and the Christian church. First, there is the inappropriateness, in terms of Christian theology, of Christians appealing to Genesis 12:3a in ways that do not take seriously the New Testament's input on the question of who should be considered a descendant of Abraham. That would be rather like a Christian making an appeal to an Old Testament conception of Davidic kingship and its implications for today without taking into account Jesus' fundamental reconstrual of the meaning of kingship in the New Testament.[18]

Second, there is an oddity about the implied stance of Christian Zionists insofar as they do not locate themselves in the place of Abraham, to whom the divine promise constitutes assurance, but rather in the place of the outsider, to whom the divine words constitute a warning. If it is part of Christian identity in the New Testament that response to God in the mode of Abraham causes one to belong to Abraham's children, then to hear the divine promise in the way that Hagee appears to, as one who may hope to receive God's blessing through appropriate response to Abraham's children, who are not identified with one's own self but as some other – that is, the Jewish people – is strange indeed. It does not strike one either as particularly Christian or as displaying a grasp of the New Testament.

Politics and Self-Interest

Finally, the Christian Zionist appeal to Genesis 12:3a also raises various issues about the relationship of religion and politics. One aspect that deserves mention is the role of self-interest. A nation's politics and foreign policy are legitimately formulated in terms of national self-interest. One of the differences that one hopes might be made by religious input on such is a deepening of moral awareness, with

---

[18] In the Synoptic Gospels, this is most obvious at Caesarea Philippi (Matt 16:13–28 and parallels) and in the crucifixion narratives, while in John, it is most striking in the trial narrative (John 18:33–38, 19:13–16).

a more searching account of what constitutes self-interest and how it is best realized. Yet the Christian Zionist appeal to Genesis 12:3a seems rather to underline *an unreflective self-seeking.* At any rate Hagee's comment on the divine words – "That gets my attention. I want to be blessed, not cursed, by God" – is wide open to a rather unsympathetic reading. How, a reader of the New Testament might legitimately ask, does this relate to denying oneself and taking up the cross, to losing one's life to find it (Matt 16:24–26 and parallels) or to renouncing the works of the flesh for the way of the spirit (Rom 8:5–8; Gal 5:16–26)?

To be sure, there are Christian Zionists who are aware of the problem. Mikael Knighton, for example, in the course of expounding "The Biblical Mandate of Christian Zionism," cites Genesis 12:3a as "the mandate" and makes the familiar claims, but then sounds a different note:

> The Scriptures are clear: We are blessed when we are a blessing to His people, and we are cursed when we curse them. History has proven this, time and time again. We are not to support and bless Israel in the hopes of some sort of "return on our investment." God knows our hearts. When we bless His people with humble, compassionate and sincere hearts, His blessings upon us will come in accordance with His perfect timetable.[19]

Nonetheless, such awareness seems not to be the norm. Moreover, even in Knighton's presentation, all the other problems with appeal to Genesis 12:3 noted previously still pertain. The wider moral and spiritual frame of reference of the Christian canon as a whole appears distinctly underused when Genesis 12:3a is the focus of Christian Zionist attention.

---

[19] www.christiansstandingwithisrael.com/mandate.html (accessed September 19, 2007).

CONCLUSION

I have discussed neither the actual politics surrounding the appeal to Genesis 12:3a nor a premillennial dispensationalist framework for interpreting scripture. So, there is more that could be said. Nevertheless, it will be clear from what has been said about exegesis and a Christian use of scripture that there are major questions that need to be put to the characteristic Christian Zionist appeal to Genesis 12:3a. Although Christian theology must indeed seek to hear the voices of the Old Testament in their own right, any authentically Christian appropriation of those voices must think and act in the light of Christ, supremely his death and resurrection. What that might mean for formulating good policies, or good responses to policies, in the Middle East today remains complex. Even so, the better one's grasp of "the whole counsel of God" as given in scripture, the more likely one is to make some genuine progress.

CHAPTER 10

Genesis 22: Abraham – Model or Monster?

Some of the central problems of theological interpretation posed by changing attitudes toward the Bible in general, and Genesis in particular, are focused with unusual clarity on the famous story of Abraham's near sacrifice of Isaac, often known by its Hebrew name, the Akedah (Gen 22:1–19).[1]

Traditionally, Jews and Christians have read this story as displaying costly right response to God on the part of both Abraham and Isaac. In the New Testament, for example, Abraham is seen to demonstrate the kind of engagement with God that is called "faith" in a Christian context. James argues that Abraham shows that genuine faith entails a total lived-out responsiveness to God (James 2:14–26), while the writer to the Hebrews sees Abraham as a model of faith in the sense of trusting God for a future as yet unseen (Heb 11:1, 17–19). For both these writers, the significance of Abraham for believers is well summarized by the words of Jesus in John's portrayal: "If you are Abraham's children, then do what Abraham did" (John 8:39).

---

[1] I have discussed Genesis 22 more fully in my *The Bible, Theology, and Faith: A Study of Abraham and Jesus*, CSCD 5 (Cambridge: Cambridge University Press, 2000), 71–183; see also my essay "Living Dangerously: Genesis 22 and the Quest for Good Biblical Interpretation," in *The Art of Reading Scripture*, ed. Ellen F. Davis and Richard B. Hays (Grand Rapids, MI: Eerdmans, 2003), 181–97.

There is also a long history of reading Paul as alluding to Genesis 22 when he speaks of God "not sparing his own son" (Rom 8:32), in a way that sets up a potent imaginative link (a typology or figuration) between Isaac and Jesus, a link that has often been developed in the history of interpretation.[2]

A good general account of the existential use of the story in late antiquity is offered by Clemens Thoma:

> The narrative found in Gen 22 had not only a significant religious and spiritual development in late Old Testament times and afterwards, but above all, it affected the history of piety. Many people, finding themselves in difficult situations, were able to sustain themselves on the strength of this account about Abraham who, confidently obeying the God who was "testing" him (Gen 22,1), was prepared to slaughter his only and beloved son, and about Isaac who was willing to be offered as a sacrifice. This expression of obedience by Abraham and submission by Isaac constitute an example worthy of imitation. The story motivated people to accept obediently and submissively in their lives what seemed incomprehensible, unendurable and contradictory and to reflect upon it.[3]

Positive construals of the story, in literature and art as well as biblical commentary,[4] still, of course, continue to appear. One of the most cited in recent years has been that of Gerhard von Rad, who had a special interest in the story. Von Rad both draws on the wider Genesis context, in which Isaac is the bearer of God's promise

[2] For an illuminating overview of ancient Jewish and Christian readings of Genesis 22, see James L. Kugel, *The Bible as It Was* (Cambridge, MA: Belknap, 1997), 165–78.

[3] Clemens Thoma, "Observations on the Concept and the Early Forms of Akedah-Spirituality," in *Standing Before God: Studies on Prayer in Scriptures and in Tradition with Essays in Honor of John M. Oesterreicher*, ed. Asher Finkel and Lawrence Frizzell (New York: Ktav, 1981), 213–222 (213).

[4] For some artistic depictions, see http://www.textweek.com/art/abraham_and_isaac.htm (accessed April 7, 2008).

to Abraham that he will become a great nation, and develops a typological linkage between Abraham and Jesus on the cross where Jesus cries out, "My God, my God, why have you forsaken me?" (Matt 27:46; Mark 15:34). So, von Rad says of God's requirement that Abraham sacrifice Isaac,

> Isaac is the child of promise. In him every saving thing that God has promised to do is invested and guaranteed. The point here is ... the disappearance from Abraham's life of the whole promise. Therefore, unfortunately, one can only answer all plaintive scruples about this narrative by saying that it concerns something much more frightful than child sacrifice. It has to do with a road out into Godforsakenness, a road on which Abraham does not know that God is only testing him.[5]

By contrast with all this, the modern period has seen a growing tendency to read the story negatively. The first weighty voice in this regard was that of Immanuel Kant who, in the course of arguing for the supremacy of the moral law, articulated a characteristic modern concern in seeing Abraham as deluded about God:

> In some cases man can be sure that the voice he hears is *not* God's; for if the voice commands him to do something contrary to the moral law, then no matter how majestic the apparition may be, and no matter how it may seem to surpass the whole of nature, he must consider it an illusion.[6]

To this general point, Kant adds an illustrative footnote:

> We can use, as an example, the myth of the sacrifice that Abraham was going to make by butchering and burning his only son at God's command (the poor child, without knowing it, even brought the

---

[5] Gerhard von Rad, *Genesis: A Commentary*, trans. John H. Marks, rev. ed., OTL (London: SCM, 1972 [German 9th ed., 1972]), 244.

[6] Immanuel Kant, *The Conflict of the Faculties*, trans. Mary J. Gregor (New York: Abaris, 1979 [German orig., 1798]), 115.

wood for the fire). Abraham should have replied to this supposedly divine voice: "That I ought not to kill my good son is quite certain. But that you, this apparition, are God – of that I am not certain, and never can be, not even if this voice rings down to me from (visible) heaven."[7]

What began as a trickle in the time of Kant has now become a torrent. Typical of many Christian commentators is Clare Amos who, in reviewing a book by Steven Saltzman, writes,

> I was particularly struck with his comments on the Aqedah – Genesis 22: "Avraham failed the test. He chose God over his son. He chose being God's servant over being his son's father. He loved God more than he loved his own son, and he made the wrong choice" (p. 56).
> When I think of the convolutions so many writers, both Christian and Jewish, get up to in their attempts to "justify" Abraham at this point, I want to give thanks for Saltzman's sanity and say, "three cheers."[8]

Or Richard Holloway, a bishop, is strongly sympathetic to Jenny Diski's bleak retelling of the Genesis narrative in his review of Diski's book:

> And the person who really fuels her anger is Abraham, the sacred monster who lurks in the fog that obscures the origins of Judaism, Christianity and Islam, who all claim him as their founding patriarch. Nowadays, someone like Abraham would end up in Broadmoor.[9] In those days he got to found a religion.

For Diski, a prime issue is Abraham's instrumentalizing of Isaac, thereby destroying his humanity; the problem with the biblical text is that making a religious point matters more than damage to a life.

---

[7] Ibid.

[8] Clare Amos, "Review of S. Saltzman, *A Small Glimmer of Light: Reflections on the Book of Genesis* (Hoboken: Ktav, 1996)," *ExpT* 108 (1997): 243.

[9] Broadmoor is a British prison for criminals who suffer from severe psychological disturbances.

Holloway sees this instrumental attitude toward people, a readiness to abuse and even murder them to further one's own "sacred" cause, as a fundamentally harmful legacy of biblical religion – as though the destruction of the World Trade Center in 2001 was, in effect, a consistent outworking of the logic of Genesis 22:

> But what happened to Isaac? That's what Diski wants to find out. She worms her way into his terror and discovers that he did indeed die inside that day, because he discovered that any son might be sacrificed to the demands of an inaudible voice. The voice could be more powerful even than the reason for hearing it in the first place – the terrible fact and fear of extinction. And the reader will understand, though Diski does not spell it out, that the Voice is still at work, calling its servants to kill their children in obedience to an allegiance that is more powerful than any ties of the heart or mind. We see it there 3,000 years ago in the pages of the Bible; and we see it here in the pages of our newspapers today. The Voice still speaks, and Abraham still obeys its command.[10]

The distance evident here from the Bible's own evaluation of Genesis 22 could hardly be greater. And since these critiques of the paradigmatic biblical story are all formulated on ethical grounds out of a concern to preserve and enhance human well-being, the moral and theological issues at stake could hardly be higher. Although the current chapter's title – "Abraham – Model or Monster?" (which might equally be "faith or fanaticism?" or "faithful father or child abuser?") – risks a polarizing oversimplification of the complexity of the issues,[11] it nevertheless starkly captures

---

[10] Richard Holloway, "Review of Jenny Diski, *After These Things* (Little: Brown, 2004)," *The Guardian*, April 24, 2004, 26. Holloway weaves Diski's own wording into his account.

[11] My positive/negative typology is heuristic for this study. For an interesting, different approach that focuses on political and cultural uses of the story, see Yvonne Sherwood, "Abraham in London, Marburg-Istanbul and Israel:

something of the conceptual and imaginative challenge that faces the thoughtful contemporary reader.[12]

INTERPRETIVE CLUES WITHIN THE BIBLICAL TEXT

How best might one proceed? In the first place, it is important to see the intrinsic difficulty posed by the story on its own terms within its Old Testament context. To some extent this is a matter of religious irregularities such as Abraham, who is not a priest, acting as a priest – although this should not be isolated from the distinctive religious ethos of the patriarchal narratives overall.[13] More important is the fact that the Old Testament prophets strongly oppose the practice of child sacrifice. Jeremiah explicitly rejects any possible in-principle acceptability of such a practice to YHWH:

> For the people of Judah have done evil in my sight, says the LORD. . . . And they go on building the high place of Topheth, which is in the valley of the son of Hinnom, to burn their sons and daughters in the fire – which I did not command, nor did it come into my mind. (Jer 7:30–31)

To be sure, many interpreters have suggested that Genesis 22 is precisely an account of Israel's rejection of child sacrifice in favor of animal sacrifice. Yet such a reading is distinctly odd, for the text questions neither God's command nor Abraham's obedience;

Between Theocracy and Democracy, Ancient Texts and Modern State," *BibInt* 16 (2008): 105–53.

[12] On the importance of disciplined historical awareness in relation to modern readings, see Jon D. Levenson, "Abusing Abraham: Traditions, Religious Histories, and Modern Misinterpretations," *Judaism* 47 (1998): 259–77.

[13] See Chapter 7.

hence, the concerns of the Genesis text may stand in real tension with the prophetic perspective.[14]

Given such intrinsic difficulty, one may reasonably suppose that the story is included in Genesis because the compilers of the book felt constrained to include it, because it was a given within Israel's traditions of its ancestors. Whether or not that is correct, on any reckoning the most fruitful approach is surely to look for indicators within the text itself as to how sense was made of this remarkable story.

One prime clue lies in the narrative context of the story. Whether or not the story (in some form) was once freestanding, and despite a tendency on the part of those who appeal to the story (both positively and negatively) to do so as though it were (in effect) freestanding, the story stands as the climax to Abraham's long journey with God. Abraham's story begins with God's promise to make him a great nation (12:1–3), yet the promise seems impossible to fulfill. Sarah is initially barren (11:30), eventually postmenopausal (18:11), and an attempt to circumvent Sarah with Hagar and her son by Abraham is sidelined by God (Gen 16–17). Against all expectation Sarah at last gives birth to Isaac (21:1–7), and it appears that the years of perplexed waiting are over and that God's promise to Abraham can now be realized through Isaac. This narrative context of Isaac as the child of promise adds to and intensifies Isaac's intrinsic value to Abraham as his beloved son (22:2), and gives Isaac enormous symbolic significance as the focus of Abraham's hope in God and the future. Yet it is precisely at this moment that God

---

[14] See Jon D. Levenson, *The Death and Resurrection of the Beloved Son: The Transformation of Child Sacrifice in Judaism and Christianity* (New Haven, CT: Yale University Press, 1993), 3–17.

tells Abraham to sacrifice Isaac. Jewish commentators have long observed the verbal resonance of God's command to Abraham to "go" – *lek-lĕkā* – which introduces both the story of Abraham as a whole and the direction to sacrifice Isaac (Gen 12:1, 22:2), and have drawn them together interpretively: At the beginning, Abraham is commanded to relinquish his past, and at the end, Abraham is commanded to relinquish his future.[15]

Another obvious clue to understanding the story is the verb used at the outset by the narrator, which tells the reader what is going on: "God tested [*nissâ*] Abraham." Hebrew has several verbs for "testing," and they are commonly used in analogy with the refining of metals, where the assumption is that as metal becomes purer and more serviceable by virtue of being refined, so too do human lives (see, e.g., Prov 17:3). Although the particular verb *nissâ* is not in fact used in metalworking analogies, it is well illustrated by its use in Deuteronomy 8, where, in conjunction with "humbling," it interprets YHWH's dealings with Israel in their forty years in the wilderness (Deut 8:2) and shows that the process, clearly unwelcome at the time, had Israel's long-term good in view (and so is analogous to the purification of metals): "He . . . fed you in the wilderness with manna that your ancestors did not know, to humble you and to test you, and in the end to do you good" (Deut 8:16). The narrator's use of this verb at the outset of Genesis 22, therefore, implies that what follows will be searing, yet positive in purpose, for Abraham.

A further clue lies in the verb that specifies the purpose of the test: "[N]ow I know that you fear God" (Gen 22:12). "Fear" is the

---

[15] See, e.g., Nahum M. Sarna, *Genesis: The Traditional Hebrew Text with New JPS Translation*, JPS Torah Commentary (Philadelphia: Jewish Publication Society, 1989), 150.

Old Testament's prime term for right human response to God. When used in relation to God, it does not indicate fright, or even (usually) awe, but rather a right attitude and obedience.[16] That Abraham should be demonstrated to be a person who fears God, therefore, is equivalent in Christian parlance to saying that he is a "true believer."[17]

It is striking to observe that these two verbs that structure the meaning of Genesis 22 occur in conjunction also in Exodus 20:20, where Moses interprets God's giving of the Ten Commandments: God has come "to test you and to put the fear of him upon you so that you do not sin." The general thrust here is that God gives Israel the Ten Commandments in order to searchingly draw them into a purer and more faithful way of living. The fact that the words that interpret the significance of the commandments for Israel also interpret God's command to Abraham to sacrifice Isaac suggests an imaginative linkage between the two contexts: Abraham's response to God models what Israel's response should be. It is not that Abraham becomes an observer of torah, but that the language of torah has been used to make sense of Abraham and to intimate that there is an analogy between Abraham's response to God and that which is expected from Israel.

A different clue to the significance of Genesis 22 lies in the geographical location it envisions. The location is clearly important, for the primary narrative sequence leads up to Abraham naming the place of sacrifice *yhwh yir'eh* (22:14a), traditionally transliterated *Jehovah Jireh* and translated "The LORD will provide." This,

---

[16] Although "fear of God" signifies terror or intimidation in contemporary English, there are still perhaps positive resonances in the epithet "God-fearing."

[17] A nice example is Luke 1:50 where Mary, using Old Testament idiom, speaks of God's mercy on "those who fear him" in a context where Christians speak and think of those who "have faith."

however, can initially appear puzzling, since nowhere else in the Old Testament is there any reference to a place with this name. However, there are two further clues to the location's identity.

First, the narrator appends to the place name a saying current in his time: "[A]s it is said to this day, 'On the mount of the LORD it shall be provided'" (22:14b). The natural implication is that the present place of YHWH's provision is the place named as such by Abraham. Since "mount of YHWH" is used predominantly of Mt. Zion (Isa 2:3; Zech 8:3), the narrator appears to envision Jerusalem as the location of Abraham's sacrifice.

Second, at the outset of the narrative, God specifies that Abraham should go to the land of Moriah (Gen 22:2). This is probably a symbolic name, like the land of Nod (literally, "wandering") where Cain is destined to be a restless wanderer (Gen 4:14, 16). Although the name Moriah can be understood in a variety of ways, in context it is readily understood in relation to the verbal root that the story elsewhere uses to indicate God's "providing" (rā'â; literally, "seeing"). Thus "land of Moriah" probably symbolizes "land of provision/providing"; the particular place of sacrifice (22:14) focuses the symbolic nature of the land as a whole (22:2). Moreover, the one other usage of "Moriah" in the Old Testament is to name the site of the Jerusalem temple (2 Chr 3:1). Thus, the place name Moriah connects to the name Abraham comes up with, and each alike apparently indicates Jerusalem.

The identity of the place of Abraham's sacrifice as the place of the Jerusalem temple is deeply established in Jewish tradition, though, for various reasons,[18] it has not generally been recognized

---

[18] In documentary analysis of the Pentateuch, Genesis 22 has usually been ascribed to the Elohist, putatively writing in and for the northern kingdom. It is a pleasing irony that a prime Old Testament validation of Jerusalem and its temple should have been ascribed to the northern kingdom of Israel that

by modern Christian interpreters.[19] If Genesis 22 is an etiology for the Jerusalem temple, its interpretation should be related to temple worship. Abraham's offering of the ram pictures Israel's offering of sacrifice, each alike a response of obedience to God. The fact that the ram substitutes for Isaac says something about the meaning of animal sacrifice – that it should represent that which is of real value to the worshiper, so much so (given Isaac's significance for Abraham) that in a sense it symbolizes the worshiper's own self-sacrifice and self-dispossession before God.

We can see, therefore, that the difficult story of Abraham and Isaac has been interpreted with the language and conceptions of (i) trust in God against all odds, (ii) the Ten Commandments, and (iii) the Jerusalem temple. In these ways, it has been drawn into the very heart of the Old Testament's theological frame of reference.

MODEL OR MONSTER? SOME FACTORS FOR MAKING PROGRESS

Although more could be said about the meaning of Genesis 22 within the Old Testament, its intrinsic positive significance should be clear. Thus the New Testament writers are fully in line with the Old Testament in their strongly positive readings, and their

---

was partially defined by its rejection of the southern kingdom of Judah and its temple.

[19] Even Brevard S. Childs, who takes Genesis 22 as a case study for theological interpretation in a canonical context, misses it. Although he looks for canonical clues to interpretation, he says nothing about Moriah, and in his section on history of exegesis, he omits any mention of the traditional Jewish understanding of the location. He offers his own positive account about the relationship between Abraham and Israel's sacrificial worship in a curiously abstracted kind of way that says nothing about any actual place of worship (*Biblical Theology of the Old and New Testaments: Theological Reflection on the Christian Bible* [Minneapolis, MN: Fortress, 1993], 325–36, esp. 327, 331, 334).

conception of faith stands in real continuity with the Old Testament conception of fear of God, though the New Testament writers do not develop the story's resonances with torah and temple.

The difficult question, however, is how this exegetical analysis should relate to the strong moral objections raised to the story. For it would not be unreasonable to say that the story may have made good and positive sense in its own context, yet it cannot do so in a contemporary context. How, then, might one make progress?

First, the interpretation offered should at the very least make some difference as to how an objection to the text is articulated, if the objection is to be responsible and more than a glorified "I don't like it." Clare Amos's resistance to "the convolutions so many writers, both Christian and Jewish, get up to in their attempts to 'justify' Abraham at this point" makes it sound like these writers are rather desperately attempting to defend the indefensible. One would not know from her way of putting it that a positive reading could just as easily be trying to understand sympathetically what is actually going on in the biblical text, nor does her remark give any indication that what stands in the text has been found by many to be life-enhancing under God.

A related issue concerns what the reader is to think about when reading the text. Although a contemporary reader may quickly come to thoughts about religious delusion and child abuse – for these are live contemporary issues, and claims to hear a divine voice that authorizes the killing of a child sound instant alarm bells in the contemporary imagination[20] – it should be clear that the

---

[20] Of course, it is not only the contemporary imagination that is so inclined, even if the inclination today is especially acute. Martin Luther, for example, reads the story with intense imaginative engagement and says, in commenting on Genesis 22:10, "I could not have been an onlooker, much less the performer and slayer. It is an astonishing situation that the dearly beloved father moves

reader who attempts to understand and enter into the narrative world of the text within its Old Testament context must be disposed to think about *the story's own concerns*, such as costly faithfulness to God or the nature of true worship. The more one attempts to *think with* the text, the less one is likely to stay with or develop thoughts about delusion or child abuse.

At this point, however, there is an obvious objection. A narrative such as Genesis 22 is open to be read in more than one way. Within the text itself, there are elements left untouched by the interpretive clues previously listed, attention to which might introduce different emphases. For example, the fact that the immediately following episode begins with the death of Sarah (23:1–2) has long led, especially in Jewish interpretation, to an imaginative linkage between Abraham's action and Sarah's demise, usually variations on the theme of her dying of shock when she found out what had happened; and this tacit role of Sarah has received renewed attention from feminist interpreters.[21] Such a move, which claims warrant from Genesis's own narrative sequence, suggests a more ambiguous reading of Abraham's action or at least its aftermath. Alternatively, there are silences within the text that are open to more than one reading, such as Isaac's demeanor as he goes to the sacrifice.

---

his knife close to the throat of the dearly beloved son, and I surely admit that I cannot attain to these thoughts and sentiments either by means of words or by reflecting on them" (*Luther's Work's*, vol. 4, *Lectures on Genesis, Chapters 21–25*, ed. Jaroslav Pelikan and Walter Hansen [Saint Louis, MO: Concordia Publishing House, 1964], 114).

[21] The most imaginative and existentially searching feminist reading of Genesis 22 of which I am aware is Phyllis Trible, "Genesis 22: The Sacrifice of Sarah," in *"Not in Heaven": Coherence and Complexity in Biblical Narrative*, ed. J. P. Rosenblatt and J. C. Sitterson (Bloomington: Indiana University Press, 1991), 170–91.

Undoubtedly, the story is open to a wide variety of readings; and anyone familiar with the history of interpretation will know that readers down the ages have rarely been slow to make many bold moves with, and imaginative reconfigurations of, the biblical story. The interpretive issues at this point are therefore at least twofold. First, how far is the reader willing to be led by the text's own priorities, insofar as these can be discerned? Second, insofar as a reader imaginatively develops the story beyond its biblical contours, what informs and constrains one's imaginative sense of the whole that influences, indeed often decides, how one construes its silences and ambiguities?

A small but illuminating example of a failure to be clear about these interpretive issues appears in the work of David Brown on the relationship between scripture and tradition.[22] After a cursory discussion of Genesis 22 in its original biblical context, where he shares the contemporary tendency to read it negatively on moral grounds – largely because Abraham's action, which displays his fear of God, "unqualifiedly flies in the face of our deepest moral sensibilities"[23] – Brown focuses on the rich history of Jewish and Christian interpretation, which, in line with his overall thesis, he considers to represent an enriching improvement on the biblical text. When underlining the deficiencies of the biblical narrative, he says, "It is [Caravaggio's] version more than any other which shows us what is so profoundly wrong with the biblical version: Abraham is shown pinning down his victim, a squirming and screaming son."[24] Where, however, does the biblical text specify "a squirming

---

[22] David Brown, *Tradition and Imagination: Revelation and Change* (Oxford, UK: Oxford University Press, 1999), 237–60.

[23] Ibid., 239.

[24] Ibid., 258.

and screaming son"? That is certainly *one possible way* of reading the silence about Isaac's demeanor; indeed, it is one that is likely to be attractive if one's overall construal of the story is negative. However, the traditional Jewish imagination readily thought of a willing, self-giving Isaac, which is, of course, more congruent with a positive construal. What is important here is how each picture is brought to the text in the light of a judgment about the whole story. Brown demonstrates how easily contemporary readers can overwhelm the biblical text with their own preconceptions, while not even recognizing that they are doing so. But real progress with the basic issues is hardly possible without serious attention both to the disciplines of exegesis and to the dialectic between classic and contemporary assumptions.

DE-INSTRUMENTALIZING ISAAC

Beyond these general issues, we must still address what has become a key sticking point within the biblical narrative: the instrumentalizing, or dehumanizing, of Isaac.

Initially, it must be acknowledged that the text does indeed make "patriarchal" assumptions in its portrayal of Abraham as paterfamilias, with the power of life and death over his child, in a way characteristic of its ancient place and time[25] (and of many subsequently). The significance of a child in this context was socially understood as contributing to the significance of the paterfamilias. Hence, for example, the loss of all Job has, culminating in the death of his children (see Job 1:13–19), is considered wholly in terms of its impact on Job; the narrator clearly thinks, and seems to want

---

[25] Cf. Genesis 38:24, 42:37.

the implied reader also to think, in terms of the devastation for innocent Job and not of the undeserved death of his children.

This understanding of children is unacceptable today. There is much within both Old and New Testaments, as well as classic Jewish and Christian traditions, quite apart from modern secular thought, to encourage a valuing of children as important in their own right.[26] To instrumentalize a child is indeed to abuse a child.[27]

What does, and does not, follow from this? First, it is clear that our moral notions are bound up with the larger social and cultural frames of reference within which we live. Principles about life that seem self-evident to us did not necessarily appear self-evident to our forebears, and vice versa. This is a point less about the relativity of our moral judgments than about their cultural complexity. Religious believers within a secular society have perhaps a peculiarly demanding task in forming moral awareness and practices that are accountable to the differing frames of reference that they inhabit simultaneously.

Second, however, many people are fully capable of engaging intelligently with, and learning from, frames of reference other than their own. Staunch believers in a republican form of government are not precluded from being moved and informed by Shakespeare's *Macbeth* or *King Lear*, even though the assumption of monarchy is intrinsic to the structure and storyline of the plays. Why, then, should the instrumental role of Isaac within Genesis 22 make constructive appropriation of the story impossible today?

---

[26] See the essays collected in Marcia Bunge, Terence E. Fretheim, and Beverly Roberts Gaventa, eds., *The Child in the Bible* (Grand Rapids, MI: Eerdmans, 2008).

[27] In a contemporary context, anxieties about instrumentalization are perhaps a counterpart to its frequent appearances in, for example, many a film and video game, or in pressures for pornography to have mainstream acceptability.

As consistently argued throughout this book, theological interpretation and/or appropriation of Genesis cannot be a matter of
all or nothing, as though one must adopt all of a text's perspectives or none of them. This is simply because the Genesis texts are
received within a wider canonical frame of reference, both biblical
and postbiblical (rule of faith, commentaries, liturgy, disciplines of
discipleship), which brings many considerations and constraints to
bear on the way a text is read and considered enduringly significant
for today.

In this regard, there is a certain oddity in the contemporary anxiety that religious appeal to Genesis 22 is likely to encourage child
abuse (or worse). The history of interpretation of the story among
Jews and Christians is both extensive and well documented.[28] It is
striking that within this literature, one looks in vain for any account
of believers considering the biblical text as a warrant of any kind for
the abuse, much less the killing, of their children. Rather, it has been
a resource for coping with some of life's worst extremities. That is
to say, Jews and Christians down the ages have instinctively (as a
result of their formation) read the text *analogically* and *metaphorically*. Identifying with Abraham comes to represent relinquishing
under God that which is most valued, even for one's own faith, a
metaphorical reading that is arguably in real continuity with the
portrayal of Isaac in the wider narrative as the symbolic focus of
Abraham's hope in God. Identifying with Isaac comes to mean, as

---

[28] For standard introductions to Jewish and Christian interpretations of Genesis
22, see, respectively, Shalom Spiegel, *The Last Trial: On the Legends and Lore
of the Command to Abraham to Offer Isaac as a Sacrifice: The Akedah*, trans.
Judah Goldin (New York: Behrman, 1979); and David Lerch, *Isaaks Opfer-
ung christlich gedeutet: Eine auslegungsgeschichtliche Untersuchung*, BZHT 12
(Tübingen, Ger.: J. C. B. Mohr, 1950). In recent years, Yvonne Sherwood has
been doing suggestive work on the use of Genesis 22 (see note 11 for an entrée).

Thoma puts it, being "motivated to accept obediently and submissively in their lives what seemed incomprehensible, unendurable and contradictory and to reflect upon it."[29]

THE NIGHTMARE SCENARIO

However, the nightmare scenario (envisioned by Søren Kierkegaard, among others)[30] has taken place recently and brings us back to Kant's issue of religious delusion. Carol Delaney tells of the trial of "Cristos Valenti," who on January 6, 1990, in California, killed his beloved youngest daughter in supposed obedience to God – "How can you say no to God? Everything is his. We all belong to him. It was an order directly to me from God."[31] A verdict of insanity was returned by the court.

In the face of such tragedy, there is no place for glib words or easy answers. I cannot here comment on Valenti's action or the trial, but I offer three brief reflections on some of the larger theological issues at stake. First, this is neither the first nor the last tragedy or atrocity carried out with appeal to God and the Bible. The higher the stakes, the more the ancient principle applies, that abuse does not remove right use. If there is a right use of Genesis 22, as already argued, then it is of primary importance to promote the conditions for that right use and not let exceptional abuses trump it.

[29] Thoma, "Observations on the Concept and the Early Forms of Akedah Spirituality," 213.

[30] Kierkegaard imagines someone returning home after a sermon on Genesis 22 and murdering his son, for "he wants to do just like Abraham; for the son is certainly the best thing he has" (*Fear and Trembling*, trans. Alastair Hannay [Harmondsworth, UK: Penguin, 1985], 58–59).

[31] Carol Delaney, *Abraham on Trial: The Social Legacy of Biblical Myth* (Princeton, NJ: Princeton University Press: 1998), 35–68 (39).

Second, Kant's psychologizing question about Abraham (or Delaney's about Valenti), as to how he could know whether a voice is from God, is unfruitful in the context of Genesis 22. Although it is important to read the text with full imaginative seriousness, one must also be able to recognize the difference between beckoning vistas and dead ends in relation to the nature of the text. As I noted in Chapter 6 with the Flood narrative, certain imaginative questions can simply lead one away from the concerns of the text, even though they relate to integral facets of the story (e.g., food for the animals); so too here. Contemporary interest in Abraham's psychology in 22:2 is a counterpart to an older embarrassed concern with seeming implications for God's psychology of "now I know" in 22:12, which has also probably never led anywhere particularly fruitful in terms of understanding the story better. Establishing criteria for the discernment of seemingly divine voices is a live issue elsewhere in scripture and classic faith traditions,[32] and progress with that issue cannot be made if one persists in questioning texts that are opaque to such concerns. Within Genesis 22 one may perhaps more profitably think of the divine voice in terms of Abraham's being led to the divinely chosen place of worship (22:2, 4; cf. Deut 12:5).

Third, Valenti's apparent use of scripture (as in his words to his wife, "But I saw it in the Bible, to make a sacrifice... "[33]) in its own way represents what seems to me a key factor within the typical modern anxiety about Genesis 22. It is, in effect, a kind of secularized reduction of the classic Protestant principle of *sola scriptura*. The principle itself, despite its polemical formulation,

---

[32] See my *Prophecy and Discernment*, CSCD 14 (Cambridge: Cambridge University Press, 2006); and Karl Rahner, "Visions and Prophecies," in Rahner, *Studies in Modern Theology* (London: Burns & Oates, 1965), 87–188.

[33] Delaney, *Abraham on Trial*, 41.

presupposed other related principles (*sola gratia, sola fide, solus Christus*) and a continuing context of faithful ecclesial (Protestant) engagement with scripture. But contemporary anxiety tends to envision a reader confronted by the bare biblical text *with its classic canonical frame of reference* – again understood to extend *beyond* the canon proper – *stripped away*. If, however, a reader has only a passing interest in the meaning of the biblical text in its ancient narrative context, is impatient with difficult historical issues of cultural difference, and sits light to a classic rule of faith that in important ways guides and constrains the understanding and use of Genesis 22, then perhaps it should not be surprising if the story seems at best weird and at worst dehumanizing. The problem, in short, may primarily reside in the contemporary way of approaching the biblical text.[34]

A CHRISTIAN EPILOGUE

When all is said and done, Genesis 22 remains a demanding and unsettling text, not least because it will not neatly fit into our preferred tidy categorizations. It is surely in this respect that, for the Christian reader, an imaginative and existential linkage between Genesis 22 and the passion of Jesus – as well as various situations today – becomes appropriate. The linkage is not a matter of details – carrying the wood/cross, the location in Jerusalem – but rather in the fact that when Jesus is at Gethsemane and Golgotha and the Easter Garden, then, as with Abraham at Moriah, all "explanations" (which, of course, abound and have a proper, if limited, role) sooner or later become inadequate to do justice to the subject matter of the

---

[34] Helpful on this whole issue is Charles M. Wood, *The Formation of Christian Understanding* (repr., Eugene, OR: Wipf & Stock, 2000), esp. 40–47.

text. The gospel narratives of Jesus' death and resurrection are no less dangerous texts than Genesis 22, liable to misunderstanding and misuse in any number of ways, which can include damage to, and destruction of, life. Nonetheless, Christians believe that, rightly understood and appropriated, these texts point to an entry into anguished darkness that can also be a way into light and life.

CHAPTER 11

Abraham and the "Abrahamic Faiths"

Interfaith dialogue is an important topic at the present time. On the one hand, secularized indifference, or hostility, toward religion can encourage members of the various religious traditions to look beyond historic controversies to see if they can find greater common ground on which to act together and resist apathy or onslaught. On the other hand, the increasing social and political profile of Islam in many Western countries, quite apart from the acute problems posed by militant Islamism, naturally leads to a desire on the part of Jews and Christians in those countries to ask afresh about the right understanding and appropriate mutual relations of their respective faiths. But whatever the reasons – and they are many and varied – interfaith dialogue, especially among Jews, Christians, and Muslims, has become an established feature of the theological landscape and is likely to remain so for the foreseeable future.

Jews, Christians, and Muslims bear certain "family likenesses," which are not shared equally with, say, Hindus or Buddhists. In general terms, their respective histories are, in certain important ways, intertwined; and in both theological conceptualities and in approaches to life under God, there are recognizable similarities. Perhaps most famously, Jews, Christians, and Muslims are all "monotheistic."[1] They are all, in one way or other, to use a classic Muslim category, "people of the book." And recently it has become increasingly common to refer to them as "the Abrahamic faiths/religions," since within each tradition Abraham stands near the beginning of a history of right response to God.[2]

This suggests that a potentially fruitful approach to the theology of the Abraham material in Genesis 12–25 is via a consideration of contemporary interfaith attempts to appropriate Abraham as a figure of foundational and enduring significance. To be sure, this will mean that many aspects of the texts will be left untouched. Nonetheless, the gain is that the discussion of the theological significance of Abraham relates directly to a major contemporary concern, where the question of what is at stake in appeal to the portrayal of Abraham in Genesis sometimes receives less attention than it merits.

Initially I will set out the argument of Karl-Josef Kuschel in his book *Abraham: A Symbol of Hope for Jews, Christians and Muslims.*[3] Kuschel is a German Roman Catholic theologian who is strongly sympathetic to the work of Hans Küng, especially Küng's thesis,

---

[1] I use the scare quotes here because "monotheism," despite its common usage and prima facie reasonableness, is in many ways a problematic term to apply to any of the Old Testament and the continuing traditions rooted in it. See my essay, "How Appropriate Is 'Monotheism' as a Category for Biblical Interpretation?" in *Early Jewish and Christian Monotheism*, ed. Loren T. Stuckenbruck and Wendy E. S. North, JSNTSup 263 (London: T. & T. Clark International, 2004), 216–34.

[2] Although Christian Zionism, as discussed in Chapter 9, shows little interest in the history and diversity of the notion of being children of Abraham, the opposite is the case in interfaith dialogue as discussed in this chapter.

[3] Karl-Josef Kuschel, *Abraham: A Symbol of Hope for Jews, Christians and Muslims*, trans. John Bowden (London: SCM, 1995).

"No World Peace without Religious Peace."[4] Kuschel's book is a contribution to Küng's interfaith project.[5] I will then consider some difficulties within Kuschel's approach, and indeed with the very concept of "Abrahamic Religions."

EXPOSITION OF KARL-JOSEF KUSCHEL'S ACCOUNT OF ABRAHAM

Kuschel's introduction gives reasons for the writing of his book with which one can hardly fail to be in some way sympathetic:

> There is "a fraternal feud in the house of Abraham" instead of ecumenical brotherhood and sisterhood: that in fact – if we look round the world – is the brutal reality of today. One need only mention Bosnia, Palestine and the Caucasus. All these scenes of bloody conflict are certainly not scenes of directly religious wars. But who could dispute that in all these crisis regions religion plays an important role and often makes things worse? . . . They are tearing one another apart, not least because by virtue of their religious self-understanding they cannot or will not make peace. (xiii–xiv)

But one does not have to choose between "violent fanaticism" and "resigned and paralysing fatalism," for there are alternatives:

> At the beginning of all three religions lies a source of peace which time and again has been and still is obscured on all sides by fanaticism and exclusiveness. This source is called Abraham. . . .
> The violent fraternal feud in the house of Abraham can only be ended by reflection on common origins. So this book dares to present an ecumenical vision: the vision of an Abrahamic ecumene of Jews, Christians and Muslims. (xiv–xv)

---

[4] In addition to Kuschel's work, see Hans Küng, *Judaism: Between Yesterday and Tomorrow*, trans. John Bowden (London: SCM, 1992), ii, xxii.

[5] See ibid., 254. Hereafter subsequent citations will be parenthetical.

This ecumenical vision matters because it relates to a sense of global responsibility:

> Those who think ecumenically thus think in universal connections, in terms of human history, human responsibility. Those who think ecumenically attach importance not only to their region, nation or religion, but to the fate of all religions, to the future of humankind as a whole. (173)

Moreover, this is no merely cerebral or armchair exercise:

> The kind of theology which will be done here is not an end in itself. The attempt at an Abrahamic ecumene made here is to be seen as an investigation of foundations which leads to action. (xv)

In the book as a whole, Kuschel's thesis is, in essence, simple. There is an intrinsic tension between particularism (God's commitment to Abraham and his descendants, whoever those descendants are) and universalism (God's commitment to Abraham and his descendants for the ultimate benefit of all others) that runs not only through the biblical portrayal of Abraham but also through Jewish, Christian, and Muslim appropriations of Abraham. Particularism leads to claims of *exclusivism* in one form or other, while universalism entails *openness* in one form or other. Within this tension the universalist pole is intrinsically superior, both morally and theologically, to the particularist. To be sure, for much of history, the particularist and exclusivist tendencies have predominated within each tradition as each has appropriated Abraham in terms of its normative categories – for Jews, Abraham becomes a pious observer of Torah; for Christians, Abraham shows the faith that alone is needed for right relationship with God; for Muslims, Abraham is the one who embodies true surrender to God. Yet today the struggle for the health of each tradition and for an "Abrahamic ecumene" is the struggle to allow the universalist strands within each tradition to make adherents self-critical about their tendencies to exclusivism so that they can truly be open to one another.

A typical expression of Kuschel's view of exclusivism as the heart of the problem is this:

> [T]he best way of demolishing intolerance and a lack of respect for others is to resist any temptation to exclusivism. For as long as any religion lays exclusive claim to the whole truth and to all the means of salvation at the expense of all other religions and thus devalues them, the gate is wide open to a latent or open arrogance about the truth and salvation. This is then used to justify feelings of superiority, militant attempts at conversion or the contemptuous exclusion of others. What is needed is a theology which makes it possible for people in the religions to maintain their own claim to truth without excluding or even vilifying other truth-claims. (181)[6]

It is crucial to Kuschel's vision of enabling each tradition to become properly self-critical, and thus open to others, that he is highlighting what is already present within them: "I have been able to demonstrate that in all three religious traditions there is a theology 'beyond exclusivism'" (193).

Thus, the goal of his work is simply this:

> [T]here will be an Abrahamic ecumene only when people in all three religions realize that none of the great traditions can claim Abraham only for itself; none can use Abraham to legitimate the superiority of its own tradition. Abraham is greater than all the Jewish, Christian and Muslim pictures of him. Abraham is a believer in God and thus poses a challenge to all traditions which make use of him to draw their own profiles. Thus Abraham is neither a Jew nor a Christian nor simply an adherent of Islam but the "friend of God" (according to Isa. 41.6; James 2.23; Surah 3.125) who can teach

---

[6] Compare Kuschel, *Abraham*, 227: "[I]t will be decisive theologically whether Jews, Christians and Muslims stop describing one another as unbelieving, apostate or superseded and begin to accept one another as brothers and sisters in the spirit, together on the way to the God who is greater, after the model of their ancestors Abraham, Hagar and Sarah."

friendship with God. And this friendship with God should not be forfeited by making Abraham exclusively a friend of the synagogue, the church or the Umma. (252)

Kuschel's handling specifically of the Book of Genesis is perhaps incipiently "canonical" inasmuch as he focuses on the biblical portrayal rather than what might lie behind it ("the original 'historical' Abraham remains once and for all in the shadows of history"), and he speaks of "the normativity of the original Abraham traditions in the book of Genesis" (204–5). Moreover, he eschews any romantic or biblicist attempts to go "back to Abraham" as though what has intervened could be set aside ("no one can leap out of the history of his or her faith community" [197]). The goal of his appeal to the biblical portrayal of Abraham can be seen in passages like this with their strong existential challenge:

> The legacy of Abraham is no deposit, no system, no dead material, but a dynamic history of faith which needs constantly new critical re-reading. Abraham's legacy needs time and again to be freed from the petrifications of tradition. Abraham is not a memorial to faith, a religious giant from distant millennia. Abraham is not a man who possesses faith, but the movement of faith; he is not the security of faith, but the quest for faith; not the arrogance of faith, but the humility of faith. (204)

Three features particularly characterize Kuschel's construal of "the original Abraham traditions" within Genesis. First, as can be seen from the passage just cited, Kuschel's Abraham is above all a person of faith. Kuschel clearly reads the Abraham traditions in the light of Paul's construal: "With a sure sense, Paul puts at the centre as his first key statement the biblical narrative about Abraham: 'Abraham believed in the Lord and the Lord imputed it to him as righteousness' (Gen. 15.6)" (82). Indeed, the way in which Kuschel polarizes "a dynamic history of faith" with "deposit . . . system . . . dead material" and "the petrifications of tradition" makes him, despite his being Roman Catholic, sound distinctly Protestant.

Second, Kuschel makes much of the distinctiveness of Abraham in relation to the mainstream norms and practices of Israel's faith. This lack of those things that typically characterize Israel provides a context in which it becomes apparently natural to highlight faith.[7] Kuschel cites Westermann, who in his Genesis commentary does much to highlight the distinctiveness and internal consistency of patriarchal religion,[8] when he summarizes his understanding of Abraham in a context of Christian–Muslim dialogue and produces his own existential account of Abraham's faith (though he eschews the specific term):

> This relationship with God was so elemental, so natural, so necessary for him that it did not yet need a special cult separate from everyday life, as theologian and priest. Where it is a matter of life and death, theories about God have to fall silent. The only thing that matters is the reality of God. So this was also a relationship with God which had no oppositions. Throughout the history of the patriarchs there is no trace of a clash with other religions, no trace of polemic against other religions.
>
> Abraham stands at the beginning. There was no greater man. He did not have to show any great achievements. But he is the father. His relationship with God was elemental, and therefore it was necessary. It was concerned with survival, survival on the way through time, survival on the way through space. On this way Abraham held firm to God.
>
> God was with him.[9]

---

[7] See Chapter 7.

[8] Claus Westermann, *Genesis 12–36: A Commentary*, trans. John J. Scullion, CC (London: SPCK, 1985 [German orig., 1981]), esp. 105–21.

[9] Claus Westermann, "Der Gott Abrahams," in *Der Gott des Christentums und des Islams*, ed. Andreas Bsteh, BZRT 2 (Mödling, Aus.: St. Gabriel, 1978), 141–43; cited in Kuschel, *Abraham*, 235.

One particular element of Abraham's distinctiveness of which Kuschel makes much is the lack of an aggressive dimension within the Abraham narratives, which contrasts with later practices:

> Indeed, if one takes the spirit of the Abrahamic capacity for integration seriously, then Jews, Christians and Muslims will never demarcate their common faith in a fanatical or intolerant way against other forms of faith.... No exclusivist and absolutist policy of religion can be carried on with Abraham. For despite the resoluteness of his confession of his God, the Abraham of Genesis does not call for any aggressive demarcation against other forms of faith, let alone the aggressive annihilation of them. (231)

Third, for the universalist dimension within the biblical text, Kuschel is dependent on von Rad's conception of the Yahwist in Genesis 12:1–3, as mediated by Westermann:

> God's blessing for Abraham is not an exclusive possession of Israel; it is not a blessing for Israel alone. God's blessing extends beyond Israel, and embraces people who do not stand in the line of Abraham, Isaac and Jacob. The "Yahwist" already conceived a theological notion which is bold in its magnitude and breadth: the power and scope of the blessing of Abraham is literally universal. Abraham is not a mediator of salvation exclusively for Israel, but the new beginning of a new history of blessing for renewed humankind which has been made possible by God (after the fall, the chaos of the flood and the building of the tower of Babel).... So we can endorse Claus Westermann's comment: "God's action proclaimed in the promise to Abraham is not limited to him and his posterity, but reaches its goal only when it includes all the families of the earth." (22–23)

In sum, when these three elements – faith, lack of aggression, and universal concern – are allowed to perform their critical function among Jews, Christians, and Muslims, there is a prospect that the source of peace represented by Abraham may become operative in our time.

PRELIMINARY CRITIQUE OF KUSCHEL

Some obvious criticisms of Kuschel's position spring to mind. For example, there is the exegetical issue, discussed in Chapter 8, about the precise meaning and scope of Genesis 12:3b. If the construal in von Rad and Westermann, on which Kuschel depends, is in fact questionable, then his thesis about the universalist dimension of the portrayal of Abraham in Genesis is also open to question – or becomes dependent on a rereading of the text in the Septuagint as used by Paul. To say this is not to deny that one can still formulate an Old Testament account of God's call of Abraham and his descendants as having the benefit of other nations in view. But such an account will require a nuanced and synthetic reading of the Old Testament portrayal as a whole and an interaction with the New Testament, and the account will not be integral to "the original Abraham traditions" in the way that Kuschel's thesis postulates.

Alternatively, there is an obvious selectivity in Kuschel's use of the text. For example, it is one thing to note the narrative space and divine blessing given to Hagar and Ishmael and to develop its possible significance for resisting too exclusive a construal of God's dealings with Abraham. But it is quite another to disregard the prohibition on Isaac's taking a Canaanite wife, with the corollary that his wife must be one of Abraham's family (Gen 24:3–4), as is also the case subsequently for Jacob (Gen 28:1, 6). To be sure, Genesis does not portray the prohibition in terms of Canaanite women posing a temptation to religious faithlessness, as is characteristic of the Old Testament elsewhere (e.g., Exod 34:12–16; 1 Kgs 11:1–8; Ezra 9–10); indeed, it does not explain the prohibition at all.[10]

---

[10] For discussion, see my *The Old Testament of the Old Testament: Patriarchal Narratives and Mosaic Yahwism*, OBT (Minneapolis, MN: Fortress, 1992; repr., Eugene, OR: Wipf & Stock, 2001), 79–104, esp. 89–91.

Nonetheless, the prohibition clearly represents concerns that are not quite as open and nonexclusive as Kuschel would like.

On a different level, some of Kuschel's conceptualities are open to question. On the one hand, he takes a rather "liberal Protestant" view of the nature and development of religious traditions: There is dynamism at the origins, which is then overlaid by the stultifying development of rituals and traditions and which requires purging by a recovery of the normative initial dynamism. Such a model is not without some truth and value, but one might still hope for a more nuanced and variegated understanding of the developing dynamics of religious traditions and of the numerous ways in which traditions, when complacent or inward looking, can be challenged to a truer realization of their essential meaning and priorities.

On the other hand, Kuschel's antithesis of exclusivist superiority versus open acceptance, with his corollary that the former needs to be renounced in favor of the latter, says less than needs to be said about the ways in which believers should understand their own tradition in relation to those of others. Although some may hold to a position of "all truth here, and only error there," many hold to a range of more variegated positions in which some truth is indeed recognized in other traditions, only that the truth in those other contexts is, in varying ways, less wide, deep, or definitive than in their own tradition. Astonishingly, Kuschel does not seem to recognize, or at least does not discuss, any of the many possible intermediate positions between "all or nothing" on issues of exclusivity and superiority. It will not do to make "exclusivism" a boo word, if one does not also recognize that the criteria by which an adherent of one faith appraises the content of another faith will necessarily be criteria rooted in and particular to one's own tradition.

It may be helpful to see how observations such as these emerge from a critique of Kuschel from a robust Jewish perspective.

JON D. LEVENSON'S CRITIQUE OF KUSCHEL

In an important essay entitled "The Conversion of Abraham to Judaism, Christianity, and Islam," Jon D. Levenson writes, "For all the transparently humane intentions behind Kuschel's proposal... the problems besetting it are legion."[11]

Levenson's initial concern about Kuschel's approach is contextual in terms of the Pentateuch: "[T]he narrative about Abraham in Genesis cannot be convincingly detached from the rest of the pentateuchal story."[12] This he illustrates via the story in Genesis 12:12–20:

> It has long been recognized that in... Gen 12:10–20, Abram and Sarai's experience foreshadows that of their descendants in the first half of the ensuing book. For the famine forces the Israelites, too, to go down to Egypt, and against them, too, a decree goes forth that threatens the males but not the females... (Exod 1:15–16). But, though it tarries, deliverance comes when the LORD strikes the offending Egyptians with plagues, and, what is more, sends the couple off with great wealth.... The typological function of Abram... indicates that something vital is lost when we detach his story from the larger narrative.[13]

Moreover, although he fully appreciates the distinctive ethos of the patriarchal context, Levenson notes that the pentateuchal text as it now stands draws out other important continuities between Abraham and Moses and Israel. In particular, Levenson discusses

---

[11] Jon D. Levenson, "The Conversion of Abraham to Judaism, Christianity, and Islam," in *The Idea of Biblical Interpretation: Essays in Honor of James L. Kugel*, ed. Hindy Najman and Judith H. Newman, JSJSup 83 (Leiden, NL: Brill, 2004), 3–39.

[12] Ibid., 3.

[13] Ibid., 6.

at length a Genesis text about Abraham that Kuschel nowhere
mentions, an oracle of Yhwh to Isaac:

> I will make your descendants as numerous as the stars of heaven,
> and give to your descendants all these lands, so that all the nations
> of the earth shall bless themselves by your offspring – inasmuch as
> Abraham obeyed Me and kept My charge: My commandments, My
> laws, and My teachings. (Gen 26:4–5; NJPSV)

This verse strikingly and explicitly portrays Abraham as observant
in what sounds like a classically Jewish (in biblical terms, Deutero-
nomic) mode. Levenson goes on to show that Jewish tradition was
by no means monolithic about the meaning of this, but rather substantially debated the sense in which Abraham's observance should
be envisaged. A maximalist view, for example, is taken by Rashi
when discussing Genesis 26:5b:

Inasmuch as Abraham obeyed Me
    when I tested him.
And kept My charge:
    The decrees for prevention of wrongdoing regarding the warnings
which are in the Torah, such as incest of the second degree, and
rabbinical prohibitions regarding Sabbath observance.
My commandments,
    Those matters which even if they were not written, would be
worthy of being taken as commandments, such as the prohibition
on robbery and bloodshed.
My laws,
    Matters that the Evil Inclination seeks to refute, such as the pro-
hibition on eating swine's flesh and on the wearing of fabrics of
mixed wool and linen, for which there is no reason, but (they are
simply) the decree of the King and His law for His servants.
And my teaching.
    This includes the Oral Torah, the laws (given) to Moses on Sinai.[14]

---

[14] Rashi as cited in Levenson, "The Conversion of Abraham," 24.

Levenson elucidates the force of Rashi's commentary as follows:

> Only Rashi's first comment, which connects Gen 26:5a with 22:18b, falls into the category of *peshat*, the immediate contextual sense of the scriptural words. As for his glosses on the four nouns in Gen 26:5b, each case represents an effort to connect Abraham's observance with one or another category of rabbinic law. "Charge" thus refers to details of laws articulated by the rabbis themselves, unattested by the plain sense of the Torah. "Commandments" denotes universally applicable moral norms that the human intellect can intuit and respect quite without the assistance of special revelation. "Laws," by contrast, refers to norms without evident rational justification, which human beings are, consequently, inclined to doubt and to disobey. Finally, "teachings," which is the plural of *torah*, includes, in Rashi's view, the Oral Torah, the deposit of rabbinic teaching that the maximalist school of rabbinic thought considered to have been revealed to Moses on Mount Sinai with all its details. The maximalist view thus interprets Abraham as observing all categories of Jewish law as the classical rabbinic tradition understood them – rational and non-rational, moral and ritual, biblical and rabbinic.[15]

By contrast, a minimalist construal is well represented by Rashi's grandson, Rabbi Samuel ben Meir (Rashbam, Northern France, ca. 1085–1174) in his Genesis commentary:

> *Inasmuch as Abraham obeyed Me*
> Concerning the Binding of Isaac, as it is written, "inasmuch as you have obeyed Me." [Gen 22:18]
> *and kept My charge:*
> Such as circumcision, as it is written about it, "And as for you, you shall keep my covenant." [Gen 17:9]
> *My commandments,*
> Such as the commandment about the eight days [until the father performs circumcision on the son], as it is written, "As God commanded him." [Gen 21:4]

---

[15] Levenson, "The Conversion of Abraham," 24–25.

My laws, and My teachings.

According to the essence of its plain sense, [it refers to] all the commandments that are [generally] recognized, such as the laws against robbery, sexual misdeeds, and coveting, and the requirement for legal order, and the laws of hospitality. All of these were in force before the Torah was given, but they were [then] renewed and explicated to Israel, and they made a covenant to practice them.[16]

And again Levenson elucidates:

The guiding principle of Rashbam's interpretation is patent. The half-verse ostensibly so supportive of the maximalist view actually refers only to norms that Abraham could have known according to a plain-sense reading of the narratives about him in Genesis itself. These are the norms that the human mind can intuit unaided by special revelation and those that were explicitly commanded to the patriarch himself. The fact that some of these directives were later absorbed into Mosaic revelation and the covenantal relationship it establishes does not make Abraham a Mosaic Jew. He remains thoroughly pre-Sinaitic.[17]

All this not only shows that rabbinic tradition is more subtle and varied than Kuschel implies, but it also shows that, on Jewish terms, at least given a minimalist reading, the way in which Abraham might be significant for non-Jews is, in essence, not distinctively Abrahamic, but rather in line with Judaism's classic category for thinking about non-Jews – namely, the Noachic commandments. The Noachic commandments are those fundamental moral requirements that are to be considered binding on all humanity, the observance of which on the part of Gentiles suffices for their good standing with God.

---

[16] Rashbam as cited in Levenson, "The Conversion of Abraham," 30.
[17] Levenson, "The Conversion of Abraham," 30.

After further discussion of the ways in which Jews, Christians, and Muslims have appropriated Abraham, Levenson concludes,

> The quest for the neutral Abraham has failed. The patriarch is too embedded in the Torah, the New Testament, and the Qur'an (and in the normative documents of the traditions they undergird) to be extracted and set in judgment upon the traditions that claim him.[18]

This brings Levenson back to Kuschel's attempt to do just this. Levenson cites a characteristic expression of Kuschel's position:

> [L]ike Abraham, Jews, Christians, and Muslims have to do with a God who calls into being that which is not and expects from human beings only *emuna, pistis, islam*: dedicated trust. In short, any talk of Abrahamic ecumene cannot be a suspension which forgets the origins but is rather a concretion of the faith of Abraham which is relevant to the present – in the light of Torah, Gospel, and Qur'an. Abraham remains a point of reference by which the later traditions of synagogue, church, and Umma can and must be measured critically...
>
> For faithfulness to Abraham is more than a slogan only if people in all three traditions are still ready to listen to the Abraham of scripture as he has been handed down in all his dimensions, neither in the Talmud nor in the New Testament nor in the Qur'an, but in the book of Genesis.[19]

On this, Levenson observes:

> The problem... is that Kuschel's Abraham is not really so ecumenical, and the underlying unity that he claims to find, not so shared, as he thinks. For this is (despite Kuschel's own Catholicism) essentially a Protestant Christian Abraham. Note that the key thing about Abraham is once again, as in Paul, his faith (*emuna, pistis*). Kuschel altogether ignores the tradition that Abraham was obedient to commandments – the Abraham of rabbinic maximalism who "obeyed

---

[18] Ibid., 37.
[19] Ibid., 37, citing Kuschel, *Abraham*, 204–5.

Me and kept My charge: My commandments, My laws, and My teachings."[20] This is, to be sure, only one verse, but, as we have observed, so is the verse that claims that Abraham had faith. Second, in Kuschel's proposal the standard by which all renderings of Abraham are to be assessed is once again the notion of *sola scriptura*, "by scripture alone," a concept familiar from the Protestant Reformation but by no means authoritative in every scriptural religion, or even in every Abrahamic religion. In Kuschel's case, unlike Luther's or Calvin's, however, the Scripture is limited to Genesis and the renderings of Abraham in the New Testament are relegated to the level of post-biblical tradition, in the manner of the Talmud of rabbinic Judaism or the Qur'an of Islam. I leave it to Christian theologians to assess the adequacy for their tradition of this proposal to locate the authoritative meaning of Abraham in Genesis rather at the expense of the New Testament. But it is surely the case that not many Jews or Muslims are likely to accept the equivalent down-playing of their own traditions and (in the case of Islam) scriptures that this requires.[21] And I find it easy to imagine some Muslims would want to question whether *islam* is really quite the same thing as *pistis* (the New Testament word usually rendered "faith" but which Kuschel translates as "dedicated trust"). That Judaism and Islam give a prominent place to "dedicated trust" need hardly be gainsaid, but the notion that this is the foundation and all else is secondary will justly meet with resistance among practicing Jews and Muslims and among many Christian communities as well. In short, Kuschel's

---

[20] This seems to me not quite accurate, as Kuschel is well aware of the Abraham of rabbinic maximalism, only not with reference to Genesis 26:5. Levenson's critique might be sharper in terms of Rashbam's minimalist construal of the verse, for this still draws attention within the Genesis context to Abraham's integrity of action, rather than his faith.

[21] I am not sure that this way of putting it quite does justice to Kuschel's overall thesis, however much it points out the shortcomings of the passage just cited. For Kuschel's overall thesis is that the respective traditions should allow the dynamic openness that is to be found in their respective foundational texts (Pauline for Christians, Qur'anic for Muslims) – an openness that stands in continuity with the Abraham of Genesis – to critique the tendencies to exclusivity that rather too readily come to the fore.

well-intentioned proposal reminds me of a person who says, "We need to stop arguing and agree on a common position: mine."[22]

Although Kuschel has continued to advance his thesis in recent writings,[23] it is unfortunate that he seems unaware of Levenson's critique and thus to date has offered no response to the concerns that Levenson raises.

SHOULD WE CONTINUE TO SPEAK OF "ABRAHAMIC FAITHS/RELIGIONS"?

Alon Goshen-Gottstein, in a recent essay that does not engage with Kuschel but reflects on the issues that Kuschel raises, is concerned primarily with the designation of Judaism, Christianity, and Islam as "Abrahamic."[24] He observes that Abrahamic is not a phenomenological description related to the study of religions as a scholarly discipline, but is rather "a suggestive category created to serve a particular interreligious ideology" whose "strength is in the eirenic suggestiveness of the term."[25] If one is seeking a genuinely descriptive approach, then one should look for other categories:

> There are many common elements in Judaism, Christianity and Islam. These include their belief in revelation, Scripture, prophecy, reward and punishment, the afterlife, and more. There is no reason to single out Abraham as the characteristic category in light of which the three religions can best be described. While all three religions

---

[22] Levenson, "The Conversion of Abraham," 37–38.

[23] See Karl-Josef Kuschel, *Juden, Christen, Muslime: Herkunft und Zukunft* (Düsseldorf: Patmos, 2007), esp. 548–623 on Abraham; in this book he also discusses Adam, Noah, Moses, Mary, and Jesus in all three traditions.

[24] Alon Goshen-Gottstein, "Abraham and 'Abrahamic Religions' in Contemporary Interreligious Discourse: Reflections of an Implicated Jewish Bystander," *Studies in Interreligious Dialogue* 12 (2002): 165–83.

[25] Ibid., 167, 177.

recognize the figure of Abraham, this is also true of their recognition of Moses as well as of numerous prophetic figures. The common recognition of Abraham is insignificant to a purely descriptive approach to the three religions. Their respective appeals to Moses, Jesus and Mohammed are of far greater significance to their self identity than their common appeal to the person of Abraham.[26]

To be sure, the "eirenic suggestiveness" of the term may be a positive strength in certain contexts, not least in on-the-ground interfaith engagements.[27] But, at the very least, it is important to be aware of what such a classification does and does not achieve. Goshen-Gottstein's anxiety is that "Abrahamic" is likely to "express the bias of one or more of the religions involved but . . . not reflect equally the theological understanding of all three religions"[28] – which is, of course, precisely the thrust of Levenson's critique of Kuschel.

Ironically, Goshen-Gottstein thinks that if one did want to try to use the figure of Abraham for interfaith dialogue, then it is the postbiblical, rather than the biblical, Abraham who is more serviceable. The famous image of Abraham as one who rejects idolatry is nowhere to be found in Genesis, but is an imaginative postbiblical development that in certain ways conforms Abraham to a Mosaic norm. The displacement of the Genesis concerns of election, covenant, and promise of land with an imaginative focus on what might have preceded God's call of Abraham in Genesis 12:1–3 can provide a possible common ground, though certainly not in the terms of the dynamism of origins that Kuschel sees as significant: "The image of Abraham the believer who discovers

[26] Ibid., 173.
[27] Note that Goshen-Gottstein's essay ends with a remarkable personal testimony about an experience of interfaith prayer (ibid., 182–83), whose implications point in a rather different direction from the main argument of his essay.
[28] Goshen-Gottstein, "Abraham and 'Abrahamic Religions,'" 166.

God, the monotheist who rejects idolatry, can obviously serve as a common point of reference for Judaism, Christianity and Islam."[29]

However, Goshen-Gottstein observes that from a Jewish perspective, the traditional way of formulating a positive interfaith approach is in terms of the "Noachide commandments," a rabbinic formulation of "a basic moral code of universal significance." These commandments have been attached to the context of God's address to Noah in relation to the whole of creation in Genesis 9, which constitutes the appropriate narrative context, though they "actually go back to God's original commandment to Adam and hence form part of a law governing creation from the outset (Bavli Sanhedrin 56b)."[30] In other words, Jews have classically approached interfaith issues in terms of natural law, whose biblical locus is Genesis 1–11 rather than Genesis 12–25.

> The figure of Abraham, by contrast, traditionally serves Judaism as a symbol for converts. Abraham is not only the father of the Jewish nation. He is also the original and archetypal convert. All converts to Judaism, lacking physical Jewish parentage, are considered children of Abraham. Thus, a convert is always called "so and so, son of Abraham." In light of these uses there is an obvious difficulty in applying the figure of Abraham to an interfaith context as a means of validating other world religions. There would be something contradictory in the same figure both enabling entry to Judaism and validating other religions outside Judaism.[31]

Goshen-Gottstein traces the modern use of "Abrahamic" for Judaism, Christianity, and Islam to the work of the Roman Catholic scholar Louis Massignon, who was influential in the mid-twentieth

[29] Ibid., 172.
[30] Ibid., 171.
[31] Ibid., 171–72.

century, not least on the Second Vatican Council. But when he analyzes ways in which one might give content to this notion, he finds them lacking. For example, is there mileage in the fact that all three religions "profess a faith in the same God, the God of Abraham"? Goshen-Gottstein observes,

> It seems to me that beyond the minimalist monotheistic sense, any attempt to describe the God of the three religions as the God of Abraham might do violence to their individual uniqueness. . . . I think particularly of Christianity. Would it be true to the Christian doctrine of God to describe Him as the God of Abraham? While from a certain perspective this is certainly true, most of what is truly unique in the Christian teaching of the triune God would be lost, were we to adopt this understanding of Abrahamic faith. A similar point, though less obviously so, can be made with regard to Judaism. Unlike the post-biblical tradition that recognizes in Abraham the true teacher of faith in the one God, it is possible that the biblical tradition itself does not consider the revelation of God to Abraham as the highest and most complete self-disclosure of the God of Israel. Exodus 6:3 is a crucial passage in this context. It may teach us that a higher expression of God is made known to Moses, in contradistinction to the knowledge of God available to Abraham and the other Patriarchs. The teaching of God that is characteristic of Judaism, as expressed in the tetragrammaton, should accordingly be referred to as "The God of Moses" rather than "The God of Abraham."[32]

These well-taken observations bring us back to the discussion in Chapter 7 about the need for theological understanding and use of Genesis to take seriously the issues posed by its being "the Old Testament of the Old Testament." The Old Testament is clear that the God of Abraham is indeed the God of Moses, yet this recognition should not obscure the substantive differences between patriarchal

[32] Ibid., 176.

and Mosaic conceptions of God, as succinctly expressed in Exodus 6:3 in terms of the differences of nomenclature, El Shaddai and Y<small>HWH</small>. It is only as the Abrahamic conception is both embraced and transformed by the Mosaic that the Abrahamic remains enduringly significant for Israel and Judaism. From a Christian perspective, the Mosaic must itself be embraced and transformed in the light of Christ in order to remain enduringly significant. For serious theological thinking, it is hardly meaningful to appeal to the Abrahamic *apart from* its subsequent transformation and appropriation.[33] The Abrahamic is not an independent norm; and so it is doubtful that it can serve as a substantive, rather than a well-meaning but potentially misleading, descriptor.

CONCLUSION

Unfortunately, the tenor of this chapter so far has been somewhat negative, arguing that Kuschel's proposal to use the Abraham of Genesis as a "symbol of hope" and "source of peace" is somewhat confused and unsatisfactory. However, negative conclusions can be significant, for they can help to prevent people from entering dead-end alleys, or to show those who may already have entered why it might be timely to retrace their steps. I conclude, then, with four remarks specifically about the theological use of Genesis in an interfaith context:

First, it is worth underlining that recent debate has followed the premodern tradition of fixing on Abraham as *the* significant figure, to the neglect of other figures within Genesis 12–50 (Isaac,

---

[33] Paul's appeal to Abraham in Romans 4 does not, I think, disprove this. For it is because Paul can find in Genesis that which anticipates what he has already come to recognize as true in Christ that Paul can appeal to Abraham in a way that sets him over against Moses and the law.

Jacob/Israel, Joseph, not to mention any of the matriarchs) or Genesis 1–11 (Adam, Noah). This focus on Abraham is slightly paradoxical. On the one hand, all those things that tend to be highlighted as distinctive of Abraham are in fact distinctive of patriarchal religion and life as a whole. On the other hand, as has been outlined in Chapter 7, it is the figure of Abraham (rather than Isaac, Jacob, or Joseph) who has most obviously been molded by the perspectives of Israel's normative concerns. So, the religious distinctiveness of the pre-Mosaic context within Genesis 12–50 as a whole tends to be heuristically applied to Abraham as significant representative, even though in important ways he is the figure most conformed to Mosaic norms. This need not be a problem for imaginative appeal to Abraham in theological debate; even so, it is important that one be critically aware of what one is doing when making such an appeal.

Second, there can be little doubt that for many contemporary readers, the patriarchal narratives have an unusual appeal. The combination of memorable stories with a religious world that is indeed less complex and more "ecumenical" than our contemporary world can give Genesis a distinctively existential and theological edge. The problem is to know how best to handle this. Sometimes the approach can be simply romanticized, aesthetic and nostalgic, in the kind of way expressed in the early twentieth century by Hermann Gunkel:

> These narratives bring the life of antiquity vividly before our eyes, a well of rejuvenation for a civilization grown old, immediately recognizable to our children, loved by them, and embodying for them lofty and eternal ideas.
>
> Think of the force with which murder is set forth as a base crime in the story of Cain; the charm of the Joseph story, eloquent with fraternal envy and love, and full of faith in an overarching

Providence.... One should imagine that linguists, historians of civilization, and everyone interested in aesthetics would vie with us in
holding up to view these golden treasures.[34]

The more interesting and difficult questions arise when one seeks to
take seriously the position of the patriarchal narratives as "the Old
Testament of the Old Testament," recognized as both foundational
and enduringly significant, yet only being so when appropriated
and recontextualized within Israel's normative perspectives, and,
for Christians, again recontextualized within a Christian frame of
reference. One is going to need a robust engagement with scripture
and tradition in general if one is to handle well the enduring
theological significance of the specific Genesis texts.

Third, it should be clear that more than one synthesized reading
of the Abraham narratives is possible. A Christian reading of the
sort articulated by Westermann and Kuschel, following in the steps
of Paul, is clearly a meaningful heuristic way of appropriating
the Genesis text. Yet the same can be said of a Jewish approach
whose accent lies on Abraham's obedient observance of the various
commands that God gives him. A Muslim approach is more distant
and focuses on the Qur'an rather than Genesis, yet, even so, its
category of submission to God's will offers a ready overall heuristic
perspective that makes sense and does not jar when one reads
Genesis. This could lead to hermeneutical relativism, but it need
not. As Levenson helpfully puts it,

> A skeptic might say that Abraham is a Rorschach card, onto whom
> each tradition projects its own convictions. I would prefer to put
> it differently. The material about Abraham in the Hebrew Bible is

[34] Hermann Gunkel, "Why Engage the Old Testament?" in Gunkel, *Water for a
Thirsty Land: Israelite Literature and Religion*, ed. K. C. Hanson (Minneapolis,
MN: Fortress, 2001), 1–30 (5). The essay was originally published in German
in 1914.

so elusive, so enigmatic, so suggestive, and so non-didactic, that it calls out, דרשני [*dorsheni*] – "Interpret me!" as the Talmudic rabbis would say.[35]

Levenson's own inference from this is not that all interpretations are equally valid, but rather that the respective traditions of Jewish, Christian, and Islamic interpretation harbor within themselves "a view of Abraham that looks more like the dominant emphasis of the other one." This means that robust engagement with the resources of one's own tradition can lead in interesting and substantive ways to the respect for others that is fundamental for interfaith dialogue.[36]

Fourth, although we noted at the outset that interfaith appeals to Abraham tend to leave many aspects of the Genesis text untouched, this frame of reference can also enable fresh reading and thinking. Consider, for example, Abraham's entertaining of Yнwн/men/angels (Gen 18:1–8). Much discussion, both ancient and modern, has unsurprisingly focused on the issue of how Yнwн, the three men, and the angels/messengers (as the men are depicted in Gen 19:1, 15) relate to one another.[37] Yet this issue should not be allowed to distract from the text's primary focus, hospitality, which

---

[35] Levenson, "The Conversion of Abraham," 39.

[36] A promising fresh approach to interfaith dialogue, in which participants are open to others yet speak from within their own traditions in such a way as to "improve the quality of their disagreements," is the Society for Scriptural Reasoning. See *The Promise of Scriptural Reasoning*, ed. David Ford and C. C. Pecknold (Oxford, UK: Blackwell, 2006).

[37] Although the traditional Christian inclination to find here an adumbration of the Trinity naturally fell by the wayside when the text was approached in a historical-critical frame of reference, there may perhaps be fresh ways of reengaging the issue in a canonical frame of reference, even if one may struggle to attain the imaginative depth and beauty represented by Rublev's famous icon of the Trinity.

was widely recognized as a fundamental virtue in premodern societies. At a time when tolerance is an overused and somewhat stale category, and also too easily confused with indifference, some are proposing that a more fruitful metaphor for the interactions of interfaith dialogue is hospitality.[38] Thereby Abraham's action can be read with fresh eyes. It can perhaps encourage members of an unduly individualistic culture to reconnect with a traditional social virtue; and it certainly reminds participants in dialogue that the issues are not solely intellectual but include personal relationships and generosity. Finally, the fact that Abraham's guests do not (presumably) fit within categories readily familiar to Abraham may gain special significance; indeed, if one reads Abraham's hospitality in the suggestive light of Hebrews 13:2, that the true significance of what the host is doing may be unknown to the host, then a genuine epistemic humility may thereby be encouraged.

[38] See, e.g., Luke Bretherton, *Hospitality as Holiness: Christian Witness Amid Moral Diversity* (Aldershot, UK: Ashgate, 2006), esp. 121–59; and David F. Ford, *Christian Wisdom: Desiring God and Learning in Love* (Cambridge: Cambridge University Press, 2007), 273–303, esp. 279.

CHAPTER 12

Genesis 37–50: Is Joseph Wise?

The story of Joseph is one of the best known parts of Genesis. The enduring popularity of Andrew Lloyd Webber's musical, *Joseph and the Amazing Technicolor Dreamcoat*, has helped make the (adapted) story a minor contemporary cultural phenomenon. Alongside a steady flow of scholarly monographs is an equally steady flow of popular studies that seek to make the biblical story accessible to any thoughtful reader.[1]

Discussion of the theological significance of the Joseph narrative tends to focus on three interrelated aspects. First is the recurrence of dreams, implicitly or explicitly sent by God, whose interpretation is not straightforward (Gen 40:8: "Do not interpretations belong to God?"), and whose outworking is central to the storyline (41:25: "God has revealed to Pharaoh what he is about to do"). Second are Joseph's statements to his brothers of divine sovereignty, both at their initial scene of reconciliation and then in the renewed context of reconciliation at the end: "You intended against me evil,

---

[1] These range from Claus Westermann's *Joseph: Studies of the Joseph Stories in Genesis*, trans. Omar Kaste (Edinburgh, UK: T. & T. Clark, 1996 [German orig., 1990]), by the author of the twentieth century's most extensive scholarly Genesis commentary, to a study written within the context of Christian ministry, Pete Wilcox, *Living the Dream: Joseph for Today: A Dramatic Exposition of Genesis 37–50* (London: Paternoster, 2007).

God intended it for good" (50:20). Third is the character of Joseph himself, traditionally viewed positively by Christians as a type of Christ, and more recently as a model of wisdom, but open also to other readings of a more suspicious nature. A particular focus for this third issue is Joseph's treatment of his brothers in Genesis 42–44. This is never explained by the narrator, and so widely differing readings are possible. These range from those that see Joseph as wisely administering a searching moral and spiritual discipline for his brothers' ultimate well-being to those that see Joseph as cruel and vengeful.

In the discussion that follows, I will try to hold all these issues together and argue that a persuasive account of one is inextricably related to persuasive accounts of the others as well.

THE JOSEPH NARRATIVE IN GERHARD VON RAD'S ANALYSIS

It is helpful to use Gerhad von Rad's influential account as an entrée to the issues. Von Rad's interpretation is primarily found in his 1953 essay, "The Joseph Narrative and Ancient Wisdom,"[2] but also in related essays and in his Genesis commentary.[3]

Von Rad begins with the distinctiveness of the Joseph material within Genesis. On the one hand is the text's distinctive *literary form*: "Whereas almost all the stories of Abraham and of Jacob are

---

[2] Gerhard von Rad, "The Joseph Narrative and Ancient Wisdom," in von Rad, *From Genesis to Chronicles: Explorations in Old Testament Theology*, ed. K. C. Hanson (Minneapolis, MN: Fortress, 2005), 75–88.

[3] See Gerhard von Rad, "The Story of Joseph," in von Rad, *God at Work in Israel*, trans. John Marks (Nashville, TN: Abingdon, 1980 [German orig., 1974]), 19–35; von Rad, "Genesis 50:20," in von Rad, *Biblical Interpretations in Preaching*, trans. John Steely (Nashville, TN: Abingdon, 1977 [German orig., 1973]), 45–48; and von Rad, *Genesis: A Commentary*, trans. John H. Marks, rev. ed., OTL, (London: SCM, 1972 [German 9th ed., 1972]).

limited in length to twenty or thirty verses, the four hundred or so verses of the Joseph narrative patently show it to be a document of quite a different literary form."[4] On the other hand is the text's distinctive *content*:

> [I]t differs from the earlier patriarchal stories that spoke much more directly about God. Where in this story do we ever read a statement like "God appeared," "God spoke," "God again went up," "God gave heed," etc.? In comparison with all these older stories, the Joseph story is distinguished by a revolutionary worldliness, a worldliness that unfolds the entire realm of human life, with all its heights and depths, realistically and without miracle.[5]

Von Rad then proposes a historical thesis to explain these distinctives: The Joseph story reflects the "Solomonic Enlightenment," a time when a new kind of consciousness pervaded Israel, a consciousness expressed particularly in wisdom traditions and literature, where Israel shared much common ground with, and indeed drew on, the wisdom literature of its wider world, especially Egypt. Joseph is a narrative embodiment of the theology of wisdom, with a didactic purpose for those who would become administrators in the royal court.

About this Solomonic Enlightenment, von Rad writes,

> The early monarchic period . . . saw a wholly new departure in spirituality, a kind of "enlightenment," an awakening of spiritual self-consciousness. Men became aware of their own spiritual and rational powers, and whole new dimensions of experience opened up before their eyes, inwardly as well as outwardly.[6]

Consequently, "[t]he appearance of these new dimensions made it possible to put on record in narrative form this whole world of

---

[4] Von Rad, "The Joseph Narrative," 75.
[5] Von Rad, "The Story of Joseph," 28.
[6] Von Rad, "The Joseph Narrative," 75–76.

the human"[7] – that is, specifically, in the novel form of the Joseph narrative.

The content of Joseph's portrayal is shown in numerous ways to represent that which Proverbs advocates. For example:

> [T]he wise men present us with a very imposing and well-found pattern for human living, which in some respects has striking points of contact with the humanistic idea of antiquity. They depict a man who by his upbringing, his modesty, his learning, his courtesy and his self-discipline has acquired true nobility of character. He is, let us say it at once, the image of Joseph! . . . The foundation on which such character is built, as Joseph himself recognizes, is "godly fear"; and the fear of Yahweh is quite simply obedience to the divine law (Gen 42:18; Prov 1:7; 15:33).[8]

Moreover, "[t]he narrative of Genesis 39 reads as if it had been devised expressly to illustrate the warnings of the wisdom writers (Prov 22:14; 23:27–28)"; also, "[i]n his relationship with his brothers Joseph is the very pattern of the man who can 'keep silence,' as described in Egyptian wisdom-lore. He is the 'prudent man who conceals his knowledge' (Prov 12:23), and who 'restrains his lips' (Prov 10:19)";[9] and so on.

The theological climax, however, comes with the issue of divine action in the world:

> Let us . . . compare Joseph's comments, both [in Gen 50:20] and in Gen 45:8, with the dictum of Proverbs that "A man's mind plans his way, but Yahweh directs his steps" (Prov 16:9). Here, too, we have a statement that Yahweh controls all things, and also a sharply drawn contrast between human plans and the divine direction of affairs.[10]

[7] Von Rad, "The Story of Joseph," 22.
[8] Von Rad, "The Joseph Narrative," 77.
[9] Ibid.
[10] Ibid., 78–79.

However, as von Rad develops this theme and its expression in the biblical text, he finds a problematic undertone within it. With reference to Proverbs 20:24 ("A man's steps are ordered by Yahweh, how then can man understand his way?"), he observes that

> [t]here is evidently another side to the wisdom-writers' impressive faith in the overriding providence of God, a side which manifests itself as a frank scepticism with regard to all human activity and purpose.... It cannot be denied ... that even in the Joseph narrative a deep cleavage threatens to arise between divine and human purposes, and that human activity is so heavily fettered by the all-embracing divine control of events that it comes dangerously near to losing all significance whatever.[11]

Thereby he posits a direct line of influence from the positive-sounding affirmations of Genesis and Proverbs to the scepticism of Qoheleth, though in this context he does not develop the point.

ANALYSIS OF VON RAD'S ACCOUNT

Von Rad's thesis is impressive. Yet it has not lasted well. Primarily this is because his Solomonic Enlightenment has been found to be a historical hypothesis for which there is no real evidence. Further, the closeness of thought between the Joseph narrative and Proverbs has been seriously questioned, as has been von Rad's construal of divine action; and the view of wisdom literature as functioning to train royal administrators is also lacking in evidence.[12] Nevertheless, I start my discussion of Joseph with von Rad's account, because there remains real value in what he says, especially if some of it is reconfigured.

---

[11] Ibid., 79.
[12] See especially Stuart Weeks, *Early Israelite Wisdom*, OTM (Oxford, UK: Clarendon, 1994).

Reenvisioning Key Elements in the "Solomonic Enlightenment" Hypothesis

First, let us consider the Solomonic Enlightenment. In essence, von Rad is doing what biblical scholars have regularly done with a wide range of biblical texts. He discerns particular concerns and emphases within the biblical text and then, on the assumption that the text is reflective of its context of composition, posits a historical context that could have given rise to what we now read. But what if one recasts the approach and changes it from a possible, but unsubstantiated, hypothesis about an ancient context of origins into a heuristic strategy for reading in a contemporary context?

Indeed, it is difficult to resist the impression that such a strategy was always integral to von Rad's historical hypothesis. The way he depicts the Solomonic Enlightenment sounds so much like an account of the modern European Enlightenment that his construal of the significance of the Joseph narrative in its ancient context looks to be a kind of transparency for its possible significance in the then-contemporary European context. When one of his Joseph essays ends with the words, "Without question, the Joseph story was for its time a modern story, and Joseph was a modern man,"[13] it is hard not to hear a tacit invitation to the modern reader of today to enter into, and ideally identify with and appropriate, the biblical portrayal. So one can surely ask whether one might legitimately abandon the historical hypothesis dimension of von Rad's proposal while retaining its heuristic ability to envision a world implied by the text, only in relation to a contemporary rather than an ancient context. If so, then one can still focus on the distinctive voice of the text – the importance of human character and responsibility, the

---

[13] Von Rad, "The Story of Joseph," 35.

sense that God's action may be hidden, Joseph's integrity within a context far removed from the ritual life and norms of Israel, and so forth – only with a view to considering how best these might be used in relation to facets of today's post-Enlightenment world.

Reenvisioning the Joseph Narrative in Relation to Proverbs
Although von Rad's historical linkage of the Joseph narrative with Proverbs has been heavily, and often justifiably, criticized, there may yet remain some real heuristic value in the linkage of these texts as a reading strategy.

One of the key issues is the didactic nature of the Joseph story. Here one must realize that there is more than one way of being didactic. A text may well have a didactic function, without being didactic in exactly the way that Proverbs is didactic. Weeks, for example, says,

> Joseph's tale-bearing (cf. Prov. 11.13), his indiscreet revelation of his dreams, and his false accusations against his brothers (cf. Prov. 12.17ff), are all of importance in the story, and in the portrayal of Joseph, but are hardly in accord with the ethical ideals of the wisdom literature. It cannot be denied that we should expect in a didactic, idealizing text not only a more lucid, but also a more consistent idealization.[14]

Leaving aside for the moment Joseph's dealings with his brothers in Egypt, and focusing on the first two of Weeks' three points, the expectation of "a more consistent idealization" might well apply to the didactic nature of Proverbs without ruling out other didactic concerns, since transformation, learning, and growth can all function didactically. Von Rad himself, in response to Otto

---

[14] Weeks, *Early Israelite Wisdom*, 94.

Procksch's depiction of Joseph as "the noblest figure in Genesis," observes that since Joseph's "portrait at the beginning of the story is not entirely irreproachable, in a certain sense one will have to speak of an ensuing purification."[15] This "not entirely irreproachable" remark depicts mildly those character flaws that most interpreters express more forcefully. As Sidney Greidanus puts it, "The young Joseph is sketched as immature, unwise, boastful, and extremely talkative";[16] or, as Pete Wilcox succinctly puts it, "He is a brat."[17] Nevertheless, Joseph's "purification" – by his abandonment of the folly of his behavior as a youth in Genesis 37 in favor of a wiser course of life – can readily function as a portrayal that teaches wisdom.[18]

Weeks also criticizes von Rad's proposal that "Gen 39 was composed especially to illustrate wisdom teachings about adultery."[19] Again, however, it may be fruitful to prescind from the historical debate about context of composition (about which we can only be agnostic) and ask about the possible fruitfulness for a reading strategy if one juxtaposes the story of Joseph and Potiphar's wife with the warnings of Proverbs.

---

[15] Von Rad, "Genesis 50:20," 45.

[16] Sidney Greidanus, *Preaching Christ from Genesis: Foundations for Expository Sermons* (Grand Rapids, MI: Eerdmans, 2007), 338.

[17] Wilcox, *Living the Dream*, 4.

[18] Compare von Rad's observation that "[o]ne does not, of course, attain such a model life as that shown by Joseph overnight. One must first learn it in the difficult school of humility. And that too is the teaching of the ancient wise men, that humility is before honor (*^{ca}nāwā*, Prov. 15.33; 22.4); and it is well illustrated in the first part of the Joseph story" (*Genesis*, 437; cf. von Rad, "The Joseph Narrative," 78). Here, however, von Rad seems to be thinking of what Joseph undergoes in Genesis 39–40, prior to his exaltation in Genesis 41, rather than of the change from prig in Genesis 37 to responsible man in the rest of the narrative.

[19] Weeks, *Early Israelite Wisdom*, 99.

Weeks usefully points out differences of outlook. Within Proverbs 1–9, "[t]he emphasis . . . is not upon the moral issues involved in adultery, but upon the difficulty of resisting the temptation and the dangerous consequences of succumbing to it." As for the portrayal in Genesis 39,

> [i]n contrast to the voluptuous seductions by *femmes fatales* in the wisdom literature,[20] the attempt by Potiphar's wife to seduce Joseph, although frequently repeated, is rather perfunctory. Joseph's refusal bears no resemblance to anything in the passages from Proverbs. He speaks of how good his master has been to him, and how he has given him everything except his wife: "How than can I do this great wickedness, and sin against God?" Here *hārā'āh haggĕdōlāh* is not simply the sin of adultery. Joseph argues not on the grounds of some inherent sinfulness in adultery, but that to take Potiphar's wife, when he has given everything else, would be wrong. . . . Joseph's reply shows none of the self-interest which characterizes the remarks of the proverbial literature on the subject of adultery. Whether we understand the "sin against God" to be a description of the ethical basis for refusal, or a second, religious basis, it too is an expression quite unknown in the wisdom exhortations against adultery.[21]

Four comments may be made. First, the brusque words of Potiphar's wife, "lie with me," are indeed less than would be expected if the admonitions of Proverbs were directly in view: If not sensual details together with assurances to overcome possible anxiety about Potiphar's return home (analogous to Prov 7:16–20), then one might expect some allure along the lines of folly's "stolen water is sweet, and bread eaten in secret is pleasant" (Prov 9:17). When the texts are read together, however, one might fill out Potiphar's wife's words along the lines of Proverbs, for nothing

---

[20] Weeks is presumably thinking here of Proverbs 7:1–27, which is the only passage to describe "voluptuous seduction" in any detail.

[21] Weeks, *Early Israelite Wisdom*, 97–98.

in the Genesis text resists such imaginative expansion; that is, the passages are readily open to intertextual reading. But if one wished to hold to the precise wording of Potiphar's wife, one consequence could be a sense of the differing ways in which temptation may be expressed, from lingering persuasion to an abrupt "just do it."

Second, another interesting difference between Genesis and Proverbs is that while Proverbs consistently warns of the possible attractions of the temptress, Genesis says nothing at all about the attractiveness of Potiphar's wife but only about that of Joseph himself. This is why Potiphar's wife lusts after him (Gen 39:6b–7). This, of course, reminds one that problems of sexual temptation run in both directions and thus usefully complements the Proverbs emphasis. Moreover, the Genesis narrative implicitly warns that personal attractiveness brings with it responsibility to use it wisely rather than selfishly and exploitatively.

Third, if one uses wisdom in Proverbs 8 heuristically for reading Joseph, there is a striking resonance between the depiction of Joseph in Genesis 39 and Woman Wisdom's words in Proverbs 8:35, "For whoever finds me finds life, and obtains favour from the LORD." Although there is no overlap in terminology, there is similar conceptuality. Joseph in Genesis 39 lacks the foolish conceit of his early days in Genesis 37 and is behaving with integrity, and the counterpart of this is that YHWH is with him and prospers whatever he does. It is no strain of text or imagination to read Joseph in Genesis 39 as one who has learned wisdom and so finds life and enjoys divine favor. Weeks' objection that "it is a strange didacticism indeed which promises a prison sentence as the reward for virtue!"[22] shows that Genesis 39 does not display the didacticism of Proverbs, but does not allow for different kinds of

---

[22] Ibid., 98.

didactic literature, where growth in wisdom may be recognized to be protracted and demanding. In any case, the Genesis narrative does not "promise" a prison sentence, for its didactic function is illustrative, rather than stipulative; not all would-be temptresses need be as malicious as Potiphar's wife.

Fourth and finally, I think that von Rad's intuitive understanding of the text is better than some of the detailed arguments that he adduces in support. For example, he says of Genesis 39 that "it shows the absolute foundation upon which the whole educational ideal [i.e., of wisdom] rests, namely, the "fear of God," i.e., obedience to his commands which is the basis of this art of life (Prov. 1.7; 15.33). Joseph also admits to this absolute obligation (Gen. 42.18)."[23] As such, this is weak. Joseph's mention of his "fear of God," when his brothers are at his mercy and fearful (Gen 42:18), is in context not a generalized reference to obedience to divine law, but rather conveys that Joseph is "fair and reliable,"[24] probably also with the specific nuance that fear of God often has: of acting with integrity and restraint toward the weak and vulnerable (cf. Gen 20:11; Lev 19:14; Deut 25:17–18.). But von Rad continues,

> The older teachers of wisdom did not cultivate a man to seek God and his revelation, but rather they cultivated him on the basis of that revelation. Thus they prescribe training and education which is not standardized by an absolute ideal above them and does not intend to lead to an ideal image. This educational ideal is much less stable and axiomatic, less doctrinaire than most of the modern prescriptions.[25]

Here von Rad's point about the approach and goal of wisdom teachers is topical in two ways. On the one hand, it bears

---

[23] Von Rad, *Genesis*, 436.
[24] Weeks, *Early Israelite Wisdom*, 101.
[25] Von Rad, *Genesis*, 436.

important resemblance to the contemporary recovery of "virtue ethics" as a way of handling ethical difficulties. Here the ethical process relativizes familiar consequentialist or deontological models, and the concern becomes to see how a morally well-formed person finds a way of doing what is right.[26] Such an approach is precisely "less doctrinaire" than its alternatives (while it does not, of course, deny or remove the need for other models of ethical thought and practice), because its focus on character makes both process and outcome relatively unpredictable.

On the other hand, there is a renewed interest in wisdom as a category for the interpretation and use of scripture as a whole. As Stephen E. Fowl and L. Gregory Jones put it, "the interpretation of Scripture is a difficult task *not* because of the technical demands of biblical scholarship but because of the importance of character for wise readings."[27] The nature of its fundamental subject matter – God and the transformation of human life into God's patterns – makes the Bible difficult to handle well in relation to that subject matter without appropriate personal formation. Moreover, if a prime purpose of the Bible within the church is to nurture the church to live in ways that are wise and faithful, then there is a sense in which the Bible as a whole comes to function in the kind of way that von Rad depicts wisdom: General formation becomes more important than precise prescription – though of course both are necessary and will always operate dialectically.

Thus, irrespective of von Rad's particular hypothesis about the origins of the Joseph narrative, there is surely still real value in seeing Joseph as a wise person who models important dimensions

---

[26] See Jean Porter, "Virtue Ethics," in *The Cambridge Companion to Christian Ethics*, ed. Robin Gill (Cambridge: Cambridge University Press, 2001), 96–111.

[27] Stephen E. Fowl and L. Gregory Jones, *Reading in Communion: Scripture and Ethics in Christian Life* (London: SPCK, 1991), 49.

of what wisdom may entail – not only the transcending of youthful arrogance and egotism through allowing suffering to have a purifying effect under God but also having the ability to live with integrity when under pressure, with a sense of accountability to God that dispenses with any kind of doctrinaire approach to living well.

JOSEPH'S TREATMENT OF HIS BROTHERS

Probably the greatest difficulty for many contemporary readers in viewing Joseph as someone who becomes a model of wisdom is his treatment of his brothers when they come to buy food from him in Egypt (Gen 42–44), prior to their reconciliation (Gen 45). In what way, if any, can what he puts them through be seen as demonstrating wisdom?[28]

Weeks sees at least a degree of revenge at work: "Given the considerable anguish and humiliation which Joseph inflicts upon his brothers, it is hard to believe that there is no element of punishment present, and this is never denied in the narrative."[29] Wilcox interestingly develops this in psychological terms:

> Even if, "remembering his dreams" ([42:]9), Joseph is setting out to establish the extent of his brothers' growth and repentance, it is not obvious that this is his role. Does that responsibility not lie with God? In other words, if Joseph did not respond at once with delight, generosity and forgiveness to the presence of his brothers, it may well owe more to an understandable resurgence of unresolved anger and a desire for some kind of revenge, than to a divinely prompted intention to assess and assist his brothers' spiritual development. Perhaps at a distance from them, Joseph had achieved some kind of

---

[28] A useful exposition and appraisal of interpretative proposals is Lindsay Wilson, *Joseph Wise and Otherwise: The Intersection of Wisdom and Covenant in Genesis 37–50* (Carlisle, UK: Paternoster, 2004), 145–49.

[29] Weeks, *Early Israelite Wisdom*, 94.

peace with his brothers for what they had done; but suddenly face to face with them it is a different matter. "Remembering his dreams" (verse 9) also meant remembering how and why his brothers acted in the way that they did. The upshot is that Joseph still has work to do before he can be reconciled to the brothers who betrayed him. Meanwhile, the path he chooses to take will bring considerable distress on his brothers and his father.[30]

Thus, for example, when Joseph instructs his steward to refund his brothers' money and also to put his silver cup in Benjamin's sack (44:1–5), "[i]t is hard to avoid the impression that Joseph is playing cat and mouse with his brothers here, manipulating them in a misguided and mean-spirited way."[31] Overall, "it becomes clear that when Joseph seemed to be trying to manipulate and control his brothers, he was really seeking to manage and control himself."[32]

Although a major alternative reading – that Joseph is wisely, even if demandingly, testing his brothers for their good and with a view to promoting reconciliation – appears to be somewhat out of fashion, we should nonetheless attend to Westermann's and von Rad's exposition of it. Westermann comments on 42:9:

> He now would have the opportunity to take revenge on them . . . however . . . Joseph, as soon as he had recognized his brothers, was resolved to try to apply healing to the breach. That cannot happen, however, unless the brothers, for their part, are first brought to "perception." This is the reason that Joseph permits them to experience the full harshness of what it means to be at the mercy of the mighty. The narrator means to say here that pardon at this point immediately after the arrival of the brothers could not have led to a genuine solution. What had happened was too serious for that.[33]

---

[30] Wilcox, *Living the Dream*, 57.
[31] Ibid., 73.
[32] Ibid., 83.
[33] Westermann, *Joseph*, 66.

Or, as von Rad puts it,

> The sufferings that come upon the brothers are not "fate." They are
> initiated by Joseph; they are not even punishment, let alone reprisal;
> they are a test. That is what Joseph says in one of those ambiguous
> statements that our narrator loves: Therein I will test you (Gen.
> 42:16). He does not test whether they are spies. He knows that they
> are not. He tests whether they are the same old brothers or whether
> perhaps an inner change has occurred in them.[34]

Both Westermann and von Rad see Joseph as seeking to replicate
the situation in which his brothers took advantage of him to see
whether they will do so again with another brother:

> There are two stages in the test; the first occurs with Simeon, the
> second with Benjamin. Both deal with the same thing: Joseph isolates
> one brother from the rest and wants to see if they will sacrifice this
> one as they once sacrificed Joseph himself. Twice . . . he creates a
> situation in which they have the opportunity to sacrifice a brother.
> The second test especially is unbelievably severe.[35]

When Judah makes his moving speech (44:18–34), a speech prefaced
by "God has found out the guilt of your servants" (44:16), which
has the same resonant ambiguity as Joseph's words about testing
(42:16), it becomes clear that "the brothers will now answer for
each other to the last man, and that they have passed the test."[36]

How might one decide between this reading and that of Wilcox?
Since the narrator is never explicit about Joseph's motives, readers
must judge in the light of their construal of the character of Joseph
and of the nature and purpose of the story as a whole. Undoubtedly either reading is possible. Even so, there is at least one factor
within the narrative as a whole that points to Joseph's acting with

---

[34] Von Rad, "The Story of Joseph," 30.
[35] Ibid.
[36] Ibid., 31.

wisdom: Joseph's famous summary statements (45:5–8, 50:19–20) that display access to the mind of God as working for good even when this was not apparent at the time. Von Rad sees this as the factor that gave Joseph the right to act as he did:

> Why did Joseph deal with his brothers in such a way...? He had authority because he alone knew something that was hidden from all others... Joseph reveals that quite openly in two speeches, first in the scene of recognition and again at the end after his father's death [i.e., 45:5–8; 50:19–20].... Here Joseph at last speaks openly of God, and here the last veil is lifted.[37]

The fact that Joseph displays definitive insight here should, I think, incline the reader to see him acting wisely in the encounters that precede, even if it cannot clinch such a reading. For a natural implication of the text is that Joseph's behavior – apparently inscrutable, yet searchingly intending good – in significant ways replicates the working of God.

A reading of Joseph as acting wisely may also perhaps be suggested by a narrative analogy in the one other Genesis narrative whose mode of telling matches that of the Joseph stories: Genesis 24, the mission of Abraham's servant to get a wife for Isaac. Here, Abraham's servant prayerfully sets a searching test of character for Isaac's wife-to-be (24:12–14): The girl who comes to the well to draw water must not only offer him a drink (i.e., be hospitable) but also offer to water his camels (i.e., be self-sacrificially generous with her time and energy). "Before he had finished speaking" (which implies that his prayer is entirely appropriate), Rebekah appears, offers a drink to Abraham's servant, and then offers to water all his camels (24:15–20). At this point, many readers might naturally expect the servant directly to recognize Rebekah as the answer to

---

[37] Ibid.

his prayer and begin to act and speak accordingly. Yet despite the girl's words and initial actions, "the man gazed at her in silence to learn whether or not the LORD had made his journey successful" (24:21), and it is only when the camels finish drinking that he acts. The point, presumably, is that the servant makes the test as searching as possible. Rebekah must not only show willingness, but she must also stay with it to the end; if she gives up halfway ("I've had it with these camels, I'm going home!"), she is not the one. The narrative analogy is between Abraham's servant and Joseph in setting a test of character that is appropriate, although more searching than some might think necessary, and then seeing it through to the end.

Certainly, if Joseph is displaying wisdom in his dealings with his brothers, then it well illustrates the general point about the nondoctrinaire nature of wisdom. However, it is one thing to admire the nondoctrinaire in principle, and another to recognize and admire it in practice. For, of course, any behavior that is wise and yet simultaneously surprising and unconventional will always be wide open to various, including negative, construals. This is why, even if the narrative implies that Joseph is wise in the way he handles his brothers in Genesis 42–44, it is unlikely that all readers will be so persuaded.

DIVINE SOVEREIGNTY AND HUMAN ACTIVITY

Joseph's statements about God's overruling his brothers' evil intentions and using their actions for good (Gen 45:5–8, 50:20) require yet further consideration in relation to the divinely sent dreams that feature prominently in the early part of the narrative. For together these give the Joseph narrative a striking dimension of divine sovereignty and guidance.

These dreams are interesting. On the one hand, in artistic terms they are impressionistic rather than naturalistic. Joseph's youthful dreams offer no hint of an Egyptian context for their outworking. Moreover, the picture of his whole family, including his mother, bowing down to him is not capable of exact fulfilment, for Joseph's mother, Rachel, is already dead.[38] On the other hand, although the youthful dreams are not symbolic or mysterious, in the kind of way that might require sophisticated interpretation – for their apparent point is instantly taken by everyone – their real significance remains open to misunderstanding. For the youthful Joseph clearly interprets his dreams egotistically: His exaltation is, pleasingly, at his brothers' expense, hence their resentment. It is only later, when he realizes that the dreams are fulfilled as he sees his brothers bowing before him (42:6–9), that he shows that he has learned (at least, on our preferred reading) that power is for responsible action toward the saving of lives during famine and reconciliation, not for an ego trip; the divine leading expressed in the dreams is therefore explicitly recognized to be for the preservation of life (45:5). In this sense one might even suggest that the dreams could be seen as a kind of microcosm of the Bible as a whole: a divine gift whose promises and warnings are easily misunderstood in superficial and self-seeking terms, and whose real significance often only becomes apparent within the context of living faithfully in the face of adversity.[39]

The central issues, however, revolve around the way in which the dreams promote the outworking of God's purposes. The dreams that Joseph receives as a youth (37:5–11) not only envision his future position of authority over his family but also help bring it about.

---

[38] Even if this narrative supposes that Rachel is still alive at the time of the dream, she does not later come down to Egypt with the rest of the family, and so the fulfilment remains inexact.

[39] Compare the proposed interpretation of Genesis 2–3 in Chapter 4.

For, Joseph's superficial construal and unwise telling of his dreams incite his brothers' resentment that leads to their action against him whereby he becomes a slave in Egypt. Joseph's interpretation of the cupbearer's dream (40:9–13) becomes the factor that causes Pharaoh to summon him because of what the cupbearer says (41:9–14). Pharaoh's dreams foretell the famine that will bring Joseph's brothers to Egypt, and Joseph's interpretation of these dreams is the reason for his promotion to high office within Egypt (41:1–57). When, therefore, Joseph tells his brothers that God, not they themselves, sent him to Egypt to preserve life, he is not making a general point about divine providence, but rather offering a specific reading of the significance of the dreams sent by God in their outworking. Thus Joseph's ability to interpret dreams is not just his ability to interpret their specific dreams to the cupbearer, the baker, and the Pharaoh, but also his ability to interpret to his brothers the way in which all the dreams indicate God's initiating, and working through, their whole history of conflict and time of famine for their good in the end.

Joseph's ability to interpret dreams also further illuminates the relation of divine and human action and the nature of wisdom.[40] What does Joseph mean when he asks the butler and baker, "Do not interpretations belong to God?" (40:8), and says to Pharaoh, "It is not in me; God will answer" (41:16)? Although one might simply depict Joseph here as "charismatic," the logic of the text deserves some teasing out. Joseph's ascription of dream interpretation to God is not a proposal that either he or the dreamer should go and pray until illumination is given. His words to Pharaoh are

---

[40] I draw here on my discussion in "Solomon and Job: Divine Wisdom in Human Life," in *Where Shall Wisdom Be Found? Wisdom in the Bible, the Church and the Contemporary World*, ed. Stephen C. Barton (Edinburgh, UK: T. & T. Clark, 1999), 3–17, esp. 6–9 and 15–16.

not an invitation to speak not to him but instead to seek illumination from God via some other means. Nor does the fact that Joseph immediately follows his ascription of dream interpretation to God with the words "tell me please" (40:8) mean that Joseph is making an outrageous claim about his personal significance. The point in each context appears to be that Joseph is saying that he is both responsive and accountable to God and that therefore his interpretation is reliable. The ascription of interpretation to God is not to deny Joseph's own human action, but rather to locate Joseph's act of interpreting within a context of divine enabling that should encourage trust on the part of his hearers. Similarly, when Joseph speaks of God's larger purposes to his brothers, each time, his words serve to give them reason, although they are fearful of him, to recognize his purposes as good and compassionate.[41]

CONCLUSION

Although von Rad's hypothesis about the origins of the Joseph narrative is open to major objection, I have suggested that many of von Rad's insights can remain helpful if they are reconceived in terms of a reading strategy. Whether or not the narrative had the particular didactic function that von Rad supposed, it is still reasonable to see the text as didactic in purpose in its portrayal of Joseph as an embodiment of the acquisition and display of wisdom. Certainly, when the narrative is read as part of scripture, then it naturally has a didactic function within the life of synagogue and church.

---

[41] So, to return to von Rad, with whom we began, we can see that his interpretation of Joseph's words about God's overruling as threatening to imperil the significance of human action is a major misreading of the text.

If it is appropriate to see Joseph in Genesis 37–50 as wise, then his wisdom is a quality with many facets: his ability patiently to learn and be purified through unwelcome and painful events; his responding to sexual temptation with a principled refusal; his recognition that power is given for responsible service of others; his nondoctrinaire approach to his brothers that, while inscrutable on the surface, intends their good in the end; his ability to understand God's sovereign ways as refracted through dreams and to act accordingly.

If wise use of the text today is to correspond to the wisdom within the text, then although there would be concern with qualities of insight, integrity, and the ability to discern God's working as enduringly important, didactic concerns should be open to perhaps displaying something of the surprising and nondoctrinaire qualities of Joseph himself.

Further Reading

COMMENTARIES ON GENESIS

Although there is a general drift in recent Genesis commentaries in the direction of theological interpretation, this drift is by no means universal, nor is there much agreement as to precisely what a theological interpretation of Genesis should look like. Notable is the resurgence of Jewish commentary, which usually draws on interpretive resources that are unfamiliar to Christian readers.

Some Recent Christian Commentaries

Brueggemann, Walter. *Genesis*. Interpretation. Atlanta: John Knox, 1982. Accessible and stimulating.

Fretheim, Terence E. "The Book of Genesis: Introduction, Commentary, and Reflections." In *The New Interpreter's Bible*, edited by Leander E. Keck et al., 1:319–674. Nashville, TN: Abingdon, 1994. Both exposition and application.

Kidner, Derek. *Genesis: An Introduction and Commentary*. Tyndale Old Testament Commentaries. London: Tyndale, 1967. Critically conservative, but pithily insightful.

Rad, Gerhard von. *Genesis: A Commentary*. Translated by John H. Marks. Rev. Ed. The Old Testament Library. London: SCM, 1972 (German 9th ed., 1972). Full of sophisticated theological insight.

Sailhamer, John. "Genesis." In *The Expositor's Bible Commentary*, edited by Frank E. Gaebelein, 2:1–284. Grand Rapids, MI: Zondervan, 1990.

Located in a series that aims to present "the best in evangelical scholarship."

Towner, W. Sibley. *Genesis.* Westminster Bible Companion. Louisville, KY: Westminster John Knox, 2001. Constructive and accessible.

Wenham, Gordon J. *Genesis 1–15.* Word Biblical Commentary 1. Waco, TX: Word, 1987.

> *Genesis Genesis 16–50.* Word Biblical Commentary 2. Dallas: Word, 1994. Some fresh analyses of the biblical text.

Westermann, Claus. *Genesis 1–11: A Commentary.* Translated by John J. Scullion. Continental Commentaries. Minneapolis, MN: Augsburg, 1984.

> *Genesis 12–36: A Commentary.* Translated by John J. Scullion. Continental Commentaries. Minneapolis, MN: Augsburg, 1985.

> *Genesis 37–50: A Commentary.* Translated by John J. Scullion. Continental Commentaries. Minneapolis, MN: Augsburg, 1987.

These three volumes constitute the fullest twentieth-century commentary on Genesis, though one sometimes has to mine it for theological nuggets.

> *Genesis: A Practical Commentary.* Grand Rapids, MI: Eerdmans, 1987. A boiled-down version of Westermann's three-volume magnum opus; one suspects that "practical" is a bit euphemistic and may just mean "accessible."

Some Recent Jewish Commentaries

Jacob, Benno. *Genesis: The First Book of the Bible.* Translated by Ernest I. Jacob and Walter Jacob. New York: Ktav, 2007. This 1934 work has only recently become available in English and has many unusual insights.

Levenson, Jon D. "Genesis." In *The Jewish Study Bible,* edited by Adele Berlin and Marc Zvi Brettler, 8–101. New York: Oxford University Press, 2004. Pithy, though all too brief.

Plaut, W. Gunther. "Genesis." In *The Torah: A Modern Commentary,* edited by W. Gunther Plaut, 1–318. New York: Union of American Hebrew Congregations, 1981. The actual commentary is thin, but the reflections can be substantive.

Sarna, Nahum M. *Genesis: The Traditional Hebrew Text with New JPS Translation.* The JPS Torah Commentary. Philadelphia: Jewish Publication Society, 1989. Thoughtful and readable.

Two Classic Commentaries

Calvin, John. *Calvin's Commentaries.* Vol. 1, *Genesis.* Edited and translated by John King. Calvin Translation Society. Repr. ed. Grand Rapids, MI: Baker, 2005. The greatest of Reformation commentators.

Rosenbaum, M., and A. M. Silbermann, eds. *The Pentateuch with the Commentary of Rashi: Genesis.* Jerusalem: Silbermann, 1972. Convenient parallel text of the greatest of medieval Jewish commentators.

HISTORY OF INTERPRETATION

A notable feature in recent scholarly work is the growth of studies in interpretive history. Although the interest in such work is often historical more than hermeneutical, the material made available offers resources for fresh contemporary reflection on the possible implications of the biblical text.

Anderson, Gary A. *The Genesis of Perfection: Adam and Eve in Jewish and Christian Imagination.* Louisville, KY: Westminster John Knox, 2001. Fresh and suggestive study of classic readings.

Kessler, Edward. *Bound by the Bible: Jews, Christians and the Sacrifice of Isaac.* Cambridge: Cambridge University Press, 2004. Seeks to demonstrate exegetical encounters between Jews and Christians in antiquity.

Kugel, James L. *The Bible as It Was.* Cambridge, MA: Belknap, 1997. Invaluable anthology, with commentary, of ancient interpretation of Genesis may be found on pp. 51–284. Still more readings can be found on pp. 43–499 of Kugel's larger edition: *Traditions of the Bible: A Guide to the Bible as It Was at the Start of the Common Era.* (Cambridge, MA: Harvard University Press, 1998).

In Potiphar's House: The Interpretive Life of Biblical Texts. 2nd ed. Cambridge, MA: Harvard University Press, 1994. Part 1 of this book contains a fascinating and readable treatment of the afterlife of the Joseph narrative.

Louth, Andrew, with Marco Conti, eds. *Genesis 1–11.* Ancient Christian Commentary on Scripture: Old Testament 1. Downers Grove, IL: InterVarsity, 2001. Anthologizes patristic interpretation. The rest of Genesis is covered by Sheridan's volume (see next entry).

Sheridan, Mark, ed. *Genesis 12–50.* Ancient Christian Commentary on Scripture: Old Testament 2. Downers Grove, IL: InterVarsity, 2002. Anthologizes patristic interpretation. For Genesis 1–11, see the volume by Louth with Conti (see previous entry).

Young, Frances. "Wrestling Jacob." In Frances Young, *Brokenness and Blessing: Towards a Biblical Spirituality,* 34–57. London: DLT, 2007. A model of constructive theological reflection rooted in classic readings.

There is also an ongoing series of essay collections, *Themes in Biblical Narrative,* published by Brill (general editors Robert Kugler, Gerard P. Luttikhuizen, and Loren Stuckenbruck). These arise from an annual conference in Groningen and are devoted to the reception history of pentateuchal texts. The following volumes on Genesis have appeared thus far:

Interpretations of the Flood. Edited by Florentino García Martínez and Gerard P. Luttikhuizen. Themes in Biblical Narrative 1. Leiden, NL: Brill, 1999.

Paradise Interpreted: Representations of Biblical Paradise in Judaism and Christianity. Edited by Gerard P. Luttikhuizen. Themes in Biblical Narrative 2. Leiden, NL: Brill, 1999.

The Creation of Man and Woman: Interpretations of the Biblical Narratives in Jewish and Christian Tradition. Edited by Gerard P. Luttikhuizen. Themes in Biblical Narrative 3. Leiden, NL: Brill, 2000.

The Sacrifice of Isaac: The Aqedah (Genesis 22) and Its Interpretations. Edited by Ed Noort and Eibert Tigchelaar. Themes in Biblical Narrative 4. Leiden, NL: Brill, 2002.

Eve's Children: The Biblical Stories Retold and Interpreted in Jewish and Christian Traditions. Edited by Gerard P. Luttikhuizen. Themes in Biblical Narrative 5. Leiden, NL: Brill, 2003.

The Fall of the Angels. Edited by Christoph Auffarth and Loren T. Stuckenbruck. Themes in Biblical Narrative 6. Leiden, NL: Brill, 2004.

Sodom's Sin: Genesis 18–19 and Its Interpretation. Edited by Ed Noort and Eibert Tigchelaar. Themes in Biblical Narrative 7. Leiden, NL: Brill, 2004.

The Creation of Heaven and Earth: Re-interpretation of Genesis 1 in the Context of Judaism, Ancient Philosophy, Christianity, and Modern Physics. Edited by George H. van Kooten. Themes in Biblical Narrative 8. Leiden, NL: Brill, 2005.

THEOLOGY

Allowing for the great diversity of understandings of what counts as theology in the study of Genesis, and recognizing that older works on the theology of the Yahwist, the Elohist, and the Priestly writers retain real value for highlighting significant aspects of the biblical text, the following are notable recent attempts to think through the theological implications of the Genesis text with varying degrees of reference to Jewish or Christian appropriation.

Bird, Phyllis A. *Missing Persons and Mistaken Identities: Women and Gender in Ancient Israel.* Overtures to Biblical Theology. Minneapolis, MN: Fortress, 1997. See esp. pp. 123–93 for feminist reflections on Genesis 1-3.

Blenkinsopp, Joseph. "Creation, the Body, and Care for a Damaged World." In Joseph Blenkinsopp, *Treasures Old and New: Essays in the Theology of the Pentateuch*, 36–52. Grand Rapids, MI: Eerdmans, 2004. Suggestive on possible insights from the Priestly writer, not least in Genesis 1, for contemporary ecological concerns.

Goldingay, John. *Old Testament Theology.* Vol. 1, *Israel's Gospel.* Downers Grove, IL: InterVarsity, 2003. Stimulating reading of Genesis as a whole is found on pp. 42–287.

Greidanus, Sidney. *Preaching Christ from Genesis: Foundations for Expository Sermons*. Grand Rapids, MI: Eerdmans, 2007. Thoughtfully moves from exegesis to homiletics.

Kaminsky, Joel S. *Yet I Loved Jacob: Reclaiming the Biblical Concept of Election*. Nashville, TN: Abingdon, 2007. See esp. pp. 1–78 for an accessible and engaging study that is indebted to Levenson's work (see next entry).

Levenson, Jon D. *The Death and Resurrection of the Beloved Son: The Transformation of Child Sacrifice in Judaism and Christianity*. New Haven, CT: Yale University Press, 1993. Perhaps the freshest and most groundbreaking study of Genesis in recent years, in which there is a profound account of election.

Trible, Phyllis. "Hagar: The Desolation of Rejection." In Phyllis Trible, *Texts of Terror: Literary-Feminist Readings of Biblical Narratives*, 9–35. Overtures to Biblical Theology. Philadelphia: Fortress, 1984. Potent feminist reading.

"Genesis 22: The Sacrifice of Sarah." In *"Not in Heaven": Coherence and Complexity in Biblical Narrative*, edited by J. P. Rosenblatt and J. C. Sitterson, 170–91. Bloomington: Indiana University Press, 1991. Imaginative and existentially charged reading.

Walton, Kevin. *Thou Traveller Unknown: The Presence and Absence of God in the Jacob Narrative*. Paternoster Biblical and Theological Monographs. Carlisle, UK: Paternoster, 2003. Suggestive historical and theological reading.

Author Index

Scripture Index

Subject Index